THE HOUSE THAT ROCK BUILT

THE HOUSE THAT
ROCK BUILT

How It Took Time, Money, Music Moguls,
Corporate Types, Politicians, Media, Artists,
and Fans to Bring the Rock Hall to Cleveland

NORM N. NITE AND TOM FERAN

THE KENT STATE UNIVERSITY PRESS *Kent, Ohio*

The Hall of Fame logo and award statue are registered trademarks of the Rock & Roll Hall of Fame.

© 2020 by Norm N. Nite and Tom Feran
All rights reserved
ISBN 978-1-60635-399-8
Manufactured in Canada

Cataloging information for this title is available at the Library of Congress.

24 23 22 21 20   5 4 3 2 1

This book is dedicated to my late father, Jim, and mother, Jean, and also to my sister, Carolyn, and brothers, Richard and Don, whose love and inspiration enabled me to develop my interest in music.

—NORM N. NITE

You'll never get the real history. You'll get the history according to somebody. Everybody has their own theory about how everything happened.

—ALBERT RATNER

CONTENTS

FOREWORD

BY STEVIE VAN ZANDT

Before you get into this excellent book about how the Rock Hall came into existence, I want to just spend a few minutes explaining the reason why it came into existence.

My generation, people born from the mid-'40s to the mid-'50s, is described as the baby boom generation. What is not said often enough, and what we should be called, is the luckiest generation.

As World War II ended, we in America found ourselves Kings of the Earth.

Our economy was as friendly as it would ever be.

Our currency had about the highest value it would ever have.

The concepts of leisure time and a middle class were really expanded. The discussion at the dinner table was not if but when we would go to the four-day work week!

And on top of all that, we grew up in the middle of what we recognize now as an artistic renaissance.

Every couple of hundred years or so the greatest art being made also becomes the most commercial.

That's what we were lucky enough to be born into.

Keep in mind it was only in the 1950s that a new alien life-form called "the teenager" had just come into existence. Before that, the human species' stages of development were considered infancy, then adolescence, then a couple of awkward years, then adulthood.

In the '60s, those couple of awkward years expanded, giving birth to teenagers, which meant a new demographic, a new market, and—America being America—new industries popping up to service them.

Rock and roll was one of them.

It turned out to be an unexpectedly satisfying means of expression, as Chuck Berry institutionalized the teenage lifestyle in song after song, giving the adults a glimpse into a world they knew nothing about, while simultaneously half-describing, half-inventing the template that defined the teenage identity, too new and hopelessly inarticulate to ever define itself. (Much as Mario Puzo's *Godfather* supplied the Book of Rules for all Mafia generations that followed!)

But while rock and roll itself was busy frightening parents to death because of its real and imagined association with juvenile delinquency, the purveyors of this new form of pop music were not taken seriously at all.

They were considered novelty acts.

The freak show in the teenage circus.

Society saw them as attention-getting gimmicks with no substance whatsoever.

"A-wop-bop–a-lu-bop–a-wop-bam-boom!" declared Little Richard!

The mother of all future Millennial acronyms?

Nah, novelty!

> Bomp-bab-a-bomp
> ba-bomp-a-bomp-bomp-bomp
> bab-a-bomp-bab-a-bomp
> a-dang-a-dang-dang
> a-ding–a-dong-ding Blue Moon . . .

What's to take seriously?

Jesters. Minstrels. That's all they were. Traveling town to town to keep the kids amused until they grew up and got jobs and took their expected places in society.

But a funny thing happened on the way to the status quo.

It was called the '60s.

Yes, the '50s kids did mostly, if reluctantly, grow up and become part of "normal" society.

The '60s kids did not.

In fact, we would be the only generation in history to *not* grow up to be our parents.

Music wasn't incidental to us. There was nothing casual about the soundtrack of our lives. It was orchestrating our every emotion and we took it quite seriously.

And so did the artists who were collectively about to become known as the British Invasion of 1964.

These groups—the Beatles, Dave Clark 5, Herman's Hermits, Animals, Rolling Stones, Kinks, Yardbirds, Searchers, Who, Hollies, and others—accidentally, unknowingly, brought three new elements that would change popular entertainment forever:

1) They introduced the "band" as the new vehicle of teenage communication, which had a very different message intrinsically—community—which would have an unexpectedly profound and lasting effect.

2) The performers became integrated into our lives not just for the music and entertainment the way the '50s guys did but as a source of information and education and mentoring and companionship and, potentially, nothing less than enlightenment.

3) They took those '50s rock-and-rolling freaky misfit novelty performers very seriously! Even more than we did.

Yeah, OK, they all had "an act"—it was still show biz, after all—but these British guys picked up on something the Americans hadn't, based on an appreciation for all things Americana we will never have.

They recognized the '50s innovators had created a very simple-to-use platform of expression that could be easily adapted and built on.

Little Richard, who invented and embodied the rock idiom as we know it, had crazy hair and crazy clothes, rolled his eyes skyward like a possessed demon, screaming incoherent lyrics—all exaggerated to become "the Act," but it wasn't an "act" when every time he opened his mouth out came LIBERATION!

And Jimi Hendrix was listening.

For his gimmicks, Bo Diddley had homemade guitars, a maraca player, a female guitarist, and crazy moves, while inventing self-promotion at the same time.

But he made the rhythm of sex commercial.

And the Rolling Stones would use it.

Chuck Berry duckwalked and clowned around.

But he brought storytelling to pop music and made his guitar innovations look like fun.

And what would soon be the two biggest bands in the world, the Beatles and Stones, became his loyal disciples.

Jerry Lee Lewis's long, pomaded hair hung down in his face as he kicked the bench over, pushed the piano across the stage, and was obviously possessed by the devil. But he represented the southern white guy as satyr, using his religious guilt thing as his source of power.

Power that the Who would harness.

Gary U.S. Bonds's name was his gimmick.

But he and sax player Daddy G taught the world what a party sounded like.

Bruce Springsteen was paying attention.

Dion and the Belmonts were white doo-wop in a black doo-wop world singing horn parts. They introduced the attitude of the street.

Lou Reed would pick up on that.

Sam Cooke was the first to demonstrate how one could be equally passionate about devotion to God and devotion to sex.

Ray Charles and Aretha Franklin would follow.

The doo-wop bird groups—Ravens, Orioles, Flamingos—would bring four- and five-part harmony to the Beach Boys and dance moves to the Temptations.

While the Everly Brothers were innovating brotherly conflict (Kinks, Black Crowes, Oasis), the Beatles were studying their two-part harmony.

James Brown would have a cape placed on his shoulders and be led offstage too exhausted to go on, only to come back to desperately testify one more time!

But he showed Mick Jagger how to dance, hip-hop stars how to rap, Prince how to funk, and everyone how to go from prison to the White House.

Elvis Presley's "thing" was that while most white performers just stood there, he naturally moved like a black performer onstage, to great gimmicky controversy.

But he would combine white hillbilly music and black blues and literally define what rock and roll was—namely, white guys trying to be black and failing gloriously!

Everybody learned from him.

And then there was one more unexpected development.

Along came Bob Dylan, turning it all into an art form.

Dylan (lyrics), the Beatles (pop structure perfection), the Rolling Stones (blues, rebellion, sex), and the Byrds (revealing the breadth—folk rock, jazz rock, space rock! psychedelic rock, country rock), would all influence each other and a new art form. And thus the rock era was born.

Those '50s circus freaks were not temporary, soon-to-be-forgotten teenage distractions after all. They were recognized correctly for what they were: pioneers of this new art form.

For the first time this social phenomena was given serious journalism, by *Crawdaddy* and *Rolling Stone* magazine.

And so it was decided.

This renaissance period should be celebrated and made accessible to future generations.

The Rock Hall was built to protect it.

The influence of those extraordinarily unique '50s and '60s artists continues to resonate in today's music and will continue to do so until new instruments are invented. And probably long after that.

The recognition doesn't stop with the renaissance artists. The Rock Hall continues to induct great artists whose work is at least 25 years old.

And yes, the decisions about who should or shouldn't be inducted will continue to be sources of discussion, passion, and frustration.

And that's how it should be.

It would be disrespectful for these conversations to be anything less than serious, life-and-death discussions every year. After all, rock and soul are my religion.

I may not take myself very seriously, but my life's work is something else again.

The Rock and Roll Hall of Fame is a sacred site to me.

Those who mistake it for some kind of self-aggrandizing move by the music industry need to come visit and learn the history it houses, because they are wrong.

In a world drowning in mediocrity, this is where greatness lives.

It is where greatness is celebrated.

And it is where greatness will continue to inspire, motivate, and inform future generations.

Forevermore.

STEVIE VAN ZANDT
Greenwich Village
March '19

Stevie Van Zandt is a musician, producer, actor, director, and activist. Recognized internationally as one of the world's foremost authorities on rock and roll, he was a founding member of Bruce Springsteen's E Street Band and went on to further success with his band Little Steven and the Disciples of Soul. Van Zandt has twice been honored by the United Nations for his political activism, costarred in the HBO hit The Sopranos, *and created* Little Steven's Underground Garage, *an internationally syndicated radio show. In 2006 he launched his record label, Wicked Cool Records, to further support new rock and roll.*

FOREWORD

BY SEYMOUR STEIN

The Rock and Roll Hall of Fame is a great institution that has stood the test of time. I'm very thankful Cleveland has proven to be the perfect home for the museum, or, as you folks call it, the "Rock Hall." I'm proud of my role overall, and most of all for helping to choose Cleveland as our home.

Music has been of vital importance to me for just about my entire life. Perhaps because I was born with a heart murmur and played little or no sports, music occupied an extra-large part of my life from the time I was six years old. Sharing a bedroom with my big sister, Ann, six years my elder, I got to listen to music very early on. That was as far back as the late 1940s; but even then, or a few years later, I could see dramatic changes. Hank Williams's songs became a tremendous influence, and when I heard R & B tunes—first and foremost "The Fat Man" by Fats Domino, "Lawdy Miss Clawdy" by Lloyd Price, "Please Send Me Someone to Love" by Percy Mayfield, "I Love You, Yes I Do" by Bull Moose Jackson, and "I Almost Lost My Mind" by Ivory Joe Hunter—I knew there was a change coming.

In the early '50s, after Patti Page spent 13 weeks at #1 on the Billboard chart with "Tennessee Waltz," and Mitch Miller started recording Hank Williams's hits with Columbia artists Rosemary Clooney, Tony Bennett, Frankie Laine, Jo Stafford, and others, I could feel the two genres coming together. Early doo-wop hits a few years later, like "Gee" by the Crows, "Sh-Boom" by the Chords, and "Hearts of Stone" by Otis Williams and the Charms, were proof positive, but it was not until 1955 or 1956 with Alan Freed wailing on the radio that I knew rock and roll was here to stay.

The fact that Alan Freed was from Ohio, and first rose to fame in Cleveland, was the main reason Cleveland was originally, and always, my first choice for the Rock and Roll Hall of Fame. To be fair, we met with many cities that we thought were viable contenders; a trip to Philadelphia to visit local politicians, a board from Chicago. We also explored Memphis and New Orleans, and even New York and Los Angeles. I was dead set against it, because both cities had so much going on that I was certain the Rock and Roll Hall of Fame could be overshadowed.

It was Suzan Evans Hochberg who first brought the idea of starting a rock and roll hall of fame to Ahmet Ertegun, who was quite enthusiastic. Ahmet got me involved, and Jann Wenner as well as Jerry Wexler and Ahmet's brother, Nesuhi. Also on the Warner side, we soon recruited Bob Krasnow, a great A&R man who, incidentally, started his career heading up the King Records branch in San Francisco. Also involved at or near the beginning was Michael Leon, representing Jerry Moss at A&M. Noreen Woods, Ahmet's trusted assistant over many years, was also tremendously important to our team. Noreen had vast knowledge of rock and roll, and rhythm and blues in particular, and joined us on many trips throughout our search and during all that went on in Cleveland.

It was my idea to bring Allen Grubman into the mix because at the time, he was the hottest music lawyer in the business and had access to all seven major labels. Allen was successful in bringing on the other six majors, including Walter Yetnikoff, the head of Columbia and Warner's chief rival. Also, early New Yorkers actively involved from the beginning were legendary music producer John Hammond, *Rolling Stone*'s legal advisor Ben Needell, and manager, writer, and producer Jon Landau, who is still very active in the Rock and Roll Hall of Fame.

On the Cleveland side, everyone seemed enthusiastically and genuinely interested, starting with the then mayor and later governor George Voinovich, Governor Dick Celeste, Al Ratner of Forest City, Milt Maltz, Mary Rose Oakar, Mike Benz, Bill Hulett, Dick Pogue, and others. The folks from Cleveland and Ohio kept their word and were totally responsible for building the Rock and Roll Hall of Fame, even as the costs doubled when we were able to bring on I. M. Pei, perhaps the greatest living architect of that time. We all owe him so much.

A later addition to the New York team was the current Rock Hall's New York–based president Joel Peresman, who has contributed mightily. I would like to thank him; also Lisa Testa for her tireless efforts; Craig lnciardi and my good friend, Lance Freed, for their continued dedication.

Norm, as Cleveland's first ambassador to the Rock and Roll Hall of Fame committee back in the day, I trust people in Cleveland, New York, and around the world know your great work in getting this started and seeing it through. For that, we are all eternally grateful.

Seymour Stein is the cofounder of Sire Records and the author of Siren Song: My Life in Music. *He was inducted into the Rock and Roll Hall of Fame in 2005, in the lifetime achievement category.*

PREFACE

I first became interested in rock and roll while growing up in Cleveland, Ohio, in the early 1950s. At that time, Cleveland got a heavier dose of music than the rest of the country, thanks to the late Alan Freed, who was a disc jockey on station WJW. It was Alan who, in concert with his good friend Leo Mintz, proprietor of Record Rendezvous in Cleveland, had the first rock-and-roll concert at the Cleveland Arena on March 21, 1952, and would go on to coin the term *rock and roll*. The late Scott Muni and I had the honor of inducting Alan into the Rock and Roll Hall of Fame on January 23, 1986. It could be said that Alan Freed moved rock and roll through its infancy and Dick Clark has a claim as its guardian during its childhood and adolescence. There is no question in my mind that Alan Freed and Dick Clark were the two most important forces in the growth of rock and roll.

In April 1973, I moved to New York City to work for WCBS-FM. Shortly thereafter I received a contract to write my first book on rock and roll, called *Rock On,* which came out in November 1974. Between then and 1992, seven other *Rock On* books would follow.

In January 1968, while appearing on the nationally televised *Mike Douglas Show,* I first met singer Lesley Gore—and I kept in touch with her over the years. In August 1983, she phoned me to get involved with a group that wanted to build a Rock and Roll Hall of Fame. This was an idea I first had in 1982, with Hank LoConti, owner of the Agora nightclub in Cleveland, and nationally known Dick Clark—an idea that never came to fruition, because of our busy schedules. If it was not for Lesley Gore calling me that summer, the Hall of Fame would not be in Cleveland—*period.* In January 1984, Seymour Stein of Sire Records invited me to be on the Rules and Nominating Committee. Then in May 1985, Hank LoConti and Bill Smith from WMMS radio called to ask me to come to Cleveland to meet with Mike Benz, who put a group of prominent Clevelanders together, after reading an article in *Crain's Cleveland Business* about a guy named Eddie Spizel, who wanted to open a music museum in Cleveland. Because Mike was with the Greater Cleveland Growth Association and Chamber of Commerce, he had done some research on rock and roll and thought that a

Community Museum Hall of Fame could be a big deal and attraction in Cleveland. Mike then got the okay to put a committee together to explore the idea.

After Mike met me and found out about the people in New York and their efforts, he asked me, on behalf of the community, to be on its committee and help its members meet the folks in New York. After our meeting, I flew back to New York and convinced Ahmet Ertegun of Atlantic Records, president of the Hall of Fame Foundation, to consider Cleveland. He agreed to a meeting with a group from Cleveland in July 1985, at the New York office. This book details the difficult task of making this all happen, which took the next 11 years.

I first thought of writing a comprehensive book on how the Hall of Fame came to be in 1996, mainly because through those 11 years, I kept copious notes on how the story unfolded. Little did I know what an immense project it would be.

In October 2015, I contacted my friend Tom Feran of the *Cleveland Plain Dealer* to work with me. It took three long years of interviews and Tom's brilliant writing to finally finish the book. My goal in this endeavor was, and is, to present the definitive book on the very complex subject of the Rock and Roll Hall of Fame. Without Tom Feran's help, this would never have happened. I want to say thanks to the late Lesley Gore, Tom Feran, Mike Benz, the late Ahmet Ertegun, Jann Wenner, Seymour Stein, Suzan Evans Hochberg, and all those involved in this project for making this book a contribution to the history of rock and roll.

May the Hall of Fame "Rock On Forever."

NORM N. NITE 2019

ACKNOWLEDGMENTS

I never could have put this work together without the cooperation of many individuals. I am grateful for all their assistance, but more than that, I am pleased at how they all extended themselves to help make this the music industry's best book about the Rock and Roll Hall of Fame. The depth and complexity of the material covered here made it necessary to interview many of the people most familiar with the Hall of Fame project. This book would never have been completed had it not been for the work of my associate and dear friend Tom Feran. I extend my deepest gratitude to some special people, all of whom gave their time and knowledge to this project.

I thank the New York group—Ahmet Ertegun, Jann S. Wenner, Seymour Stein, Allen Grubman, Joel Peresman, Suzan Evans Hochberg, and Benjamin F. Needell. Also, John Hammond, Jon Landau, Doug Morris, Bob Krasnow, Michael Leon, Lenny Kaye, Bob Altschuler, Frank Barselona, Jerry Wexler, and Nesuhi Ertegun.

I am grateful to the Civic Committee, which brought the Rock and Roll Hall of Fame and Museum to Cleveland—K. Michael Benz (chairman of the Cleveland Civic Committee and executive vice president of the Greater Cleveland Growth Association), Mike Belkin, Jules Belkin, Ernie Anderson, Gary Bird, William Burgess, Richard F. Celeste, George V. Voinovich, Gary Conley, Paul David, Joseph P. Ditchman Jr., Nolen M. Ellison, Dale R. Finley, Richard Fleischman, George L. Forbes, David Freed, John Gorman, Timothy F. Hagan, Marsha Hughes, Lawrence C. Jones, Mary Ann Jorgenson, J. Richard Kelso, Tim LaRose, Hank LoConti, Peggy Mathna, George I. Meisel, George N. Miller, Mary Rose Oakar, Jane Scott, William T. Smith, Michael Stanley, Patrick A. Sweeney, Leo "Kid Leo" Travagliante, William Wendling, Helen Williams, Larry Robinson, Tommy LiPuma, and Steve Zamborsky.

Heartfelt appreciation to Milt Maltz, Albert Ratner, John M. McMillion, Morry Weiss, Stu Brostoff, George Sipl, Chris Fahlman, Richard Amendola, John Moore, Evan Hopkins Turner, Laurence G. Isard, Pete Zaremba, Thaxter Trafton, Lowell G. Chrisman, David Gockley, Lawrence S. Dolin, William Bryant, Frank Joseph, Shelley Roth, Lawrence J. Wilker, Keith Rathbun, Gerald Gordon, Steven A. Minter, Richard W.

Pogue, Esq., Robert Broadbent, Harry R. Horvitz, Thomas Vail, Ruth Miller, Connie Edelman, Vivian Goodman, Kim Colebrook, Phil Locascio, Theodore Sande, Don Webster, William Weller, Lonnie Gronek, Billy Buckholtz, Curtis Shaw, C. David Whitaker, Dick Lumenello, John Llewellyn, Roger Turner, Hubert Payne, Fred Anthony, Joe Marinucci, Walter A. Tiburski, Zemira Jones, Art Caruso, Xen Zapis, Bruce Felder, John Zoilo, Louis Stokes, Dennis Kucinich, and Mike White.

Special thanks to Joel Peresman, president and CEO of the Rock and Roll Hall of Fame Foundation; former Cleveland Hall of Fame and Museum directors Bill Hulett, Dave Abbott, Chris Johnson, Larry Thompson, Dennis Barrie, K. Michael Benz and Terry Stewart; and current president and CEO Rock and Roll Hall of Fame and Museum Greg Harris. Deep thanks also to Andy Leach, Sharon Uhl, Avery Friedman, Larry Morrow, Alice Glick, "Big Chuck" Schodowski, "Li'l" John Rinaldi, Billy Bass, Bill Younkin, Bernard Karr, Bill Randle, Cindy Barber, Barry Gabel, Chuck Collier, Carolyn Lascko, "Cousin Brucie" Morrow, Denny Sanders, Deanna R. Adams, Dale Solly, Don Durma, Dick Clark, Kari Clark, Bernard Sokolowski, Mike Zappone, David Spero, Anastasia Pantsios, Chuck Rambaldo, Donna Mathers, Ed "Flash" Ferenc, Jeff Kinzbach, Harlan Diamond, Mark Avsec, Frank Lanziano, Jack Soden, Jim Henke, Jose Feliciano, James Tusty, Tom Locke, Mike Sokolowski, Rick Fryan, Bruce Mielziner, Amy Feran, Jim Davison, Jerry Silecchia, Tim Hays, John Lanigan, Jimmy Malone, David Moss, Jim Hooley, Joe McCoy, Joe Corace, Joe Contorno, Jim Paponetti, Lynn Toliver, Leon Bibb, Carl Monday, Lance Freed, Mary Jarosz, Michael Lynne, Nick Kostis, Richard Durma, Rick Rhein, Richard Lorenzo, Ray Prokorym, Steve Popovich, Stevie Van Zandt, Ted Henry, Martin Savidge, Tony DeLauro, Jeff Maynor, Donna Gould, Henry Niedzwicki, Bill McGrath, Tim Taylor, Bob DiBiasio, Tina Ludwig, Chris McDonald, Paul Shaffer, Eric Carmen, Suzy Phalin, Tom Embrescia, Linda O'Connell, Lisa Spies, Marc Lascko, Tony Vitanza, Jim Swingos, Angelo Sidari, Diana Gornick, Al Sutowski, Ricky Durma, Freddy Cannon, Teri Hare, and the citizens of Cleveland. Thanks to curator Matthew Benz and the staff at the Ohio History Center.

And special thanks to those who supplied me with priceless photos, among them Janet Macoska, Jim Davison, James Toncar, Robert Golubski, Lance Freed, and Stu Mintz.

And finally, we extend our appreciation to our designer, Christine Brooks, and our editor, Will Underwood, whose effort, patience, and dedication made this book a reality.

"Mr. D.J."

—ARETHA FRANKLIN

Alan Freed belonged in the Rock and Roll Hall of Fame; no one doubted that. He was the disc jockey and showman who popularized the term *rock and roll,* who championed the music so vigorously he became its personification and was called its father. Ultimately, some would say, he became a martyr to it.

Without Freed, the Rock and Roll Hall of Fame, opened 30 years after his death, would not have made its home in Cleveland. So it was only fitting that Freed would be recognized and remembered in the glittering music shrine.

The surprise was that his mortal remains were interred there, behind glass, on public display.

Terry Stewart, the executive director who approved the installation, said, "I thought it was kind of a rock-and-roll thing to do. And if there's one linchpin to the museum being in Cleveland, it's Alan Freed."

Freed's son Lance offered the family's perspective.

"Dad loved an audience," he said.

Freed began to find his biggest audience a few blocks south of the Rock Hall in July 1951, in the studios of WJW radio, playing rhythm-and-blues records in the fringe hours around midnight. Leo Mintz, owner of the big Record Rendezvous store, supplied the idea, the sponsorship, the records, and the words *rock and roll.* Freed, who had grown up in northeast Ohio loving music and had worked his way up from stations in New Castle (Pennsylvania), Youngstown, and Akron, supplied the energy, the enthusiasm, and ultimately the passion.

Sounding older than his 29 years and adopting the "black sound" employed by other white announcers playing "race records" in that era, he spun the discs, pounded the beat on a phone book, rattled a cow bell, and called himself the Moondog, the King of the Moondoggers. He called the show a party and developed a following among an underserved African American audience.

Then Freed, Mintz, Akron booking agent Lew Platt, and Milton Kulkin (Mintz's brother-in-law and store manager) dreamed up the Moondog Coronation Ball, a 10:00 P.M. to 2:00 A.M. Friday night gala at the Cleveland Arena, for March 21, 1952. Freed, urged on by Mintz, told his listeners to "come down and rock and roll." They did, and the crowd far exceeded the arena's capacity of 11,000. "The result," Cleveland's daily *Plain Dealer* reported, "was a near brawl as thousands of angry ticket

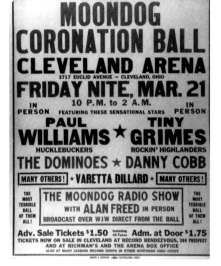

Moondog Coronation Ball poster, March 21, 1952 (Author's collection)

After four executive directors in four years, the search for a permanent director of the Rock and Roll Hall of Fame in 1998 seemed to come to a choice between a heavy-hitting business executive or someone with standing in music and the arts.

They got both with **Terry Stewart**, 52, who earned undergraduate degrees in engineering and education, an MBA, and a law degree; had worked in banking and corporate

mergers and acquisitions; and then became president of Marvel Entertainment Group. He had a personal collection of more than 200,000 records, a storehouse of knowledge, and a conviction that rock and roll was the most impactful art form in the history of mankind.

In 14 years, he smoothed the fractious relationship between Cleveland and the New York board, steered the museum from deep trouble to

financial health, opened the Library & Archives, and—crediting a million-dollar backing commitment from Mayor Frank Jackson—brought induction ceremonies to Cleveland.

Fate brought him to town. A friend called him from Pittsburgh about the job opening, he recalled, after seeing a story about it in the *Wall Street Journal*—the three-star edition. The story wasn't in Stewart's two-star paper in Connecticut.

Record Rendezvous, where rock and roll was born, with owner Leo Mintz on Cleveland's Prospect Avenue (Courtesy of Stuart Mintz)

Cleveland has the distinction of being the place where **Leo Mintz** introduced Alan Freed to the term *rock and roll* and where Freed popularized it on the radio. But there is more to the origin story that is less well known.

Blues singer Trixie Smith made a recording released on the Black Swan label in 1923 that was titled "My Daddy Rocks Me (With One Steady Roll)."

"That's the first record with rock and roll in the title," according to Terry Stewart, longest-tenured CEO of the Rock and Roll Hall of Fame. "The song was so popular it caused those words to become conjoined.

"The first white cover version of that blues record was, of all things, recorded in 1925 by Harold Ortli and His Ohio State Collegians—in downtown Cleveland. It's just remarkable that it happened in this town." He died November 4, 1976, at the age of 65.

holders milled about outside and others demanded admission, breaking down a door in the rush. Police ended the ball at 10:45 P.M., observing the place was so filled that nobody could dance or hear the music."

Eventually, it would be recognized as the first rock-and-roll show. At the time, it was a scandal. But it made Freed front-page news, and he turned it to advantage. Two months later, his Moondog Maytime Ball at the arena went off without incident. More stage shows followed. WJW gave him more airtime.

Rival WSRS hired Buffalo's "Hound Dog," George Lorenz, to compete. "When all the hip black people heard what we were doing on the radio, they went crazy," Lorenz said, years later. "That's where rock and roll as everybody knows it got started."

Something more happened. Leo Mintz saw it at his store, nicknamed "the Voo." "The listening booth in the back of Leo's store was the first around, and he had loudspeakers promoting what was being heard,"

recalled Jay Trattner, who worked for him and became his son-in-law. "He noticed that white kids were starting to buy this 'race music.' And he watched them rock-and-roll down the aisle to the listening booths. That's how [he] described it."

And that's how Freed began to describe it. His audience was growing, and his influence grew with it. Promoters, performers, and producers flocked to him. Cleveland was a breakout market, a place where records were tested and where hits happened first. Freed was at the center.

He took the act to New York and WINS in 1954, bringing the big beat to the nation's biggest market and exploding like a firecracker. In a lawsuit, he lost the Moondog name to a wildly eccentric musician who'd used it first, so he tried unsuccessfully to trademark *rock and roll* and settled for being King of the Rock and Rollers, Mr. Rock and Roll. "Mr. Rock 'n' Roll" eventually became the title of one of the movies—with *Rock Around the Clock; Don't Knock the Rock; Go, Johnny, Go!;* and

Rock, Rock, Rock—in which Freed played himself, surrounded by a who's who of performers.

His star-packed stage shows got bigger, were sensations in New York, and traveled to dozens of cities. CBS Radio syndicated him nationally, and Radio Luxembourg brought him an international audience by airing tapes of his *Rock 'n' Roll Party*. Decades later, Ringo Starr remembered being 17, gathering with friends in Liverpool for the show every Sunday afternoon and hearing Little Richard and Jerry Lee Lewis for the first time. The ABC network gave Freed a weekly TV series, *The Big Beat*.

Freed was the most visible and vocal proponent of rock and roll in the world. But pioneers get the arrows. He became a lightning rod for attacks on music that was dismissed as garbage and condemned for encouraging rebellion, race-mixing, violence, and promiscuity.

His network TV show was canceled after it briefly showed Frankie Lymon dancing with a white girl from the audience, stirring a storm of complaints in the South. Freed was arrested and charged with inciting

Alan Freed's 1952 Cleveland Record Hop
(Courtesy of Stuart Mintz)

to riot after fights broke out outside one of his shows in Boston, which led authorities to cancel concerts in other cities.

Then came the scandal that erupted in 1959 over payola—paying disc jockeys, in money or other considerations, to push records on the air. This practice, then legal in most of the country, was neither new nor confined to rock-and-roll records. But recent scandals over rigged TV quiz shows and an infamously debauched disc jockey convention had put broadcasters in a harsh public spotlight. And suspicion would later linger that the payola disclosures were aimed at the small, independent

WJW poster featuring Alan Freed
(Courtesy of Lance Freed)

record labels that were mainstays of rock and roll and of black artists, which had to struggle for radio exposure.

The US House of Representatives Subcommittee on Legislative Oversight opened hearings. Freed, the unapologetic and even defiant face of rock and roll, insisted he received only consulting fees. But he was the investigation's biggest target and, many would say, the scapegoat and sacrificial lamb. He eventually pleaded guilty to two counts of commercial bribery, received a suspended sentence, and paid a $300 fine.

Rock and roll survived the scandal. Freed was destroyed. Blackballed in New York broadcasting, he tried starting over at smaller stations in Los Angeles and Miami but could not escape the shadow or the scandal. A federal grand jury indicted him for income tax evasion. Broke and broken, all but abandoned but still dreaming of being on top again in New York, he died in Palm Springs, California, on January 20, 1965. He was just 43. The autopsy said the cause of death was massive internal bleeding caused by cirrhosis.

Some said he drank himself to death. His brother David saw it otherwise. He said, "Alan Freed died of a broken heart because they took his microphone away."

He was cremated in Los Angeles. Inga Freed, his widow and third wife, had his ashes interred in Ferncliff Memorial Mausoleum in Hartsdale, New York, because she returned to the city and wanted them nearby.

The ashes remained there until 2002. As Terry Stewart recalled it, "Lance called me and said the kids [Freed's four children] would like to bring Alan home. I thought that would be appropriate. So we started arranging to get him out of the mausoleum."

Stewart first thought of putting the ashes under one of the stones in the plaza outside the Rock Hall, as a sort of symbolic cornerstone. But municipal prohibitions against such an interment, outside the building and not in a cemetery, brought the decision to go inside.

A piece of wall was cut out under the big escalator in the main lobby. After a small religious ceremony, the brushed brass urn was sealed inside. The exact location was not made public, but the marble plaque from the Hartsdale mausoleum, reading "FREED—ALAN 1921–1965," was hung in the lower lobby.

The urn was moved again, a few months later, largely at the instigation of Judith Fisher Freed, Lance's wife and the keeper of Freed's archives, who wanted it to be part of an exhibit.

"At first I was uncomfortable with the idea, really," Lance said. "But I talked to my brother and sisters and Inga and said, 'You know, Dad was a public figure. If you asked, he'd probably get a kick out of it. Dad loved an audience.'"

Stewart said, "We went from putting him in the wall to 'Why don't we put him on display?'" But he wanted to honor the wishes of the

WINS promo photo of Alan Freed
(Courtesy of Lance Freed)

family members, who had been good friends of the Rock Hall. Besides, he said, "I thought it was kind of a rock-and-roll thing to do."

So an alcove was cut on the second floor. After another religious ceremony, the urn was placed inside, behind glass, and under a small light. "You had to go to the guide to know what it was," Stewart said.

"It wasn't ostentatious, it wasn't terrible, it was just a nice touch," Lance said. "Some people just passed by it. Other people stopped and looked. I didn't know at that time whether or not it would stay there forever."

It stayed until 2014, when Greg Harris, who succeeded Stewart as executive director, decided Freed would be better honored in a different setting.

"Museums in general no longer exhibit human remains," Harris explained. "What was happening was that visitors would look at these things, and they wouldn't quite know what they were, and when they figured out what they were, they weren't learning anything about Alan Freed. They were learning his remains were here. They were just on loan to us. We wanted to tell his story a different way."

He called Lance and suggested interment in Cleveland's Lake View Cemetery, a sprawling and verdant park that was the final resting place of such notable Clevelanders as President James A. Garfield, John D. Rockefeller, Eliot Ness, and writer Harvey Pekar.

Initially hurt by the request, the family agreed and then warmed to the idea. Officials at Lake View Cemetery were pleased.

After months of planning, the reinterment was held May 7, 2016. Lance Freed and the family wanted the event to be a celebration of life, with "a little bit of fun." About 400 people—family members, fans, and the curious—watched on the lawn behind the cemetery's Wade Chapel.

Left: Lance Freed at Alan Freed's gravesite, May 7, 2016 (Jim Davison photo)

Right: The Freed family at Alan Freed's gravesite, May 7, 2016. *Left to right:* Colleen and Lance Freed, Alan Freed Jr., and Sieglinde. (Jim Davison photo)

Left: Stevie Van Zandt speaks at the Alan Freed dedication while Norm N. Nite looks on, Lake View Cemetery, May 7, 2016. (James Henke photo. Courtesy of the *Heights Observer*)

Right: Jimmy Clanton at the Alan Freed reinterment, May 7, 2016 (Jim Davison photo)

I served as master of ceremonies, an honor that carried its own significance, and not only because of my long friendship with Lance. I had inducted Alan Freed into the Rock and Roll Hall of Fame with its first class of honorees on January 23, 1986, on the stage of the Waldorf Astoria Hotel alongside legendary disc jockey Scott Muni, who'd worked at Freed's station in Akron, WAKR, before moving to New York. Growing up in Cleveland, I had listened to Freed and knew even then that something special was happening.

Jimmy Clanton, who starred in *Go, Johnny, Go!,* sang his hit "Just a Dream" and remembered Freed bringing him to New York from Louisiana when it was on the charts in 1958. The reconstituted Drifters sang "This Magic Moment," "Stand by Me," and "Smoke Gets in Your Eyes." Hall of Fame songwriter David Porter of Memphis credited Freed for opening the doors that integrated the music industry and made his career possible.

Stevie Van Zandt, Lance's longtime friend who had suggested the design of the memorial stone, was keynote speaker. He noted that Alan Freed was not the first white disc jockey to play black music, "but he was the one who sold it. There was something new he introduced. It was called enthusiasm, and his enthusiasm was colorblind."

"What's important to understand," Van Zandt said, "is that rock and roll was not inevitable. Black music crossing over to the white world in

Left: Alan Freed's headstone, Lake View Cemetery, Cleveland, May 7, 2016 (Jim Toncar photo)

Right: The reverse side of Alan Freed's headstone, flanked by son Lance Freed and rocker Stevie Van Zandt, May 7, 2016 (Amy Feran photo)

a segregated society was not inevitable. I don't believe in inevitability when it comes to history or when it comes to greatness. . . . Rock and roll was not inevitable. Neither was civil rights. It was the obsession of great individuals that caused both of these revolutions to take place. Alan Freed was one of those revolutionaries. He played black records for white kids and changed the world for the better, and our country crucified him for his accomplishments. But he sure got the last laugh. There's some evidence right down the street called the Rock and Roll Hall of Fame."

The event opened in bright sunshine, but a soft spring rain began to fall—"like teardrops," one watcher whispered—as Freed's children spoke.

The youngest, Alan Jr., who was nine when his father died, said his strongest memories of Freed involved his feelings about "how we should treat each other and how the races should get along."

"Rock on, Dad," said daughter Sieglinde, known as Sigie, who wondered "how much more Dad would have been able to accomplish had he lived a long and healthy life."

Lance said, "The fact that we're all here today is living proof that he did carry on." He said that the odyssey of his father's ashes, from

California to New York to the Rock Hall and now Lake View Cemetery, echoed the concert tours that kept him on the road in the 1950s.

"Dad," he said, "what I want to say to you is 'Welcome home. You don't need to travel anymore.'"

Then Lance pulled the cover from a massive, gleaming granite monument in the shape of a jukebox, with Freed and his story on one side and the jukebox etched on the other.

At the Rock Hall, Greg Harris said, "In place of the ashes, we hung his microphone that he used at WINS. Through that microphone, he spoke to hundreds of thousands of teenagers across the country and brought the message of rock and roll. He really changed their lives and all of our lives. We wanted that to be the story and not some ash and bone inside of an urn. We want to tell the story of Alan Freed by his accomplishments and impact. His story will always be told here."

Gone was any idea that the Rock Hall was a place of entombment. "It's intended," Harris said, "to be a living, breathing space that has the DNA of rock and roll."

It could be called the House That Freed Built—though he'd been dead for 20 years when the planning for it started and though building it took as long as Freed's journey from pariah to icon.

The project drew on a groundswell of street-level, can't-stop-rock support from fans that Freed would have recognized. But far from being

Songwriter David Porter, Stevie Van Zandt, and Norm N. Nite at Alan Freed's headstone, Lake View Cemetery, May 7, 2016 (Amy Feran photo)

the work of a kids' crusade, the Rock Hall was built only through the fierce and unflagging efforts of a local establishment that would have looked askance at Mr. Rock and Roll in his day. Some tough politicians, determined businesspeople, and shrewd bureaucrats were the improbable true believers who got it done.

Behind the scenes there were gambles, bluffs, battles, and betrayals. Call it rock and roll. It's the House That Freed Built. It rocks on.

CHAPTER 1

"Wouldn't It Be Nice"

—THE BEACH BOYS

Lesley Gore was 17 years old in 1963, the last summer before Beatlemania and the British Invasion, when her sweetly defiant "It's My Party" rocketed to number one and made her America's most famous teenager. A year later, after three more top 10 hits, she was a headliner with one of the longest sets in the legendary *T.A.M.I. Show,* a who's who of pop music that featured the Rolling Stones, the Supremes, James Brown, the Beach Boys, Jan and Dean, Smokey Robinson and the Miracles, and Marvin Gaye, among others.

She attended college, kept recording and performing, and, as Catwoman's sidekick Pussycat, even introduced her song "California Nights" on an episode of ABC's *Batman* in 1967.

It was to be Lesley's last top 20 record. After five years, the hits stopped coming. It happened to a lot of artists. By 1983, at age 37, she was a nostalgia act, the answer to a trivia question, but still a talented and ambitious dynamo writing songs and performing. She was a wonderful person.

We had been friends for many years. We first met on the nationally syndicated *Mike Douglas Show* in January 1968, during a week when Bobby Darin was the cohost, when the topic was the roots of rock and roll.

Early rock and roll was my passion. It had been the world-changing, mood-making soundtrack of my life growing up in Cleveland's Tremont neighborhood, which was the uncredited setting for the movie *A Christmas Story*. I built a huge record collection and listened to guys on the radio like Alan Freed, Tommy Edwards, Bill Randle, Jockey John Slade, and Pete "Mad Daddy" Myers. When I got to Ohio University, I switched my major from business to broadcasting, went on the air at the campus station, and produced a tape-recorded thesis that I later expanded into a narrative album, *Rock and Roll—Evolution or Revolution?*

The album, issued on Laurie Records in 1967, was the first recorded history of rock and roll. To make it, I had to track down 41 artists whose songs I sampled for interviews and permissions, from the Crows—whose "Gee" charted in 1954—to the Music Explosion—whose "Little

Bit O' Soul" went gold in 1967. Some of the artists were still performing. Others worked in various trades. About a dozen were penniless.

That's rock and roll. When the album put me on *The Mike Douglas Show*, I was fresh out of the army and selling cars. But the passion for music soon put me on Cleveland's WHK and WGAR with my *Nite Train* oldies show and then in 1973 brought me to WCBS-FM in New York. My research for the album would later become the foundation for my *Rock On* encyclopedia series of books and for the one-hour radio specials I called "rockumentaries."

Moving from Cleveland to New York put me closer to a lot of the performers I'd come to know. Many became regular listeners and guests. Lesley was a favorite. I would call her up to put her on my show, and we both enjoyed it. Jay Black, of Jay and the Americans, once kidded me on the air by loudly demanding that I tell him Lesley's shoe size. I was known as "Mr. Music" by then, and I reinforced my reputation as a serious historian on rock when the first *Rock On* book came out in 1974.

When Lesley called me out of the clear blue sky on August 2, 1983, she said, "Listen, some people are talking about doing a Rock and Roll

The Mike Douglas Show, January 22, 1968. *Left to right:* Ellie Frankel, Mike Douglas, Norm. N. Nite, Bobby Darin, Lesley Gore, and Guy Marks. (Author's collection)

Hall of Fame, and we're going to have a meeting, and because you're a music authority we'd like you to be at that meeting."

I agreed to go. The meeting, on August 10, was in a loft apartment on East 28th Street in Manhattan. Lesley wasn't there. I looked around and saw someone from Radio City, someone from *Billboard,* and a guy who was a singer with the Dovells. They had big ideas, but they were lightweights in the music industry.

There was also a smart young lawyer named Suzan Evans, who was involved with a group called the Black Tie Network. She said she was there so we could put together something called "The Rock and Roll Hall of Fame with the Black Tie Network" for a TV special on its induction ceremonies. It would be comparable to Dick Clark's American Music Awards shows.

We had several other meetings, and then I decided not to go to any more because I didn't think anything was going to happen, not sitting around talking with this group. My impression was that there was no one who was a mover and shaker. I was not going to be involved.

Suzan didn't come after the first meeting. I told her afterward that I thought the other people were lightweights and that it seemed nothing was going to happen. I wondered if she was sounding me out and had reached the same conclusion. She didn't tell me anything else was going on.

Unbeknownst to me, it was.

⚜ ⚜ ⚜

Alan Freed would go on to wider fame, but it was his Cleveland contemporary **Bill Randle** whom *Time* magazine proclaimed America's "top jock" disc jockey in 1955. As cool as Freed was hot, he came to Cleveland's WERE in 1949 from his native Detroit. He demonstrated an uncanny ability to pick hits and new artists—*Time* said he did it better than anyone else in the country—and pioneered music research, making Cleveland the era's "breakout" market for new records. He had an incredible 54 percent share of the radio audience tuned to his daily show on WERE by the mid-1950s, and he commuted on weekends to a show on WCBS in New York.

He booked and emceed Elvis Presley's first appearance in a pop music show in suburban Brooklyn, Ohio, and helped launch and build the careers of Elvis, Tony Bennett, Johnnie Ray, Sam Cooke, Fats Domino, the Diamonds, the Crew-Cuts, Bobby Darin, and Rosemary Clooney, among others. It was Randle who introduced Elvis on his first national TV appearance in 1956 and whom Ralph Kramden and Ed Norton wanted to play the song they'd written on an episode of *The Honeymooners.*

A high school dropout who earned eight degrees, wrote books, worked as a lawyer and college professor, raced cars, and flew planes, he walked away from radio in 1961 and said he went back to WCBS a year later for fun "and for money" while teaching at Columbia. He returned to Cleveland and WERE in 1965. He told *Billboard,* "Somebody said, 'Why are you leaving the Big Time?' I said, 'Cleveland is the Big Time. There've been only three or four personalities who've really had impact in the nation and none of them have been from New York.'"

He died in Cleveland at 81 in July 2004.

As she explained it later, the woman who would become Suzan Evans Hochberg was a New Yorker who got into the entertainment business because she was miserable practicing law. A graduate of Boston University and Brooklyn Law School, she had been working in the profession for about 18 months when she had dinner with a friend, a woman who was also an attorney, and said she was thinking of taking time off to consider another direction.

It was a fortuitous conversation. The friend represented the Black Tie Network, a television production company interested in building a pay-per-view business, and represented an independent producer, Bruce Brandwen. He had the idea of creating an entity called the Rock and Roll Hall of Fame, so he could use it to produce an awards ceremony and concert for pay-per-view television.

Suzan recalled, "He needed somebody to make it happen. One of the people who worked with him on his team was a cousin of Lesley Gore. He had talked her into using her name as a proponent of this Rock and Roll Hall of Fame. And he also retained a lawyer from Los Angeles who was well known in the music industry, David Braun.

"It sounded like an interesting idea and a challenging project," she said. So Evans quit her job, left the law, became executive director at a sizable pay cut, moved into an office with Black Tie, and did the legal work of incorporating the company. The group next planned to form a board of directors and a nominating committee, come up with rules for nomination, "and figure out a way to give it some gravitas," she said. "This was all an idea so there would be an entity called the Rock and Roll Hall of Fame and this producer could produce a concert for pay-per-view."

Braun introduced them to leaders in the music industry to pitch the concept. One of these was Ahmet Ertegun, with whom Evans would meet many times, trying to convince him that he should be chairman of this Hall of Fame.

Ertegun was an inspired and ambitious choice. The cofounder and president of Atlantic Records, he had been a producer and songwriter whose eclectic taste and ear for talent had helped shape American pop music since the 1950s. His mastery of relationships, in a business built on them, created the presence that had led the *New Yorker* to call him "the Greatest Rock-and-Roll Mogul in the World."

Respected even by rivals, he was almost invariably described as royalty in the music industry, and with good reason. Born in Turkey of aristocratic heritage, at age 12 he moved with his family to Washington, DC, when his father, Munir, was appointed ambassador to the United States for the Turkish Republic. (They lived in a mansion, later to become the Turkish embassy, that was built during the Gilded Age by a millionaire businessman from Cleveland, Edward Hamlin Everett.)

AHMET ERTEGUN WAS ALMOST INVARIABLY DESCRIBED AS ROYALTY IN THE MUSIC INDUSTRY.

In the often dodgy record business, **Ahmet Ertegun** was literally like royalty. Born in Turkey to an aristocratic family, he had developed his taste for jazz and rhythm and blues in Washington, DC, where he moved at age 12 when his father was named ambassador to the United States.

He cofounded Atlantic Records, building it to the nation's premier R&B label while producing or coproducing most of its releases. After he was approached to join the advisory board of the Rock and Roll Hall of Fame pay-per-view event, Suzan Evans Hochberg recalled that he said, "If it's going to be a nonprofit, it should be nonprofit and not an excuse to produce a television show."

Ertegun recruited a group of industry leaders and established the Rock and Roll Hall of Fame Foundation with himself as chairman. The memory of his early years plugging records on the road would open him to hearing Cleveland's bid to establish a significant bricks-and-mortar structure, and his interest in Turkish politics would reinforce it.

He was inducted into the Hall of Fame in 1987, and the museum's main exhibition hall was named for him in 1995. He died in 2006 at age 83.

Washington helped nurture Ahmet's lifelong interest in politics and policy, especially involving Turkey. He and his older brother, Nesuhi, explored the segregated city's neighborhoods, becoming devoted regulars in its jazz clubs and record stores. Their father opened the embassy to African American musicians they invited to brunches. The brothers staged jazz concerts, growing in the passion that led them both to the record business.

Cultivated, complex, impeccably dressed, and gentlemanly, Ertegun was, as biographer Robert Greenfield described him, "a creature of his own creation."

Now he was interested in the Rock and Roll Hall of Fame.

"He kept requesting to meet with me to talk about it and throw ideas around," Suzan recalled. "He called one day and said, 'I think I'll be very interested to do this and become chairman and grow this thing. But if this is going to be an institution which is going to be respected by artists and by the industry, and if I'm going to donate my time and do this as a charity, I just don't like the idea that the reason for this institution is so that some producer could produce a TV show and make money from it. It doesn't sit right with me. If it's going to be a nonprofit, it should be nonprofit and not an excuse to produce a television show.' So with that, he and I kept meeting. He kept saying, 'It's going to be a respected institution, we have to have the music industry participate, and these are the people I think we should approach to be on the board and on the nominating committee.'

"Ahmet put together a board made up of leaders in the music industry. He said, 'We need to have that kid who runs Sire Records.' He gave me the kid's name and numbers." She laughed at the memory. The kid was Seymour Stein, who was becoming a legend for putting Sire at the vanguard of new wave rock.

"I walked into Seymour Stein's office," Suzan said, "and there was Madonna on the telephone in her black bra. This is 1983. I saw 'the kid,'

Seymour, sitting behind his desk, and at that time he was probably 41 years old. To Ahmet, who was almost 60, he was a kid."

"Ahmet called me, and I was very excited," Stein said. "Ahmet was one of my heroes. I knew him fairly well, but this would really bring us very, very close together."

They also reached out to Allen Grubman, who was considered the most important entertainment lawyer in the music industry. His clients and contacts ran deep among both talent and record labels.

And Ertegun called Jann Wenner, enormously influential in music, journalism, and pop culture as the cofounder, publisher, and editor in chief of *Rolling Stone*. Wenner was intrigued, and he recalled agreeing "that there should be a rock and roll hall of fame—but not with these people [Black Tie] and not just as an adjunct to a TV show. I thought it had to be a true hall of fame, as opposed to a television show. It had to be nonprofit and be respectful of music."

Ertegun invited the group to lunch at Pearl's Chinese restaurant near Times Square. "Ahmet was the visionary," Grubman said. "Jann had *Rolling Stone* magazine. Seymour ran Sire Records. I was the business/ legal head. Suzan basically was the administratrix of the whole thing. And it was the four or five of us meeting and talking about the fact that there's a Baseball Hall of Fame, and there's an Academy Awards, there's all these halls of fame, but there's no hall of fame for rock and roll. It was created at Pearl's restaurant."

On April 30, 1983, they established the Rock and Roll Hall of Fame Foundation.

"We wanted to let the industry know what we were doing and try to get them excited," Grubman said. "I had relationships with all the record companies, but so did everybody else—everybody else being those four people."

"It became a labor of love for them all," Evans said. "With Allen Grubman, we approached heads of all the major record labels and put together a pretty prestigious board of directors."

Ertegun gave the new organization office space in Atlantic Records and said Atlantic would underwrite initial expenses. Evans, who moved into an office two doors from his, said she was never on the Atlantic payroll, because each of the major labels agreed to pay annual dues, "which was just seed money for the institution."

The group grew, adding Bob Krasnow, who had just taken over as chairman of Elektra Records; Jon Landau, the former *Rolling Stone* rock critic who produced and managed Bruce Springsteen; and Noreen Woods, vice president and executive assistant to Ertegun at Atlantic.

"Ahmet used to joke it was like a *Saturday Night Live* show," Evans said, "because all of these guys had a lot of laughs while we were creating this, creating the rules."

The cover of **Seymour Stein**'s autobiography, *Siren Song: My Life in Music,* calls him "America's greatest living record man." It's often said he has the best ears in the business, and he knew at a young age how he wanted to use them. A native of Brooklyn, New York, he was still in high school when he spent a couple of summers interning at King Records in Cincinnati, where storied old-school label owner Syd Nathan became a mentor.

Stein cofounded and led the legendary Sire Records and, he notes, is "the man who signed the Ramones, Talking Heads, Madonna, the Pretenders, the Dead Boys, the Replacements, Ice-T, Brian Wilson, k.d. lang, Lou Reed, Throwing Muses, and many more."

One of the first people Ahmet Ertegun reached out to in 1983 to form the Rock and Roll Hall of Fame Foundation, he became one of the most important people in the Rock Hall's history. He was inducted into the Rock and Roll Hall of Fame in 2005, in the lifetime achievement category.

I got involved again after getting a letter from Seymour Stein and a call from Suzan Evans in January 1984, inviting me to join the new nominating and rules committee. If I had any doubts about what I was getting into, they were erased at the first meeting, on July 16, in the boardroom of Atlantic Records in Rockefeller Plaza. I saw who was at the table and knew this was really going to be something. These were special individuals. I knew somehow, some way, with these people something was going to happen.

Ertegun's "*Saturday Night Live* show" continued as we got together in 1984 and 1985. The meetings lasted an hour or two and always started with stories about the old days; then we got to discussing the first Rock and Roll Hall of Fame induction: who was eligible for induction, what the criteria would be, who we would nominate, how many would be inducted each year—and where would we have an induction ceremony and who would be part of it. It was in late 1985 that we decided to hold it Thursday, January 23, 1986, at the Waldorf Astoria.

"At that point we hadn't even thought too much about where the Hall of Fame building would be," Evans said. "I guess in the back of our minds we envisioned buying a small townhouse someplace in New York and having a physical presence there."

"Possibly we would buy a brownstone," Stein said. "We were dreaming about it. That was the height of our expectations at that time."

When the subject of a building came up, limitations were accepted. The group realized you couldn't just acquire and tear up 10 blocks of real estate in Manhattan. It came down to, "So let's get together and have a party once a year, and maybe we can hang plaques up in a hallway in this little building."

CHAPTER 2

"This Magic Moment"

—THE DRIFTERS

Ahmet Ertegun and his board had named it and claimed it by establishing the Rock and Roll Hall of Fame Foundation. They had the power and prestige to make something happen with what they'd created. But if rock and roll is like a river, fed and deepened by streams and tributaries, the same could also be said for its Hall of Fame. Despite the Black Tie Network's claim of authorship, the idea of a rock and roll hall of fame wasn't new or even especially novel.

Before I. M. Pei or Ahmet Ertegun or anyone in a New York boardroom thought about a Rock and Roll Hall of Fame, **Henry J. "Hank" LoConti Sr.** had the architectural plans for one on the West Bank of the Cuyahoga River in Cleveland's Flats. The year was 1978, and LoConti was thinking about a bigger new home—with more parking and what he called a Rock and Roll Hall of Fame—for the Agora, the legendary concert club he founded in 1966.

Visionary LoConti was one of the principal people behind Cleveland's reputation as a rock-and-roll city. The Agora at its peak hosted more than 200 shows a year, and it helped launch the careers of Bruce Springsteen, U2, Todd Rundgren, ZZ Top, Joan Jett, Pat Benatar, and Kiss, among others. He built a recording studio, created a record label, and produced local and national broadcast series, including *Coffee Break Concert* and *Live from the Agora*. *The Agora, Cleveland 1978,* a live album by Springsteen and the E Street Band, was called their greatest live LP by *Rolling Stone*. LoConti would open 11 clubs in all as far away as Texas, plus one later in St. Petersburg, Russia.

He changed his plans and was considering buying the huge Cleveland Masonic Auditorium for a hall of fame and performance venue by 1982. When he was told of New York's plans, in spring 1984, he set up the meeting at which Norm N. Nite was asked to intercede for Cleveland.

LoConti, who never lost his interest in breaking new music, died at 85 in July 2014.

By the 1980s, the music was 30 years old, old enough to have a recognized history, mythology, and icons. Graceland, Elvis Presley's Memphis home, opened to the public in 1982, immediately drawing fans on visits that sometimes resembled reverent pilgrimages. In Detroit, Motown's Hitsville U.S.A. facility began opening to visitors, and by 1985 it would become the Motown Museum. In Los Angeles, there was talk of a Grammy museum. In San Francisco, rock promoter Bill Graham was talking about opening a shrine to rock and roll.

In Cleveland, my friend Hank LoConti, an impresario and owner of the Agora, had talked since the 1970s about relocating his concert club to the city's funky Flats district, in a complex with what he called a Rock and Roll Hall of Fame. He showed me the architectural plans he had drawn up.

I had raised the idea of a hall of fame on WCBS-FM, after doing a show in March 1982 celebrating the 30th anniversary of the Moondog Coronation Ball. The response was so enthusiastic that several promoters talked with me about doing a concert at Radio City Music Hall in support of a hall of fame. I even put together a proposal for the show, with a producer from NBC and an attorney from CBS, pitched it to CBS-FM, and discussed it a few weeks later with Dick Clark, who gave it his blessing. Hank and I talked about it when I was visiting Cleveland in the summer of 1982. By that time, he was considering buying the landmark Cleveland Masonic Auditorium for a rock hall. Miami Steve Van Zandt, who was in town playing the Agora, loved the idea and wanted to get involved. Ultimately, however, nothing came of it. Anybody can have an idea, but putting the pieces together takes sustained commitment and work. It takes time. People are busy with other things.

Then, in the spring of 1985, Eddie Spizel returned to Cleveland. Edgar S. Spizel, 62, was an advertising and public relations consultant who generated ideas and made commercials at such a breakneck pace he once was called "the closest thing to a perpetual motion machine the city has yet produced." He had left Cleveland in 1974 for San Francisco, where he built a successful ad agency.

When he heard about Bill Graham's plans to build a hall of fame there, however, his reaction was close to outrage. Cleveland was Spizel's hometown, and he knew it as the place where rock began to roll.

Sounding a bit like he was first to come up with the idea, he proposed that Cleveland strike first. Still well connected and well regarded in Cleveland's business community, Spizel made his pitch to friends in the media, winning a full-page interview in the weekly *Crain's Cleveland Business* and then a couple of short articles in the entertainment pages of the *Plain Dealer*.

Spizel said Cleveland needed a new sense of identity, with "something for tourists to see." He imagined a hall of fame as something like a gallery, in the office building that once housed Alan Freed's WJW radio studio. Spizel, whose promotional clients had included the Super Bowl, also envisioned a week of concerts and parties leading to a national TV show on which inductees would be announced, after a popular vote on nominations from the music industry. He told *Crain's* he would talk with "all the movers and shakers who can make it happen."

The story became a call to action.

At WMMS, one of the country's leading rock stations and an immense presence in Cleveland, operations manager and programmer John Gorman set up a staff meeting with Spizel on the day the *Crain's* story appeared. The station had been talking for years about starting a hall of fame, and the idea it could happen first in San Francisco rubbed the staff the wrong way. As Gorman recalled it in his radio memoir, *The Buzzard,* Spizel "made an impassioned pitch from the heart: Cleveland needed to beat Graham to the punch." WMMS, which had been breaking new acts and music nationally for more than a decade, took up the cause. Gorman and his staff started making phone calls to find support.

Spizel's hall of fame idea was also noticed at the Greater Cleveland Growth Association and Chamber of Commerce. Michael Benz, its young executive vice president, "saw this story and said 'Whoa!'" he recalled later. "I thought a hall of fame could be an economic development engine. If we put some people together, get some people behind it, this could be a big deal."

Benz went to Bill Bryant, his boss at the Growth Association. "Bill said, 'No problem, if you want to go do this thing. But don't spend a lot of money.'"

Benz reached out to the station manager of WMMS, Bill Smith, a media acquaintance who invited him to a meeting about the effort there.

WMMS HAD BEEN BREAKING NEW ACTS AND MUSIC NATIONALLY FOR MORE THAN A DECADE

He and the station also contacted Tim LaRose, president of the House of LaRose, the area's Budweiser distributor. The company sponsored numerous local concerts and events, and it advertised and staged promotions with radio stations. LaRose was one of the hippest and most plugged-in businesspeople in town. "No problem," he said. "I'm in. Let's do it." He started making his own calls to lobby for a hall of fame.

In Columbus, Ohio, Governor Dick Celeste got a call in his office from his 14-year-old daughter, Noelle. "She said, 'Dad, what are you going to do about this rock-and-roll museum?' I said, 'What rock-and-roll museum?' She said there was a story in the paper that a group of music executives want to build a museum and hall of fame for rock and roll, and it should be in Cleveland. I said, 'Why?' She said, 'Because the phrase *rock and roll* was coined in Cleveland. Alan Freed was a disc jockey there.'

"When I got home for dinner that night, we had this conversation," Celeste recalled. "She was saying, 'You know this belongs in Cleveland.' I called Al Dietzel, who was my head of economic development, and said, 'Al, we need to make a pitch for this Rock and Roll Hall of Fame for Cleveland. I want you to set aside $5 million for a potential site.' That's how it began."

There was just one problem. John Gorman might have discovered it first. Sounding out friends in the music industry to see what support he could rally for a hall of fame, he called Tunc Erim, Atlantic's vice president in charge of artist development, who had strong relationships with rock radio and was close to Ahmet Ertegun.

As Gorman recounted in *The Buzzard,* Erim said, "It's funny you bring this up, because Ahmet is starting a rock and roll hall of fame."

Hank LoConti confirmed the story—and, because of Ertegun's clout and head start, said he doubted Cleveland had a chance. But Hank knew I was involved with Ertegun's group in New York. He told Mike Benz at the Growth Association, and then called to ask me to come to Cleveland to talk. I flew in for a meeting at the Growth Association

In the days before big promoters took over the business, individuals would invest in concerts, sometimes teaming up with disc jockeys for promotional purposes. **K. Michael "Mike" Benz** was a junior at Wickliffe High School outside Cleveland when the owner of the nearby Dari-Pride shop told his father he was bringing the Beach Boys to town for an afternoon show over Thanksgiving weekend and could use some help setting up chairs at the arena.

"He said, 'I'll make sure he gets to meet the Beach Boys,'" Benz recalled. "I'll never forget it." He brought his father's big Wollensak to tape-record the meeting, and he played it back in choir class. "That's how I got an A in that course."

Some of the same excitement hit him, 20 years later, when he was executive vice president of the Greater Cleveland Growth Association and saw a newspaper interview proposing a Rock and Roll Hall of Fame. "I

thought a hall of fame could be an economic development engine. If we put some people together, get some people behind it, this could be a big deal. . . . It's like putting a band together."

Benz led the effort that brought the Rock and Roll Hall of Fame and Museum to Cleveland. Six years later, with nothing built, he was strong-armed unhappily into returning, this time as executive director, "to try to bring it from third base to home."

offices with Benz, LoConti, Bill Bryant, Bill Smith, and Jules Belkin, the Cleveland-based music promoter whose credits included staging the massive World Series of Rock concerts with WMMS at Cleveland Stadium in the 1970s. Yes, I told them, what they had heard about New York and the Hall of Fame was true.

"They're moving along with this thing," I said. "They've been working on it a few years, and I've been working on the advisory committee.

"But maybe," I said, "we can get you guys introduced to the guys in New York."

New York was still focused mainly on hall of fame nominations and inductions, things that would support a TV special. The Cleveland group was thinking about something more. Its members asked if I'd consider doing a pitch to get them an audience with New York.

Cleveland is my hometown. I said I'd try.

It was just before Memorial Day in May 1985. I flew back to New York, called Ahmet when I landed at LaGuardia Airport, and asked if I could see him. I went to his office the next day and said, "I just came back from Cleveland, and there's a group of people who are interested in building the Rock and Roll Hall of Fame there. Would you consider Cleveland as a site?"

No, he said emphatically. "Absolutely not, because we're committed. Mayor Koch has given us a location on 42nd Street, and when we get this thing under way we're going to put it here in New York."

That was the magic moment. Had I gotten up and shaken his hand and said thank you and walked out the door, the Rock and Roll Hall of Fame might be on 42nd Street, in a four-story brownstone, a place with some plaques and records on the wall.

Something clicked. With nothing to lose, I stood up and gave Ahmet my pitch. Consider, I told him, the fact that Cleveland is a neutral city—it doesn't have a sound it's identified with, like New Orleans, Memphis, Philadelphia, or the West Coast. Consider the fact that it's centrally located between New York and Chicago, meaning it would be a lot cheaper and easier for visitors to get to. Consider the fact that it would be just another building in New York, but a prime attraction in Cleveland. Consider that with the cost of real estate in New York, you could never duplicate in Manhattan what you could do in Cleveland.

And I asked Ahmet to consider that Alan Freed did the first rock-and-roll show in Cleveland on March 21, 1952. That seemed to turn on a light with him. He had known Freed. He had done a lot of business with Freed and Leo Mintz. He knew how important Freed was to the birth of rock and roll.

I went on for six or seven minutes. I threw a lot of things at him, and maybe one of them got his attention. He smiled in concession and called out to Suzan Evans in the outer office, "When is our next meeting?"

Ohio governor **Richard "Dick" Celeste** in 1985 was an energetic Yale graduate and Rhodes scholar from Cleveland who had assembled the most diverse and youthful cabinet the state had ever seen. But he learned about the Rock and Roll Hall of Fame from his 14-year-old daughter, who had seen a newspaper story about the idea. "She said, 'Dad, what are you going to do about this rock-and-roll museum?' I said, 'What rock-and-roll museum?'"

He immediately agreed it was something that belonged in Cleveland, instructed his economic development director to get behind it, and became intimately involved in the effort—talking frequently with Jann Wenner, whom he knew socially, and even flying back to Cleveland from an official trip to Asia to join a lunch meeting with members of the New York Rock and Roll Hall of Fame Foundation.

Celeste's involvement diminished only after he left office in 1991, because he was limited by law to two four-year terms.

It was his children who convinced Cleveland mayor **George Voinovich** to support the city's bid to build the Rock and Roll Hall of Fame in 1985, telling him, "You're going to have something no other city has."

Voinovich was an unpretentious opera lover who was so "fiscally prudent" that he once famously picked a coin out of a urinal, but he quickly came to believe in the project for his city. He built a public-private partnership to make it happen. He won the respect and ultimately the affection of the Rock Hall's New York board. His support—enthusiastic, unwavering, and, on occasion, fierce—continued after he became Ohio governor in 1991. He was Ohio's senior US senator by 2010, the Rock Hall's 15th anniversary, when its main atrium was named the George V. Voinovich Atrium in recognition of his efforts.

He died in his sleep at his home in Cleveland in June 2016 at age 79.

She said it was July 18. He said, "Put down Norman's name, because he wants to bring in some people."

I went back to Cleveland, met with the committee, and said, "I got your foot in the door—you've got to take it from here."

"We can't," they said. "We don't know these people. You've got to work with us." They made me an official member of their group. For the next two months, I flew back every week to guide them through questions about the individuals on the Hall of Fame committee, what they were looking for, what they hoped to achieve.

Benz, chairman of what would become the Hall of Fame Committee, reached out to Steve Zamborsky, a partner in the consulting firm Laventhol & Horwath, who developed business plans for the leisure industry.

"We always had an agenda." said Benz. "We started strategizing. What are we going to say? How much time are we going to have? We came out of each meeting knowing what we wanted to accomplish. Most things that get done in Greater Cleveland, it's like putting a band together. It's not one person or organization or company, it's a group. And this was a public-private partnership, which was very prominent at that moment, because George Voinovich was mayor."

George Voinovich seemed an unlikely champion for a rock and roll hall of fame. Elected mayor in 1979, after more than 15 years in public office and not long after Cleveland became the first big city since the Depression to default on its bank loans, he was a fiscally prudent—or penny-pinching, some would joke—moderate Republican who worked hard and successfully to right the city's finances and boost its image.

Utterly unpretentious, tough-minded but compassionate, he was a devout Catholic and devoted family man. Joe Eszterhas, the Hollywood screenwriter who grew up in Cleveland, described him as "a sensitive and caring man who viewed his stewardship of the state in the manner of secular priest," and added, "if there was one honest politician left in America, he was it."

Voinovich initially dismissed the idea of building a rock hall, especially with the help of public money. He credited his children—George, Betsy, and Peter—for convincing him it would be a "significant prize" for Cleveland. Once on board, he became a tenacious backer whose support was invaluable and unwavering. He brought credibility and respectability to the effort, and he opened doors.

He joined a committee being assembled by Benz whose seriousness was shown by the people who joined it. One was Richard Kelso, the president and chairman of the East Ohio Gas Company, a community leader who sat on numerous local boards and moved easily between the worlds of business and nonprofits. Dick Kelso became a dedicated and vital partner.

Another was Milton Maltz, the founder and head of Malrite Communications, owner of WMMS. Maltz went on to make a larger mark as a philanthropist, but his business interests made him especially important to the Rock Hall campaign. Two years earlier, in 1983, he had bought a weak and low-rated easy-listening FM station in New Jersey, moved its transmitter to the Empire State Building, and changed its format to Top 40 rock. As contemporary-hit Z-100, WHTZ rocketed from worst to first in the New York ratings in a mere three months. In the record business as well as radio, Maltz was a force to be reckoned with.

Benz and Zamborsky enlisted the support of leaders of Cleveland's arts community and cultural institutions. The committee started brainstorming, coming up with potential sites that could be donated, talking about financing and fundraising, and developing a concept for the Hall of Fame.

We believed New York's focus on the nomination process and induction ceremony gave us an opportunity to do something more. We were proposing a true museum for an American art form, with a legitimate educational component, something I thought would be important to the New York committee.

We compared our conception to the Pro Football Hall of Fame in Canton, an hour's drive south of Cleveland. We thought the comparison helped our case. Why, after all, was professional football's shrine located in Canton? Because it's where the NFL was founded. And why, for that matter, was the National Baseball Hall of Fame in tiny, out-of-the-way Cooperstown, New York? Because of the claim, however apocryphal, that Abner Doubleday invented the game there.

Origin stories are important. The ghost of Alan Freed seemed to grow.

Cleveland's presentation began coming together. Its centerpiece would be a video. "We knew we couldn't have a typical chamber of commerce tape," Benz said. "It had to be so impactful it would blow them away." He enlisted local public relations and advertising executive Bill Wendling to produce it.

Wendling got Ernie Anderson to do the voiceover. Reputedly the highest-paid announcer in the world, Anderson was the main promotional voice of ABC-TV, famous and often imitated for his deep, rich intonation of "The Lo-o-ove Boat." In Cleveland, however, he rated as a legitimate icon for his run on TV in the 1960s as Ghoulardi, an irreverent and spectacularly popular horror movie host. He agreed to do the work for the Rock Hall committee as a favor.

Cleveland-based American Greetings, one of the world's largest greeting card producers and the company behind characters including the Care Bears and Strawberry Shortcake, came up with the characters Rollie and the Rockers for the video and designed the cover for a presentation book.

Amazingly, the work was all done quietly, without publicity. "We swore everyone to silence," Benz said, remembering how Tim LaRose had dismissed him from one meeting to speak privately to a group from several radio stations. "Timmy said, 'I'll pull ad money from your station if you break the code on this.' We didn't want this out there. We wanted it very under the table.

"There was no competition. We figured we'll just steal into town, and we'll be so good we'll steal it."

They left nothing to chance. Benz and Zamborsky set the order in which committee members would speak during their presentation. Zamborsky wrote their talks and oversaw a rehearsal.

The Cleveland committee flew to New York on July 18, 1985. We—the members of the New York committee—were upstairs at 75 Rockefeller Plaza, in the boardroom of Atlantic Records, ready to have our meeting at 3:30 in the afternoon.

What happened with the meetings we had was that they were usually two-hour gatherings about 80 percent filled with good-old-boy stories. "Remember with the payola?" "Remember when Chess had Muddy Waters painting his house?" "Remember when we had this guy working for us?" It was a lot of fun, it was great, but it had nothing to do with the Hall of Fame. Then, in the last 15 minutes, when everyone was looking at their watches, they'd say, "OK, let's wrap it up."

When we were informed the Cleveland group members were downstairs, ready to have their meeting, Ahmet said, "Well, look, tell them to wait. And when we're done, they can come up."

Wow, I said to myself, they'll be dead in the water then. They need at least 45 minutes. They've got a video presentation. I said to Ahmet, "Listen, consider the fact they're here—bring them upstairs, let's get them up here, give them a chance to say what they have to say."

They came up and walked in. The two groups didn't know each other. It was the very first meeting of both cities. As the unofficial liaison, I had to make introductions.

The New York group included Ahmet Ertegun, Seymour Stein, Jann Wenner, Suzan Evans, Atlantic Records vice president Noreen Woods, Elektra/Asylum chairman Bob Krasnow, MTV programmer and former Atlantic executive Les Garland, CBS Records executive Bob Altshuler, record producer John Hammond, and me. The Cleveland group was Mayor George Voinovich, Jules Belkin, Dick Kelso, Bill Bryant, Bill Smith, Malrite Communications president Carl Hirsch, Greater Cleveland Convention and Visitors Bureau president Dale Finley, New Cleveland Campaign executive director George Miller, and Benz.

Suzan Evans recalled the meeting with a smile. "In 1985," she said, "Ahmet was the only person who wore a suit every day. Here were ten people from Cleveland walking in, all in suits, like aliens."

Mike Benz handed out folders with copies of the presentation booklet. The group got down to business with a brief explanation of its proposal, then played the video.

Ernie Anderson's commanding, growling voice filled the room: "Let me tell you about rock and roll." Then Alan Freed's voice, from "Rock Around the Clock," and ending with Starship's "We Built This City."

Ahmet, sitting with his back to the screen, spun in his chair and watched.

"We wanted to convince them to come to Cleveland and get them on our turf," Benz said. "We wanted to fuzz up their thinking."

The Clevelanders made it clear they weren't thinking about a tourist trap designed to sell memorabilia. Nor were they proposing an institution that would be, as Benz put it, "so legitimate that nobody would go to it, something to justify this art form that didn't need justification. Rock and roll is life. It's a language. It's what's going on. It's what you're living right now."

"In Cleveland," we said, "we can make it a big deal. In New York it wouldn't be a big deal. It would get lost. We promise it will be one of the biggest deals."

They were so effective that Ahmet stood up and applauded when the presentation ended.

"At that point, we hadn't even thought too much about where the hall of fame building would be," Suzan Evans said. "I guess in the back of our minds we envisioned buying a small townhouse someplace in New York and having a physical presence there. And they made that initial presentation, which was something like $25 million that they would raise if we would agree to build the museum in Cleveland. We were blown away.

"Noreen passed me a note: 'Pack your bags, you're going to Cleveland.'"

Noreen Woods, Ahmet's right hand, knew how to read the room, or at least her boss. The committee agreed to come to Cleveland. Benz said the Cleveland group would arrange transportation.

"Oh crap," he said to himself. "They're coming to Cleveland. Now what'll we do?"

"IN CLEVELAND,"
WE SAID, "WE
CAN MAKE IT A
BIG DEAL"

CHAPTER 3

"Searchin'"

—THE COASTERS

Now what? It was a good question. Cleveland had invited New York to the ball. New York had accepted. Now Cleveland had to put on the ball.

I thought my work was done. It was only beginning. I was in touch constantly with Seymour Stein and other board members and flew back to Cleveland almost weekly to meet with Mike Benz, discussing where the hall might go, what it would look like, what it might cost, and where to get the money.

"We had to get land donated, public land from the state or city or from private sources," Benz said. His committee got the

Ostendorf-Morris real estate brokerage to approach the developer Forest City Realty and assemble a list of 18 different parcels as possible sites. Those sites would be part of the itinerary for the board's visit. It would help demonstrate, Benz said, that "we can make it a big deal, that in Cleveland it will be one of the biggest deals.

"We wanted to wine them and dine them. We wanted them to be impressed from the moment they hit the ground until the moment they left."

Almost by accident, the plan to do it all quietly went crashing down.

In New York, our priority on the nominating committee was the Hall of Fame inductions—who would be eligible, what were the parameters, how many inductees should there be—and we were moving forward.

In August 1985, the Rock and Roll Hall of Fame Foundation announced that the votes of more than a hundred industry insiders were being counted on ballots assembled by the nominating committee. (In addition to me, it included Ahmet Ertegun, Jann Wenner, Seymour Stein, Bob Krasnow, *Los Angeles Times* critic Robert Hilburn, *Rolling Stone* senior editor Kurt Loder, John Hammond, and producers Jerry Wexler and Nile Rodgers.) The first induction, based on those votes, would be held January 23, 1986, at the Waldorf Astoria Hotel in New York. And near the end of the news release was the passing mention that Cleveland would like to be the site of the Hall of Fame and Museum.

"You might as well have flipped a switch," Benz said. "Rock and roll is everywhere. Eighteen or twenty cities jumped in after we did all this work. They all wanted to be the home.

"It was totally inadvertent. Frankly, for a long time in the process I don't think New York really understood what they had in their hands. They understood the induction, we didn't know crap about that, but they had no idea of the significance."

For the Hall of the Fame Foundation, it was an awakening to new possibilities.

"As a result of that publicity," Suzan Evans said, "we were approached by many other cities who wanted the Rock and Roll Hall of Fame, . . . including Philadelphia, Memphis, Chicago, Los Angeles, and, to some degree, New York.

"We said, 'We have a fiduciary responsibility to this nonprofit corporation, we have to play this out and see where we could get the best offer to build this museum,' which we hadn't even envisioned. We hadn't even yet had our first induction ceremony."

"Now there was no hiding," Benz said. "It was 'We're going to have a competition. Keep throwing your jewels at us.' We had to be so good, so perfect, so compelling, that we got into the finals."

ALMOST BY ACCIDENT, THE PLAN TO DO IT ALL QUIETLY WENT CRASHING DOWN.

With its proposal out in the open, the Cleveland group decided to capitalize on the publicity and turn a possible setback into an opportunity.

Benz credited Bill Smith and Carl Hirsch of WMMS for the idea of staging a petition drive. It would be a stunt without any real power, but it would also be a way of letting the community show its support.

Benz loved it. He related it to the scene in one of his favorite movies, *Miracle on 34th Street,* where Kris Kringle, the old man claiming to be Santa Claus, gets a court hearing to prove his sanity. As evidence, his lawyer submits three letters, addressed simply to Santa Claus, that the US Post Office has delivered to Kringle. When the judge asks for more evidence that the agency has acknowledged him as the "one and only" Santa Claus, workers haul 21 bulging mailbags to the bench. Case dismissed.

"That was in my brain," Benz said. "We wanted this to be the one and only Santa Claus, the one and only Rock and Roll Hall of Fame."

Radio and television stations put aside their customary and sometimes bitter rivalries to cooperate and push the campaign. Petitions circulated everywhere, and not only at concert venues and clubs. They were at supermarkets and malls, the Cuyahoga County Fair and the annual Cleveland National Air Show, 3,000 savings and loan offices, and thousands of establishments served by the House of LaRose beverage distributorship.

In about a month, more than 660,000 signatures were collected.

Lawrence Travagliante, the WMMS afternoon disc jockey and music director known as Kid Leo, used his connections in a different sort of petition drive. A recognized force in the music industry who had been proposing a rock hall of fame for years, he asked top performers to write letters in support of Cleveland. The A-listers who did included Michael Jackson, Bruce Springsteen, Pete Townshend, the Beach Boys, Sting, Tina Turner, Neil Young, B. B. King, Daryl Hall and John Oates, Cyndi Lauper, Bobby Rydell, the Everly Brothers, Gladys Knight and the Pips, the Kinks, Foreigner, and Heart.

The performers took up the argument: Cleveland had a reputation far surpassing other cities as a launch pad for breaking new artists and music, on the radio and in its performance venues, and that the city supported the artists by buying more records per capita than any other city.

"We had good ears," Leo said.

More than a place where hits happened first, Cleveland was where performers happened first—going back at least to early 1955, when disc jockeys Tommy Edwards and Bill Randle brought Elvis Presley to town for one of his first shows outside the South, the Hillbilly Jamboree at the

Circle Theater. Randle, "the Pied Piper of Cleveland," brought him back for another show in the fall, then introduced him when Presley made his national TV debut, in January 1956, on Jackie Gleason's *Stage Show*.

It was not all ancient history. David Bowie started his first US tour in Cleveland in 1972. "When we came here," Bruce Springsteen said, "we got some respect."

Before other places knew their names, Clevelanders knew the words to their songs.

"Cleveland always had the coolest rock fans in the country," Ian Hunter said. "I wrote 'Cleveland Rocks' for them because they were always so great to me."

Huey Lewis, leaving Blossom Music Center in a band bus, mused that rock's heart was in Cleveland. The thought became inspiration enough for him to write "The Heart of Rock 'n' Roll," with its nod to Cleveland.

Brian May of Queen knew Cleveland as "a regular port-of-call for us. It was well known as one of the rock capitals of the world, and we felt at home there."

Over and over, Clevelanders heard visiting rockers greet them with a British-accented "Hello, Cleveland!" after the line was immortalized in *This Is Spinal Tap,* the 1984 rock mockumentary.

"It is a rock-and-roll town," said Michael McKean, one of the film's stars and creators. "You can't deny it."

Cleveland was also drawing on other connections. Governor Dick Celeste, it turned out, was friends with Jann Wenner—they'd met through a college friend—and found him "not unsympathetic" to the city. The two would talk regularly.

And there was Margaret "Peggy" Mathna, chief of staff to Congresswoman Mary Rose Oakar of Cleveland, who had a uniquely useful background.

As the daughter of the mayor of Lorain, the industrial port just west of Cleveland, Mathna had grown up in politics. She worked on national and state campaigns in Ohio after getting a political science degree at the Ohio State University and became a skilled operative who seemed to know everyone. Celeste asked her to work for him in Columbus, after she worked on his 1982 campaign, but Oakar, who had risen to a leadership position in the House of Representatives, asked her to come to Washington.

"Washington or Columbus?" Mathna recalled with a chuckle. "I mean, come on."

She made the move in 1984—professionally as well as geographically, because she had spent most of the previous seven years in Los Angeles after traveling there to to see a former roommate open for Mort Sahl at the Comedy Store. Mathna, a classically trained violinist, spent a summer playing with Stan Kenton, began working as a studio session musician, and became the producing partner of jazz drummer Jackie Mills at his Larrabee Studios.

"That was the real heyday of the studio thing—big productions, string sections, horns, real musicians," she said. "String sections always in the morning, horns in the daytime, too, I guess because we were more traditional people. Overdubs at night, rhythm tracks at night, vocals at night. They spent fortunes on recording sessions. Those were fun days. It was a great time."

It was also when she met Ahmet Ertegun. "I think the first time was when they were mixing Laura Branigan, 'Gloria,' at Jackie's studio," in 1982.

"We had a lot in common because Ahmet came from a very political family in Turkey. He had the mixture of music and politics. I was an unusual personality because I was in the music business and knew politics, because in LA nobody gives a shit about politics. I always got along really well with Ahmet. We always were friends."

While she was working for Oakar in Washington, she recalled, "Somebody from her Cleveland office sent a fax and said people are talking about a rock hall. I asked who was behind it. They said Ahmet Ertegun. I said to Mary Rose, you better get involved because anything he does is fabulous. That's who he is, and everybody in the industry respects [the] hell out of him."

Mathna reached out to Ertegun. She expected he would enjoy meeting Oakar, a popular and effective Democrat who was the first woman of Arab American ancestry to serve in Congress. A relentless Cleveland booster, Oakar began meeting and talking regularly with Voinovich, Benz, Celeste, and Ohio representative Patrick Sweeney of Cleveland. Sweeney—a skilled politician and master of policy who also knew his music, theater, and literature—held one of the state's most powerful positions as chairman of the Ohio House Finance and Appropriations Committee. He was passionate about Cleveland, and he worked tirelessly to bring projects and money to the area. He believed the Rock Hall would be a game changer for the city.

Benz continued working out details for the New York board's visit. He found the members could rent a corporate jet for a round-trip from New York for $18,000. "How did we get the money? I would pick up the phone," he said, "now that it was public, not that it was easy. But we called the leadership of the community, and they kicked in the money for the greater good of the community."

On Friday, October 4, Benz and I flew on a jet rented from American Cyanamid to New Jersey's Teterboro Airport, a dozen miles from Manhattan. Ertegun arrived by helicopter from his home to join the board members and Wenner's lawyer, Ben Needell.

Spirits apparently were high.

Right: Ahmet Ertegun at Cleveland's Burke Lakefront Airport on October 4, 1985, when he received the key to the city from Mayor George Voinovich. *From left:* Bill Bryant, Mary Rose Oakar, Norm N. Nite, Suzan Evans, Ben Needell, Ertegun, Allen Grubman, Voinovich, Seymour Stein, Michael Leon, and Jann Wenner. (Margaret "Peggy" Mathna photo)

Below: River Street in the Flats during the late 1950s (*The Cleveland Press* Collection, Cleveland State University)

As they were taking off, Benz recalled, "Jann says, 'How far does this plane go?' I asked the pilot. 'Fully fueled we can go to Geneva, Switzerland.' I said, 'Mr. Wenner, we can go all the way to Geneva, Switzerland.' He goes, 'Really? Screw Cleveland! We'll give you the Hall of Fame, let's fly!' Straight faced."

Benz sat near the front. The board, sitting aft, called him on the intercom and asked him to come back to answer a question. Are there any drugs on board? No, Benz said, he didn't think so, but there was alcohol. No, he was told, that's OK, but thanks. Fifteen minutes later, he was summoned again. Are there going to be women in Cleveland? "Uh, let me see what I can do," Benz replied uncomfortably.

He went back to his seat. No sooner had he sat down than he was summoned again. Now what, he said to himself, returning to his guests. This time they were laughing, and this time Benz could join in.

Marquees on Playhouse Square on Euclid Avenue in 1969 (*The Cleveland Press* Collection, Cleveland State University)

Mayor Voinovich, who had proclaimed it Rock and Roll Hall of Fame Day, led the delegation with City Council President George Forbes that met the plane at Burke Lakefront Airport around 1:00 P.M. Voinovich gave Ertegun a key to the city, and everyone climbed aboard a charter bus to tour a few points of interest and potential Hall of Fame locations: Tower City Center, on Public Square, which Forest City was expanding and renovating into an upscale mall; Playhouse Square, the theater district where Alan Freed broadcast on WJW; the Gateway District, where a new arena and stadium were being envisioned; the Flats, the industrial river valley transforming into an entertainment district; the lakefront; and the lot on the edge of downtown where the Cleveland Arena, site of the Moondog Coronation Ball, had stood.

Celeste flew back from a trip to Asia to join a lunch meeting at the private Clevelander Club atop Erieview Tower, a choice not everyone

View of Terminal Tower (*The Cleveland Press* Collection, Cleveland State University)

Above left: Ahmet Ertegun speaks during the New York group meeting at the Clevelander Club in October 1985. (Margaret "Peggy" Mathna photo)

Above right: Jann Wenner and Mary Rose Oakar greet each other at the Clevelander Club in October 1985. (Margaret "Peggy" Mathna photo)

Left: As Ahmet Ertegun looks on, Mary Rose Oakar holds a pennant boosting Cleveland's effort to win the Rock Hall in October 1985. (Margaret "Peggy" Mathna photo)

was pleased with. John Gorman of WMMS was uncomfortable that the room overlooked the bus station, not the lakefront or city center. Tim LaRose didn't think it was rock and roll. It was not Windows on the World, Peggy Mathna said, adding, "I would have taken them to somewhere in the Flats. Instead the chamber of commerce guys were trying to impress these jet-setters with their middle-class sense of what they thought was proper."

But the purpose was business, and the lunch went well. Celeste and Tim Hagan, one of the three Cuyahoga County commissioners, kept the presentation focused. There was another video from Bill Wendling and a presentation book.

Top: Billboards on the corner of East 21st and Prospect Avenue (*The Cleveland Press* Collection, Cleveland State University)

Above: Sex workers on Cleveland's Prospect Avenue (*The Cleveland Press* Collection, Cleveland State University)

But Peggy Mathna might have had a point, judging from the most memorable part of the five-hour visit.

"They wanted to see the gritty Cleveland," she said. "Ahmet and Jann said, 'Hey, take us to Record Rendezvous.'"

Her boss, Mary Rose Oakar, laughed, remembering what happened next.

"On the bus I said, 'Mike, we're turning right, we're going down Prospect.' And we got them to stop the bus. The business guys were kind of mad at me and Benz for directing this. He was caught in the middle."

Prospect Avenue, on the backside of glittering Tower City, was then a notorious seedy home of dive bars, strip joints, pawn shops, surplus stores, hookers, and vagrants. But 300 Prospect was the address of the legendary 'Vous, where Leo Mintz and Alan Freed once watched teenagers rocking and rolling. It was where Ertegun, running his fledgling record label, had peddled new 78s to Mintz from the trunk of his car. Those were the days, Ertegun said, when record guys with new product might double-team a disc jockey—one of them schmoozing the jock while the other scratched rival releases with his keys, leaving only their platters playable.

Leo Mintz was gone, dead at 65 almost a decade earlier, but his son, Stuart, was still at the store when the tour rolled up.

"We got them to stop the bus," Oakar said. "They were like cloistered before that with this homogeneous bus tour. Now they get out, they see fans signing petitions. Ahmet says to Stu, 'Do you have any tapes of the Rolling Stones' early work?' He says, 'Yeah, there's this file cabinet where we keep real old tapes.' Ahmet finds this tape that he could not find anywhere of the audition he gave the Rolling Stones to be part of his Atlantic Records. He says to me, 'Oh my God, I've been looking all over!'

"It was like the Holy Grail," Benz said. "We wanted to win. At the end of it all, Ahmet and Jann told us, 'We'll let you know, but you can pretty much guarantee you'll be in the finals.'"

Wenner agreed. "I remember our trip to Cleveland as they really knocked it out of the park. It meant a lot to them, and a lot of preparation had gone into it."

The estimated cost of Cleveland's pitch, at that point, was about $100,000. Most of it had come from private sources, especially people like Tim LaRose and Milt Maltz.

The trip seemed worth it. And Peggy Mathna had guessed right about Ertegun and her boss. The Turkish-born music executive and the congresswoman of Lebanese descent had hit it off.

After the trip, Oakar said, "I'm back in Washington and get a note in the mail from Ahmet Ertegun. He said, 'I met you in Cleveland, we went to Record Rendezvous and we had a wonderful time.' And he said, 'I noticed that you are a parliamentarian to NATO.'" It was an unusual observation, but she would soon learn its significance.

CHAPTER 4

"Money"

—PINK FLOYD

The remarkable thing about the competition for the Rock and Roll Hall of Fame was that it created itself. The New York foundation never issued any request for proposals or invitations to bid. The board never even announced that it was looking for a home for the Hall of Fame, beyond the passing acknowledgement that Cleveland was interested. It set no parameters or guidelines. Cities acted on their own, typically at the instigation of local disc jockeys and fans, to enter the sweepstakes.

"The upshot," Jann Wenner said, "was that myself, Ahmet, Suzan, Grubman, and Seymour traveled to Cleveland, Philadelphia, Chicago, maybe Memphis, for presentations from the local power structure—what they would offer in terms of incentives, where they would build it, that sort of thing. Some were just plain pathetic, ill thought out. Philadelphia was well thought out—that would have been the alternate, was to do it in Philadelphia."

Philadelphia greeted the board with a rally at city hall. Mayor Wilson Goode wined and dined them and led a campaign that made a serious and attractive proposal and offered a variety of potential sites.

Chicago also made an offer serious enough to qualify it as a finalist, talking about locations that included the touristy Navy Pier. But the Windy City effort was months behind Cleveland and, we would learn later, might have suffered from a memorable slip in presentation.

Memphis was the home of Beale Street, Sun Records, and Graceland. Sun founder Sam Phillips, one of the true fathers of rock and roll, was a vocal advocate for the city, finding it almost unthinkable that the Rock Hall would be located anywhere else. But the city was unable to unite in a plan or come up with the sort of financing Cleveland promised.

Nashville, "Music City," already was home to the Country Music Hall of Fame and Museum. Bernie Walters, founder of the International Rock and Roll Music Association in Nashville, led a lobbying effort that rallied the local music industry. But it was late to the game. By the end of 1985, months after the process started, Nashville had made no proposal to the New York foundation.

In San Francisco, promoter Bill Graham led a bid that built heavily on the city's history with psychedelic rock and the 1967 Summer of Love, using Starship's "We Built This City" as a theme song.

New Orleans was a favorite of Seymour Stein, then president of the foundation. But, he said, the Big Easy did not make an offer that showed serious interest. Board members received feelers from places like Orlando and San Antonio.

One "really impressive proposal came from the Smithsonian, who wanted us [as] part of that institution," Suzan Evans said. "So Ahmet, Jann, Seymour, Noreen, and I traveled to Washington."

Some ideas were little more than fantasies. At one point, someone suggested building the Hall of Fame on Strawberry Fields—the two-and-a-half-acre section of New York's Central Park that was dedicated as a memorial to John Lennon on what would have been his 45th birthday, October 9, 1985.

New York City, in fact, was both a fallback and a nonstarter. Wenner didn't even recall an offer from the city, which "just doesn't need another attraction" anyway. Stein said he was never in favor of New York, or Los Angeles, for much the same reason, though New York had been the starting point of Hall of Fame discussions.

"We were dreaming about it," he said, "possibly a brownstone we would buy, like Bill Paley from CBS," whose original Museum of Broadcasting, later to become the Paley Center for Media, occupied two floors of an office building on West 53rd Street. "That was the height of our expectations at that time. Ahmet was really specific that it would be no bigger than the Television and Radio Museum. We both thought along the same lines, but we were dreaming. Then Norman—Norm N. Nite—came in, and that was it. I think it really got us going."

Stein kept his own list of places, including cities that weren't in the running.

"In terms of music, all the towns are very important," he said. "I think Cleveland was ahead of it because of Alan Freed and the audience there. I had Philadelphia because of Dick Clark and all the little labels they had. I had New Orleans and a couple of other cities, possibly Nashville, but I felt it would have been overcrowded by the Country Music Hall of Fame."

He listed Cincinnati because it had been the home of Syd Nathan, one of his life-shaping mentors. Nathan founded King Records, whose pioneering work in roots music and early rock and roll once made it a force in the industry and made Cincinnati an important regional music center. He included Detroit, "which I didn't want because it was so synonymous with Berry Gordy and with Motown.

"Nobody paid any attention to my list, I think," Stein said. "It was a wish list."

As the visits went on, Evans said, "you can imagine how exciting this all was to us. At the end of the day, Ahmet said you know this is not going to cost $25 million, this is not going to cost less than $100 million. Wow—we came a long way from that townhouse."

As the visits went on, Cleveland "went back to the drawing board," the committee's Mike Benz said, with the political leadership and business community lining up strongly in support. "We said, 'How much is this going to cost? Let's make it a 100,000-square-foot building,' figuring $100 a square foot. We can have it really cool for $100 a square foot in 1985."

Richard Fleischman, a visionary architect whose innovative work had been recognized with a Cleveland Arts Prize for its "clean geometric lines, vast expanses of glass and light-filled open spaces," agreed to work on the project for free. His design added moving walkways and elements of sound to his signature touches.

In the state legislature, Pat Sweeney was developing a plan to fund the education aspect that was important to members of the New York

ONE REALLY
IMPRESSIVE
PROPOSAL
CAME FROM THE
SMITHSONIAN

board. Benz's committee decided the concept for the Hall of Fame and Museum would be "edutainment," combining the museum legitimacy that the foundation wanted with the need to represent and reflect a popular art form.

"This is not the Guggenheim," Benz said. "This is rock and roll. It's got to be electric. It had to be sexy and exciting.

"We didn't vote, we just did it. Eventually we put a bid together."

They started playing with numbers. At $100 per square foot, they figured the building would run at least $10 million. They guessed another $5 million would support the foundation, and they put the cost of operating the offices at $1 million.

"When we added it all together, we said we're going to bid $26 million," Benz said. "This would lead to the final finals."

Bill Bryant, Benz's boss at the Growth Association, wanted the bid in a book "that'd make a noise." And he wanted to present it to the board in New York, not send it. He wanted to make sure the proposal was read. Benz went to Cleveland-area Traveler's Shoppes, bought all the board members $180 briefcases with their initials embossed, and put the proposal and another video from Bill Wendling inside each briefcase.

"We wanted them to visualize," Benz said. "This is their baby—if they're going to send their daughter to Bela Karolyi for gymnastics in another city, it better be compelling. We had to make it a big deal and come shooting in with money."

On December 4, a group that included Mayor Voinovich, Representative Sweeney, and Congresswoman Oakar gave its presentation to the New York board with Bryant and Benz. The board was impressed.

The night before they went, however, Bryant called Benz at home, noted the bid of $26 million, and asked, "Where are we getting the money?"

Benz mentioned donations and development money and TV rights for induction ceremonies. "But frankly," he said, "I don't know. Let's win this and figure it out later."

The Hall of Fame was taking increasing amounts of Ahmet Ertegun's time, but it was far from the only matter on his mind. He took more than a casual interest in politics, and he was more than an observer when it came to Turkish-American relations.

Through the fall of 1985, he took particular interest in a resolution in the US House of Representatives that called for the proclamation of a National Day of Remembrance of Man's Inhumanity to Man—and "especially for remembering the Armenian genocide by the governments of the Ottoman Turkish Empire." It would officially recognize as

---

"THIS IS NOT THE GUGGENHEIM," BENZ SAID. "THIS IS ROCK AND ROLL."

genocide the massacre of as many as 1.5 million ethnic Armenians in the Ottoman Empire between 1915 and 1923, before the establishment of the Turkish republic.

The resolution was a lightning rod. Armenian Americans, survivors and their descendants, passionately sought acknowledgment of the terrible events. The modern Turkish government argued the killings were a consequence of conflict more akin to civil war than a centrally planned genocide aimed at destroying an ethnic group. Some feared the recognition could lead to demands for reparations and more attacks on Turkish diplomats.

Ertegun called and visited Washington to lobby against the resolution. He met especially with friends in Congress like Stephen Solarz of New York, who became a leader opposing the resolution and later a lobbyist for Turkey, and Mary Rose Oakar.

"It was very important to Ahmet," aide Peggy Mathna said. "We had conversations about Turkey."

Oakar did not want to go against the Armenians, but she was sympathetic to Ertegun's views and did not want to jeopardize the United States' relationship with Turkey, which was exceptionally pro-Western and secular. And she was recognized as an expert on the intricacies of parliamentary procedure and was part of the House leadership.

"I compromised about this," she said. "Steve Solarz stopped the ball on the Armenian resolution. I got together with Steve and said, 'Look, you have to bring the resolution up. But here's what you should insist on—a rule,'" which would set the terms for debate and amendment under House floor procedures. "I said, 'Your focus should be on the rule, not on the content. Because if the rule is defeated, the bill doesn't come up.' He focused on the rule, and the rule was defeated. So we never voted on the resolution."

The resolution was, in effect, defeated.

"Mary Rose was really tight with Tip," Mathna said three decades later, referring to Speaker of the House Thomas "Tip" O'Neill. "She was in the Democratic leadership of the House. She was able to pull in a lot of guys."

Did the Hall of Fame have anything to do with it?

She laughed. "Totally. Absolutely. The Turkish thing was all because of Ahmet. He asked, and we delivered. Turkey was all about the Rock Hall."

CHAPTER 5

"Celebration Day"

—LED ZEPPELIN

Members of the foundation board said the decision on the Hall of Fame wouldn't be based on a popularity contest. That didn't stop someone from holding one.

Enter *USA Today*.

In January 1986, the board was focused largely on the fast-approaching inaugural induction ceremony, which some observers speculated might include the announcement of a site selection.

RADIO STATIONS MADE

THE POLL AN ALL-DAY

CRUSADE

A reporter from *USA Today* supposedly saw board members in a New York restaurant, wondered what they were doing—and learned they were talking about the Hall of Fame. Ready to build on its slogan of being "the Nation's Newspaper" and the paper of the people, the three-year-old daily decided to give readers a voice in where the hall should be built—inviting them to vote for one of eight cities, by phone, at 50 cents a call.

USA Today reporter David Zimmerman called Mike Benz to tell him it was coming.

"I thought, Now what are we going to do? After all this work and effort?" Benz said. "So we started organizing again. We've got to get Clevelanders to turn out. We've got to get radio and TV.

"Somebody identified a guy in the repeater station printing the regional edition who would alert us what day the poll was going to be in the paper. I got a call at like four in the morning, 'It's going to be today!' We had built a phone tree ahead of time like you do for school closings. All the stations were alerted ahead of time. So everybody was beating the doors down to dial this number."

It was Monday, January 20, a cold winter day. Radio stations made the poll an all-day crusade, pushing listeners to dial the Cleveland number. Downtown merchants put signs in their windows inviting people to come in and vote, offering, "We'll pay for the phone call." WMMS set up a phone bank for listeners in the lobby of the Statler Building, downstairs from its studios.

When the phone lines closed, Cleveland had almost 50,000 votes. Memphis, in second place, had fewer than 2,300.

"At the end of the day," Benz said, "I'm sitting in my office and I get a call from Zimmerman. 'Mike, you're not going to believe this. The response was unbelievable, this was the biggest edition we've ever had! We're going to run it a second day!' I'm going, 'What?!' We thought it was going to be a one-day competition! But we had a dedicated group of people dedicated to winning. We went all the way back to the beginning, the same telephone tree."

From the start, the phone poll, to a lot of Clevelanders, had seemed like a way for other cities to match Cleveland's huge petition drive. Running it for a second day was putting time on the clock after the game was over. By then, however, the quest had become a crusade. Clevelanders went back to the phones. Businessman and philanthropist George Gund III, co-owner of the Cleveland Cavaliers and an avid supporter of the Hall of Fame campaign, set up speed dialers to register support.

When the phones closed, Cleveland had 110,315 votes. Memphis, still second, received 7,268. San Francisco had 4,006, Nashville tallied 2,886, New Orleans registered 2,500, New York had 2,159, Philadelphia totaled 1,044, and Chicago had 1,030. Cleveland had well over five times the number of the other cities combined.

The results could not be ignored. Even detractors who said Cleveland benefited from an organized effort had to admit that other cities had the same time and opportunity to mobilize.

The results also raised hopes in Cleveland that an announcement might be coming soon—maybe even the following night, at the first Hall of Fame induction.

The current Rock Hall logo (Courtesy Rock and Roll Hall of Fame)

Arena-scale induction ceremonies still lay far in the future. What everyone remembered about the inaugural induction was its intimacy and the excitement of its being the First Time. That happens only once.

The celebration actually started the night before the poll results were announced, on January 22, with a reception hosted by the foundation for inductees and presenters at Mortimer's, the tony Upper East Side café where even a normal night's seating of boldface names appeared to have been cast theatrically. Part reunion and part meet-and-greet, the reception was an icebreaker to a night we thought could make history. We had worked a long time toward it, and no one really knew exactly what to expect.

At noon Thursday, the next day, I checked into the Waldorf, where the lobby and coffee shop were giddy with the arrivals and meetings of stars. Cocktails got going around 6:00 P.M. outside the grand ballroom, dinner started at 7:15, and the ceremony began at 9:30. Each person in that crowd of a thousand paid up to $1,000 a plate to attend.

They weren't paying for the food: the fare was meatloaf, with lumpy mashed potatoes and gravy, peas and carrots, and ketchup on the table. With Oreo cookies for dessert. The menu was part of a 1950s theme, "something down-home and funky," Suzan Evans said, and it proved so popular it was repeated four years later.

Rock Hall award statue (Courtesy Rock and Roll Hall of Fame)

I was broadcasting live on WCBS-FM from 10 to midnight, and I split my time between the ballroom and the quieter lobby, where program director Joe McCoy and I had set up a table to work. I buttonholed people like Ray Charles and Fats Domino for interviews, and we did a play-by-play of the inductions.

It was no ordinary dinner when the houselights went down, starting from the moment Ahmet Ertegun, cohosting with Jann Wenner, introduced Keith Richards, who would make the first induction. That was Chuck Berry, very appropriately, though the honorees were presented in alphabetical order.

"It's very difficult for me to talk about Chuck Berry, because I lifted every lick he ever played," Richards said, before peeling off his tuxedo

jacket to reveal a garish yellow leopard-print coat. "This is the gentleman that started it all as far as I'm concerned." Then Berry duckwalked onto the stage as the house band—Paul Shaffer and the World's Most Dangerous Band from NBC's *Late Night with David Letterman*—played his signature "Roll Over Beethoven."

The tone for the evening was set: authentic, appreciative, and exciting.

Taking the stage to induct Ray Charles, Quincy Jones drew shrieks and shouts when he said, "You know, Cleveland may become the ultimate home of the Rock and Roll Hall of Fame"—before holding up his hand to add, "Wait a minute, I said *possibly*. But I tell you one thing for sure, only New York could start it.

"I can't believe after all these years," he continued with a grin, "I thought I'd seen everything. And here we come with ham hocks and chitlins and rock and roll at the Waldorf."

The induction pairings spanned generations and genres. James Brown was presented by Steve Winwood, Fats Domino by Billy Joel. Neil Young presented the Everly Brothers, and Hank Williams Jr. presented Jerry Lee Lewis. Little Richard couldn't attend because he was recuperating from an October car accident. His brother-in-law Marvin Blackmon accepted for him after he was inducted by Roberta Flack—the only female presenter on a night when none of the inductees were women.

"All of my heroes are being honored tonight," she said with a smile, "with the exception of some people whose names I'd also like to call: Tina Turner, Big Maybelle, LaVern Baker, Janis Joplin. And maybe next year will be the year for women."

The posthumous inductions were presented in order with the rest, avoiding any "in memoriam" pall.

Al Green presented Sam Cooke; Herb Alpert, whom Cooke had once mentored and who wrote his hit "Wonderful World," accepted for him. Jann Wenner, beaming proudly, introduced John Fogerty to induct Buddy Holly, whose widow, Maria Elena, accepted. "I'm not going to say I wish Buddy was here tonight," she said, "because I know he is."

John Lennon's sons, Julian and 10-year-old Sean, presented Elvis Presley's award on behalf of their late father. "Our father was a big fan of Elvis's," Julian said, "and, of course, Elvis was loved all over the world, and we are all influences from him. I think a lot of people in the world get a lot of pleasure from listening to him and love him greatly." Then he read something his father had written: "Elvis was a thing, whatever people say, he was it. I was not competing against Elvis, rock happened to be the media I was born into—it was the one, that's all. Those people who picked up paint brushes, like Van Gogh, probably wanted to be Renoir or whomever went before him. I wanted to be Elvis."

Jack Soden, the president and CEO of Elvis Presley Enterprises and Graceland, read a statement of thanks from Elvis's daughter, Lisa Marie Presley, and introduced Memphis broadcaster George Klein, Elvis's close friend since boyhood, to accept.

"Elvis Presley wasn't a star, he was a damn galaxy!" Klein said, remembering his talent, charisma, and humility and that he had sold 1 billion records. "Death is a very short thing," he concluded. "I ask all of you not to think how Elvis Presley died, but please, think how Elvis Aaron Presley lived."

Norm N. Nite interviews Fats Domino at the first Hall of Fame induction, January 23, 1986. (Author's collection)

I put down my microphone and went inside to join broadcaster Scott Muni inducting Alan Freed. His son Lance accepted.

"Showman that he was, he would have loved to hear your applause," Lance said with a grin. "It's no secret that a lot of people predicted rock and roll was nothing more than a passing fad. My father never believed that for a minute. In a sense, there's no finer tribute to his memory than to know that rock-and-roll music is not only alive and well, but it keeps on getting better and better. That was his dream."

Sam Phillips, the other nonperformer inducted, said the event was "the culmination of something I hoped I would live to see," remembering his discovery at Sun Records of Elvis, Jerry Lee Lewis, Carl Perkins, Johnny Cash, and others.

John Hammond—the legendary producer, talent scout, and critic—received the first Lifetime Achievement Award from Ahmet; he had just suffered a stroke and could not attend. Three Early Influences of rock and roll also were honored: bluesman Robert Johnson, inducted by critic Robert Palmer; piano man Jimmy Yancey, inducted by Ahmet Ertegun, and singer Jimmie Rodgers, inducted by producer Jerry Wexler.

At midnight, magic happened. It wasn't planned. Honorees and presenters—Chuck Berry, Fats Domino, Jerry Lee Lewis, Keith Richards, Steve Winwood, Billy Joel, Neil Young, John Fogerty, Julian Lennon, and Ron Wood of the Rolling Stones took the stage with Paul Shaffer's band for a jam session that lasted until 1:10 A.M.

The night got longer for most of us, because we didn't want it to end. I went upstairs for afterglow with Jack Soden and George Klein, and then a bunch of us went to the China Club on Columbus Avenue until 4:30. Hank LoConti and Mike Benz were there, part of a large contingent from Cleveland that bought tables for the inductions. They were a conspicuous presence.

"During the induction ceremony," Benz said, "I got the word, 'Don't do anything more. We get it. We understand Cleveland wants it. You've done a fabulous job.'" The word, he said, came from Suzan Evans.

To some people, especially from cities already out of the running, Cleveland was looking like a done deal. But the foundation board still had meetings and trips scheduled with Philadelphia and Chicago. Nothing was a sure thing.

Norm N. Nite interviewing Ray Charles at the first Hall of Fame induction, January 23, 1986 (Author's collection)

It wasn't surprising that no decision about the Hall of Fame site was announced at the inductions. Even apart from the fact that the board wasn't ready, the announcement would have taken attention from the inductees and the event itself.

More surprising for an affair that had been conceived as a pay-per-view TV special was that the inaugural inductions were not televised, although they were filmed for the future Hall of Fame museum. Ahmet Ertegun said televising it would "take away from the dignity of the event," underlining the seriousness of purpose of the Hall of Fame's foundation.

It wanted legitimacy, and that included an educational component, possibly in partnership with an established institution.

State Representative Pat Sweeney was determined to make it happen. From his powerful perch as chairman of the Ohio House Finance and Appropriations Committee, he also wanted to find funding to help seed a Hall of Fame. It wasn't easy.

"I went to legislators who were good pals of mine," Sweeney recalled. "They said, 'Great idea, can't vote for it. I can't put eight million into the Rock and Roll Hall of Fame and go back to Morgan County with $150,000 of capital improvements. I'll get my ass kicked.'

"I'm using higher education funds. That's where I can get the money. If there's not a higher education component, I'm not going to do it. Cleveland State didn't want it. I called Nolen Ellison," the president of Cuyahoga Community College. In 1980, six years earlier, he had created the Tri-C JazzFest with the aim, according to the college, of fostering the history and nurturing the future of jazz.

Talking to Ellison, "I said I can't get anybody," Sweeney said. "It's a political hot potato. He said, 'I don't want it either.' He said, 'What I want is a Center of Contemporary and Popular Music.' I said, 'Thank you!' So I changed the name of it. So the bill is out, there's no Rock and Roll Hall of Fame.

"I got a couple of the things going. It was hilarious—nomenclature. It covers those guys who want to vote for it and did vote for it—because this sounded like a university function, it didn't sound like rock and roll."

When Governor Celeste unveiled his capital improvements bill in March 1986, the biggest share of the two-year budget went to higher education. Included was $4 million for a "Center for Contemporary Music" at Tri-C.

Pat Sweeney, with Dick Celeste and Nolen Ellison, had delivered proof of the state and city's seriousness and commitment to winning and establishing the Hall of Fame.

The longer the search process stretched on, however, the more nervous Clevelanders grew. Other cities had seemed to be falling by the wayside, but a few had gained time to press their cases or simply to run down the idea of choosing Cleveland.

I had started to become concerned once the word got out to other cities. I did not know what kind of power markets like Memphis, New Orleans, Chicago, or Los Angeles would have or what kind of energy they would put into the effort. And I didn't know how Cleveland would respond. In sports, Cleveland always fell short of winning a World Series or Super Bowl. I thought, Uh-oh, this could be the same scenario. I started to get more confident about Cleveland being able to do it when I'd talk with Seymour Stein in New York. The board would visit another city, and he would call me up and say how he was unimpressed.

Even though Suzan Evans had told Mike Benz there was nothing more the city could do, it seemed like something more still could be done. I think the turning point for me came during a meeting in early 1986 with Benz and his committee at the Growth Association.

Did they realize, I asked, that the first-ever rock-and-roll concert took place on March 21, 1952—Alan Freed's Moondog Coronation Ball at the Cleveland Arena? It was where rock began to roll. That was the line I used at the meeting.

"Twenty-five hundred people were supposed to show up," I said. "Instead there were more than 10,000, and they almost had a riot on their hands."

Benz said, "That must be the day rock and roll was born. We gotta restage it." He proposed a citywide event.

John Gorman, the operations manager overseeing both WMMS and WHK, its AM oldies sister station, jumped on the idea. Finding that

Rally on Public Square, March 21, 1986. Mary Rose Oakar and Dick Celeste hold a plaque honoring the birth of rock and roll in Cleveland. (Janet Macoska photo)

the name *Moondog Coronation Ball* was not under copyright, he and his staff began plotting a flat-out sequel, Moondog Coronation Ball II, for the 34th anniversary, on what fortuitously happened to be a Friday night. To sweeten the deal, they planned to make it a free concert.

Right: Rally on Public Square, March 21, 1986. Governor Dick Celeste and Congresswoman Mary Rose Oakar. (Janet Macoska photo)

Below: Rally on Public Square, March 21, 1986 (Janet Macoska photo)

Rally on Public Square, March 21, 1986. Politicians line up for support. *Left to right:* State Senator Lee Fisher, Voinovich aide Claire Rosacco, Congresswoman Mary Rose Oakar, and Gov. Dick Celeste. (Janet Macoska photo)

Rock 'n' Roll Birthday Celebration rally on Public Square, March 21, 1986. *Left to right:* Michael Stanley, Barry Gabel, and Mike Belkin. (Janet Macoska photo)

Other stations, including WGCL, WZAK, and WMJI, planned their own Moondog anniversary shows and parties. All of it worked, and more.

On the first official day of spring, with the temperature in the 20s under gray skies, the Rock 'n' Roll Birthday Celebration started with a noontime outdoor rally on Public Square, emceed by Denny Sanders of WMMS. The band Wild Horses warmed up the crowd until cold-numbed fingers stopped them. Governor Celeste, wearing a red jersey proclaiming "The Rock Stops Here," joined Mary Rose Oakar in unveiling a plaque honoring Alan Freed, which would be installed at the site of his old WJW studio on Playhouse Square. Celeste and

Oakar danced. A plane towed a banner overhead, reading, "Happy Birthday, Rock & Roll from WMMS."

The evening celebration started with a unique broadcast collaboration. At 7:58 PM, nine radio stations—WBEA, WDMT, WGAR, WGCL, WHK, WLTF, WMJI, WMMS, and WZAK—and five TV stations—

Right: Michael Stanley performs at Cleveland's Rock 'n' Roll Birthday Celebration, March 21, 1986. (Janet Macoska photo)

Below: Rally on Public Square, March 21, 1986 (Janet Macoska photo)

Rally on Public Square, March 21, 1986. *Left to right:* Congresswoman Mary Rose Oakar, John Gorman, Kid Leo, Gov. Dick Celeste, and Eric Carmen. (Janet Macoska photo)

Rally on Public Square, March 21, 1986 (Janet Macoska photo)

WKYC, WEWS, WJW, WOIO, and WCLQ—played Bill Haley's "Rock Around the Clock."

Then the shows started. Chuck Berry headlined Moondog Coronation Ball II inside Tower City Center. Typically, I had predicted, you'd be lucky to get 30 minutes from Chuck. He played an hour and 20 minutes. Eric Carmen, first known for fronting the Raspberries and in 1986 a year away from "Hungry Eyes," took the stage with Cleveland's Beau Coup, after Wild Horses and the Innocent. Celeste led the crowd in chanting, "The Rock Stops Here," the title of a song Carmen had written with his brother Fred for the Hall of Fame campaign.

WHK sponsored an old-school sock hop at Brooklyn High School, where Elvis Presley had played probably his first concert north of the

Mason-Dixon Line in October 1955, opening for Bill Haley & His Comets, Pat Boone, and the Four Lads. Clubs in the Flats, downtown, around Cleveland State University, and in the suburbs held tie-in rock parties.

I played records with Chubby Checker and Eric Carmen in the Rock 'n' Roll Birthday Bash at the Palace Theater on Playhouse Square. *Go, Johnny, Go!* the 1959 movie that starred Alan Freed, Chuck Berry, and Jimmy Clanton, had a midnight screening at the Hanna Theatre.

Fireworks in the Flats, sponsored by WMMS and WKYC-TV, capped the celebration. Police estimated 50,000 people were downtown for the evening.

It was a long way from the original Moondog Coronation Ball, which was stopped early by police and was a local scandal before it became a legend. This one drew notice of a better sort, on ABC's *World News Tonight,* the *CBS Evening News,* and NBC's *Today* show and from the *New York Times, Variety,* and wire services.

ABC hired a limo to take Benz to city hall early the next morning to talk about Cleveland and its bid for the Hall of Fame. *Good Morning America* set up its cameras outside on the roof. "At this point I'm way beyond my pay grade," Benz said.

"Then I got the call from Suzan—'Look, enough is enough. We don't want you to do anything more. We get it. You're putting pressure on us, and that's not going to go well for Cleveland. Back off; we'll let you know.' She said, 'I'll tell you what, I'll make you a deal. I'll call you after our meeting and I'll give you a signal whether you won or lost.'"

The meeting was scheduled for the end of April, more than a month away.

I had publicly predicted at the Moondog celebration that there would be a decision on the home of the Hall of Fame within three weeks and that I'd put my money on Cleveland—a good bet but not a sure thing. Two days after Moondog Night in Cleveland, the *Chicago Tribune* reported that Chicago was still in the running and that members of the city's Hall of Fame committee were "modestly optimistic" after meeting with the foundation in New York.

CHAPTER 6

"(We're Gonna) Rock Around the Clock"

—BILL HALEY & HIS COMETS

With March coming to an end, Congress was nearing spring vacation and Mary Rose Oakar was "dying to go home" from Washington. "But there was a NATO meeting in Istanbul, Turkey," she said, and she was a congressional delegate to the NATO Parliamentary Assembly, which includes every country in the alliance. Before she could send regrets, Ahmet Ertegun called.

"Ahmet said, 'They're honoring my father, who was the ambassador from Turkey to the United States. I grew up in Washington, and my dad always wanted me to be a diplomat. I wonder if you could come, go to the event, and talk to the Turkish businessmen as a congresswoman.'

"I wanted to go home," Oakar said. "I was so tired. I called Mike Benz and said, 'You're not going to believe this.' Mike said, 'What do you mean you can't go, you gotta go!'

"The reason this was special was when Ahmet's father died, President Truman sent his body back to Turkey on the USS *Missouri*. Ahmet told me that this changed Tukey's point of view from pro-Soviet to pro-West. Then Turkey ultimately joined NATO. Ahmet said, 'It's the anniversary of his death, and I'd like you to be there and speak to these people.'

"I had no choice. I was able to take a couple of my staff people [among them Peggy Mathna] to help. He invites me to stay with him and his wife, Mica, a Romanian interior designer, at their home in this Turkish village. 'If you stay, I will take you on a tour of Turkey.' I said I could do it because we were on recess, and when will I ever do this again?

"I go to his little place on the Mediterranean. He's Muslim. There's a little mosque and this adorable one-story home Mica had furnished beautifully. He took me all over Turkey. To where they think James took the Blessed Mother to live, to ruins, to the capital. We'd go to the market, he'd make fish on the grill, and I got to know him and Mica. He was just fabulous.

"Finally we're eating one night, and I thought, I gotta bring this up. So I said, 'What'd you think of Cleveland?' And he said, 'When I saw those kids, I knew—signing petitions.' He said, 'I'll tell you a story. I love jazz. My whole idea was to have the Rock and Roll Hall of Fame and another something for the history of jazz, a jazz museum'—because when he was a kid living at the embassy, he and his brother, Nesuhi, would get the guys from Blues Alley, a place where jazz musicians usually went, an all-black nightclub. And they would invite them to the Turkish embassy and record them. The *Washington Post* chastised him for it. Washington was below the Mason-Dixon Line. And that did it for him. He went to all the right diplomatic schools but got interested in recording. Both brothers went into that industry.

"Ahmet said, 'You know, Chicago's the place where jazz was created,'" noting that the Hall of Fame board had visited Chicago after Cleveland. "I thought, 'Oh, he's going to choose Chicago, damn it.' He said, 'But we didn't choose Chicago, and I'll tell you why. We get off the plane, and there's a video of Mayor [Harold] Washington, and he says he couldn't be there, he was in Europe trying to do a trade deal. All his top lieutenants were with him. He says, "You know I love rock and roll, Chicago is the home of jazz, that's where it came from, blah blah

blah. And I want you to know my favorite singer is Bruce Springtime.'"
Ahmet said, 'That was it for us, we didn't even want to tour anything.'

"So I said, What about Cleveland? He said, 'I'm for Cleveland.' I wanted to kiss that guy. Mica said, 'Yes, we like you, Mary Rose, because you're Middle Eastern.' He said, 'You can't tell anybody, because I have to convince Jann Wenner.' He said Wenner wanted three townhouses for different eras. He said, 'I want to get I. M. Pei, who did the Louvre. He's from New York, and he's a friend of mine. I want him to design the building.'"

Peggy Mathna also remembered the dinner. "Ahmet said, 'My board doesn't know it yet, but I want the Rock and Roll Hall of Fame to be in Cleveland.'

"I don't think anybody else wanted it there," she said. "It was all him, because he thought it would be very important to Cleveland. It would be a big deal. He thought it would just be another museum in New York. He liked the way the community got together and the political people got involved. George [Voinovich] was fabulous. As straight as he was, he got it. Ahmet was very fond of him."

Oakar and Mathna kept quiet. Ertegun may have made his decision, but the board had yet to vote. Cleveland was still on shaky ground. As late as April, Seymour Stein said we might lose.

The weekend before the board met, however, Seymour called and told me he thought it was a done deal. He called back on April 29, a Tuesday, and said the board would meet to vote the next day. On April 30, word of the outcome started to leak out.

"The phone rings in my office," Mike Benz said. "I hear, 'Mike, Suzan Evans. Wink, wink.' And she hung up. Five minutes later, Voinovich's office calls. He gets on the phone. 'Mike, I just got the word. We won, but you can't say anything. We're going to have a press conference in New York. We'll try to get the governor's plane.' Ten minutes go by. Now it's Dick Celeste. 'The governor would like to speak with you.' 'Holy crap, we won this thing! But you can't say anything.' I had a bag

Left: Governor Dick Celeste, May 6, 1986 (Author's collection)

Right: "We won!" May 6, 1986. *Left to right:* Governor Dick Celeste, George Meisel, Mayor George Voinovich, and Mike Benz. (Janet Macoska photo)

phone, no cell phone then. It rings. I hear, 'Mike, it's Norm N. Nite. What do you think? We won! But you can't say anything.'"

I had a meeting with Ahmet and Nesuhi Ertegun and Seymour Stein that day. They talked about how Cleveland got it. Ahmet was the one who said that after they discussed the pros and cons and the other cities in the running, and talked about the enthusiasm and the history, it was going to be Cleveland.

I think the board never thought Cleveland would get it, that the city wouldn't be able to come up with the enthusiasm and the money. But the board members were wrong on all counts. Every time the Cleveland committee was asked to do something, it did it. If Cleveland had been at the bottom of the list in the *USA Today* poll, that would have been it. But the board couldn't dismiss the fact that Cleveland overwhelmingly dominated it. The Alan Freed Moondog weekend really sealed the deal.

Looking back on the decision, Jann Wenner later said, "Cleveland made the effort and wanted it so badly because they needed it. And it worked to our advantage."

On May 1, 1986, a *USA Today* headline proclaimed that Cleveland had won the Rock Hall. The front-page headline in the *Plain Dealer* quoted a source that declared it "looks real good for Cleveland." The decision had not been officially announced.

That came on May 5, a Monday. Celeste, Voinovich, and Oakar led a contingent that flew to New York. Benz had commemorative hats and T-shirts made up for everybody on the plane, "like when you win a national championship."

Ahmet Ertegun made the announcement at a crowded news conference. "We're confident that we have made the best possible selection," he said. "The quality of the people in Cleveland and the enthusiasm made the selection almost an inevitable choice."

Anticipating objections from other cities, he said, "As we all know, rock and roll did not emerge in just one place at one time, and Cleveland has played as significant a role as many other cities in the development of this music."

"Rock and roll really belongs to all America," Ertegun continued. "It really doesn't belong to one city. This was a difficult decision because many cities have a claim that rock started there."

Jann Wenner validated Cleveland's approach and the work of Pat Sweeney and Dick Celeste. "Cleveland alone among the competitors seemed to understand the character of what we want this to be," he said, promising a "major museum and archive and scholarly institution."

"We won!" May 6, 1986. *Front row, left to right:* Gov. Dick Celeste, George Meisel, Norm N. Nite, and Mike Benz. (Janet Macoska photo)

"We won!" May 6, 1986. *Left to right:* George Miller, unidentified person, Bill Smith, Tim LaRose, Mike Benz, Norm N. Nite, and unidentified person. (Janet Macoska photo)

Above left: "We won!" May 6, 1986. *Left to right:* Tim La Rose, Lynn Tolliver, Norm N. Nite, and Mike Benz. (Janet Macoska photo)

Above right: "We won!" Cleveland Mayor George Voinovich at the podium, May 6, 1986. (Janet Macoska photo)

Right: Victory! May 6, 1986. *Left to right:* Governor Dick Celeste, Kid Leo, Bill Smith, and John Gorman. (Janet Macoska photo)

"This will be no Disney World," Ertegun said, but rather a place that would host "serious scholarship and study."

Wenner's lawyer Ben Needell, a member of the foundation's board of directors, joined Ertegun in saying that the decision had been "essentially unanimous."

The unanimity might have reflected a final consensus and desire to speak with one voice. Milt Maltz, an important member of the Cleveland committee, later said he'd received a phone call after the board's meeting in New York, "and Cleveland won by one vote. That's how close it was."

Close or not, the decision had been made.

When the news conference ended, the group flew to Cleveland for the local announcement and welcoming celebration at Burke Lake-

"We won!" *Left to right:* Mike Benz and Kid Leo. May 6, 1986. (Photo by Janet Macoska)

front Airport—including music from Wild Horses, thawed out from the March Moondog rally.

"In the end," Suzan Evans said, "what we realized was that rock and roll was American music. Each city laid claim to a certain aspect of rock and roll and its genesis. So we realized that we can't base our decision on one thing because rock and roll is an American institution. We decided to build the museum in Cleveland because Cleveland was the best offer. If we wanted it to be built and to be successful, Cleveland was the answer. They wanted it the most, they were great people to work with. We became very fond of their business and political leaders."

The deal was done. Or almost done. Cleveland was chosen, Ertegun said, "contingent on fulfillment of certain requirements," which included financing, choosing a site, and setting operational plans.

CHAPTER 7

"We Can Work It Out"

—THE BEATLES

The story goes that Benjamin Franklin, emerging from the Constitutional Convention of 1787, was asked what sort of government the new nation would have. Franklin immediately answered, "A republic, if you can keep it."

Anyone sounding a similar note of caution during Cleveland's victory celebration—"A Hall of Fame, if you can keep it and build it"—would have been the proverbial skunk at the picnic. But they wouldn't have been wrong.

The selection of Cleveland was not popular everywhere. Sam Phillips, the inaugural Hall of Fame inductee, eventually came around and had generous, even warm, words for Cleveland—but not before raging that it was a take-the-money-and-run betrayal to put the Hall of Fame anywhere but Memphis.

He was not alone, recalled Jack Soden, who oversees Graceland in Memphis as president and chairman of Elvis Presley Enterprises and was an early friend of the Rock Hall. "Everybody was stomping around here, going, 'This is an outrage! If there's a Rock and Roll Hall of Fame, it's got to be in Memphis! Maybe we can get together $6 or $7 million. Other than Alan Freed and the Raspberries, what did Cleveland have to do with rock and roll?'

"They were almost mad at me," Soden said. "Cleveland was going to rebuild itself, use their lakefront redevelopment money; $30 or $40 million they were throwing around. I said, 'Come up with $30 or $40 million and we can compete with Cleveland.' Memphis couldn't compete. It was years and years, and I'd still have people go, 'I can't believe it.' Then Memphis should have had a check of $50 or $60 million dollars. That's where the money was."

The money was not cash on hand, however. Public announcements to the contrary, the deal wasn't done. Cleveland was chosen, as Ahmet Ertegun said, "contingent on fulfillment of certain requirements."

The New York board came back to Cleveland in late July for a couple of days of meetings and visits to sites. It began to clarify its preferences.

"Ahmet called me," Peggy Mathna remembered about the visit, "and said, 'Can you get a boat? I. M. Pei is going to send some of his guys and he wants to look at things.' I got a sailboat, and we went up the river. I. M. Pei wanted it on the water." Pei hadn't yet been publicly identified with the project.

The directors looked at several sites during the visit and indicated they envisioned a freestanding building and wanted the freedom to design it, eliminating the thought of refurbishing an existing structure like the five-floor Post Office Plaza building next to Tower City Center. Within those constraints, the Cleveland group preferred the site be downtown or in the Flats. Milt Maltz, an important committee member, continued to build his good relationship with Ahmet Ertegun, and, he recalled, "He and I walked the length of the Shoreway, about a mile on each side."

Mathna hosted a relaxed dinner and party for the group afterward in rural Concord Township, 35 miles from downtown, at Pease Hollow Farm, the retreat of restaurateur John Saile, an Ohio City neighbor and friend of Mary Rose Oakar. It was a good time. They all stayed past midnight.

The directors also attended a thank-you lunch staged by the Growth Association at Stouffer's Inn on the Square to recognize the people who helped bring the Hall of Fame to Cleveland. Ertegun, who was among the speakers, told the crowd of more than 200, "We are absolutely convinced Cleveland is the right choice," and "there was really nobody running close to you." Before it was over, 31 individuals and 43 companies and organizations were given awards for their contributions.

Ohio budget director William Shkurti, standing in for Governor Celeste, presented Ertegun and Growth Association president Bill Bryant an oversized prop check for $4 million, representing the state's opening contribution to the Hall of Fame. The check was made out to Cuyahoga Community College, however, to establish the Center for the Study of Contemporary and Popular Music—just as Pat Sweeney had shrewdly arranged months earlier in the Statehouse.

Sweeney quipped, "You didn't think we'd put a line item called 'Rock and Roll Hall of Fame' in the budget, did you?"

Some felt the congratulatory lunch was premature—especially when Mike Benz said fundraising and management decisions could be three years in the future, and even though Bryant said he hoped construction could start in 15 to 18 months.

As much as anything, however, the luncheon was a demarcation line as the whole Hall of Fame effort moved into a new phase.

The Hall of Fame in Cleveland got its first full-time staff member, 29-year-old Christopher O. Johnson, who was named project manager and also would be called coordinator and director. Indicating the importance of the state's role—and the power of the governor, because the seed money for day-to-day activities came from the state pass-through money Sweeney had secured for Tri-C and the development money Celeste had earmarked—Johnson came from the Celeste administration, where he'd been assistant deputy director for business development for the Ohio Department of Development. From a small office in the Leader Building in downtown Cleveland, Johnson had the thankless job of developing fundraising strategies.

Ertegun, as chairman of the Rock and Roll Hall of Fame Foundation, announced a 55-member board of trustees for the separate Rock and Roll Hall of Fame and Museum. Headed by George I. Meisel, the chairman of the Growth Association and a senior partner in the law firm Squire, Sanders & Dempsey, the board included 27 recording industry executives and lawyers, mostly New Yorkers. Among them, significantly, were friendly and not-so-friendly rivals in the music business. Bringing them together was seen as a testament to the persuasive skills of entertainment lawyer Allen Grubman.

I was among the 28 Cleveland members of the board. Some of the heaviest hitters in the local business community joined key players in the campaign to win the hall, like Tim LaRose and Milt Maltz, and political leaders—including the governor, the mayor, Mary Rose Oakar, Pat

SWEENEY QUIPPED, "YOU DIDN'T THINK WE'D PUT A LINE ITEM CALLED 'ROCK AND ROLL HALL OF FAME' IN THE BUDGET, DID YOU?"

Richard W. "Dick" Pogue
had never been to Cleveland before he was recruited by the law firm Jones, Day, Cockley & Reavis in 1957. By the time he became managing partner in 1984, the firm was known as Jones, Day, Reavis & Pogue. It became the nation's second-largest law firm and expanded to a worldwide presence during the years of his leadership.

In 1988, *Cleveland Magazine* named him "the most powerful man in the city." He served as a director of a number of major companies, and he chaired or served as a board member of dozens of civic groups. He shunned the spotlight and self-promotion but was unfailingly generous with time and money in service to the community, remaining active and involved into his 90s.

When Cleveland was threatened in 1989 with losing the still-unbuilt Rock and Roll Hall of Fame, three years after "winning" it, Pogue led the behind-the-scenes effort to develop a plan to raise the money to save it. He cared little and knew less about rock and roll, but he thought the Rock Hall would be important for Cleveland.

Sweeney, county commissioner Tim Hagan, and city council president George Forbes.

People like Mike Benz, who had spearheaded the campaign to win the Rock Hall, stepped into the background. Lead roles shifted to civic leaders who were driven by their interest in the community rather than rock and roll.

One of the most influential was Richard Pogue, who, as managing partner, headed the nation's second-largest law firm, Jones, Day, Reavis & Pogue. He was also a trustee for the Rock Hall.

"I got called in because they knew there would be some legal aspects," Pogue said. "I had no knowledge of rock music, no interest. Voinovich kind of pleaded that this was an important thing for Cleveland. It was something that would make Cleveland unique."

When a reporter once asked him for his favorite rock song, he recalled with a chuckle, he couldn't even name one. "The only thing I could think of was 'You Ain't Nothin' but a Hound Dog.' I didn't know if it was a rock song or not, but it was the closest I could come." Even years later, he said, when the Rock Hall had become reality, "a guy onstage introduced himself—'I'm Chuck Berry.' I'd never heard of Chuck Berry. When I told my kids that, they were very embarrassed. People from all backgrounds contributed to this thing."

Albert Ratner, chairman of Forest City Enterprises, the giant real estate company that was developing Tower City Center, said, "There was almost a disconnect between the guys who got it here and the guys who got it done. It couldn't have happened without both of them. But there wasn't a lot of crossover, because it was two different things."

Jann Wenner, with his lawyer Ben Needell, was acting as point person for the foundation in day-to-day talks with Cleveland. "I had a good relationship with Dick [Celeste] and George [Voinovich]. Then, very fortuitously, I was dealing with a friend of mine who was raised in Cleveland and said he was friends with Bruce Ratner," Albert's cousin who ran Forest City's New York City subsidiary. "He said I should meet Al Ratner, who's a real pooh-bah in Cleveland.

"I said [to the Cleveland trustees], 'I want you to put Albert Ratner in charge of this project.' I had them recruit Albert. Albert didn't really want to do it, but he took it on as a civic duty. The minute he got involved, things started to move and shake. Doing what I'm sure he's done a hundred times. He was somebody I could work with. I recruited the guy who could put the project together, and that was Albert, and we got to be terrific friends."

"I very much liked music," said Ratner, who'd played music as a disc jockey at junior high and high school dances with his friend Bart Wolstein, who became another prominent Cleveland developer. They called their partnership "Musical Art by Eddie and Bart."

"But I wasn't a big fan of rock and roll," Ratner said. "We ended up winning the Rock and Roll Hall of Fame, which I thought was fine. We started talking to them about . . . where it should go, and I didn't pay a lot of attention to that. I think what happened was, my cousin Jimmy Ratner"—then director of Forest City Realty Trust—"had a friend who was involved with the rock-and-roll people. He came to me and said, 'We're going to lose the Hall of Fame.' This was very early on. I said, 'That's fine.' He said, 'No, we can't do that.' He said, 'I want you to go to New York with me and make a presentation for where the Rock and Roll Hall of Fame should go and why it should be in Cleveland.' So I said, 'You know, we're building Tower City, we have enough on our plate, I really don't want to get involved.' He said, 'You have to go with me.' I had never met any of the rock-and-roll people. So Jimmy and I got on a plane and we went to New York. I think we were in Jann's office, in a room in which the members of the New York board were assembled to talk about the Hall of Fame in Cleveland, about Tower City, and where you could locate." This would have been late in 1986.

"The meeting started about an hour late, because I found out they did not necessarily show up on time for meetings. One of the people, whose name I won't mention, said, 'I don't know why you're here, the Rock and Roll Hall of Fame shouldn't go to Cleveland. I don't know why they asked you to come.' Which was music to my ears. So I said to my cousin Jimmy, 'Let's pack everything up and go.' We packed everything up. We started to walk out. And Ahmet Ertegun and Jann followed us out of the room, and [Ahmet] said, 'Don't pay any attention to that; Jann and I are committed to see this go to Cleveland. Please come back to the room and let's continue the conversation.' So we went back into the room, and we had the conversation. And that was the first real contact that I had with the Rock and Roll Hall of Fame."

Despite the public face of unanimity and support for Cleveland, Pogue met similar resistance trying to work out an operating agreement with New York.

"Once they agreed it would be in Cleveland, the arguments started," he said. "Almost every detail. There was still this lingering unhappiness among some of the New York group that Cleveland had been selected. The majority of them were against it. Ertegun and Wenner were able to overcome that negativity, fortunately. Ertegun and Wenner kept it in Cleveland, no question—they didn't think it should be in New York."

Working with Bill Roj, a young partner in his firm who did the drafting work and served as secretary for the Cleveland trustees, Pogue explained, "My main role was to negotiate the agreement, which took three years. It was an endless negotiation. We couldn't agree on anything. Fortunately, the other side selected Ben Needell as its lawyer. He was easy to work with and pretty close to Jann Wenner.

Albert Ratner was prepared to shoot down the Rock and Roll Hall of Fame in a Saturday meeting with local power brokers. But his son, Brian, told him it would be a great thing for Cleveland, and his daughter, Deborah, agreed. "I said if that's what you think, I'll reconsider," Ratner said.

"He took it on as a civic duty," Jann Wenner said. "The minute he got involved, things started to move and shake."

No one was more respected than Ratner, who was chairman of the family business Forest City Enterprises— a giant urban developer and real estate company that evolved from a lumber supply company—and was known for his community leadership and philanthropy.

He was the absolutely essential figure without whom Cleveland would not have the Rock and Roll Hall of Fame, said former Ohio governor Richard Celeste. His involvement gave Wenner the confidence to support Cleveland's effort, and Wenner came to rely on him and his wisdom.

"It was endless drafts going back and forth. Minor points. They were very focused on making this upscale and having a museum. They insisted on the name *and museum,* Rock and Roll Hall of Fame and Museum. We thought that was kind of silly at the time, but in the end it was a positive contribution.

"To Cleveland, this was a great opportunity to showcase and build up Cleveland. The New York people wanted to rehabilitate the art form in the public mind. They had different missions than we did."

Without any operating agreement, progress on the project seemed to stall. Six months after Cleveland "won" the Rock Hall, the New York group's Seymour Stein warned us that we could lose it. On January 14, 1987, Dick Celeste and Mary Rose Oakar led a group to New York to provide reassurance, and they showed they "really know how to get things done," Wenner said. The presence of Al Ratner and his sister, Ruth Miller, the president of Tower City Center, didn't hurt. Tower City was emerging as the favored location.

The New York board made it official in March 1987, after making another bus tour of potential sites, this time with I. M. Pei. It picked Tower City Center.

Tower City was already a happening place. Its core was known originally as the Cleveland Union Terminal complex, opened on Public Square in 1930. Ranked in size as an excavation project second only to the Panama Canal, it encompassed a railroad station, three office buildings, three connected other buildings, and the 52-story Terminal Tower, which was North America's tallest building outside of New York City until 1964. Forest City Enterprises renamed the complex Tower City in the 1980s, for the massive project that added two more office towers and turned the former train station into The Avenue, a 110-store underground mall.

With the site selected, the Rock Hall was moving forward. But the wait for Pei's design became a trap.

CHAPTER 8

"It's Now or Never"

—ELVIS PRESLEY

The Founders Club seemed like a good idea at the time. It was a fundraising campaign that turned into the first real blunder of the nonprofit Rock and Roll Hall of Fame and Museum, Inc.

Launched in June 1987, the campaign asked individuals to make tax-deductible contributions ranging from $15 to $500. Its goal was to raise $2.6 million by Labor Day—about 10 percent of the $26 million that the Cleveland group had committed to raise. At that point, projections of the hall's cost had risen to $35 million, and the balance of the building money was to come from corporate contributions, foundation grants, and government money.

Following the model of the petition drive that had collected more than 600,000 signatures in a matter of weeks, the Founders Club was promoted with billboards, counter displays in stores, and information tables at events. The hope was that at least 100,000 people who had signed petitions would also be willing to sign checks.

The strategy was the opposite of what major fundraising campaigns normally do, which is to make public appeals near the end, to take the drive over the top after the big donors have committed.

The Founders Club aimed to maintain enthusiasm, tap grassroots support, and give Clevelanders a real stake in the hall. It also projected the idea that some sort of activity was going on, while the Cleveland group put off an appeal to corporations and foundations until the building had been designed and cost estimates were more definite.

The danger was that the public appeal wouldn't work, which would kill momentum and send out a signal of failure. In its first week, the Founders Club raised $25,000. After six weeks, it had $150,000 from 7,000 contributors, an average of about $21 apiece. By its target of Labor Day, it had raised $250,000, less than 10 percent of the goal.

Instead of public enthusiasm, fear spread that Cleveland was in danger of losing the Rock Hall. Ben Needell offered words of reassurance— "Leaving Cleveland is not even on the agenda," he said—and made a statement of realism.

"Nobody's pleased with the level of fundraising in Cleveland," he said. "If the deal fails to go ahead in Cleveland, it would be because of the failure to raise the money—not a dissatisfaction with Cleveland."

The Cleveland foundation began to regroup to prepare a major fundraising campaign. But it was hamstrung. It could not plan the capital campaign without a cost estimate for the project. Impatience and anxiety grew as the foundation awaited Pei's design.

I. M. Pei came with both an international reputation and a certain fear factor. "With I. M. Pei," went a pun on his name, "you will pay."

Jann Wenner was aware of it. "We wanted to be very ambitious, very special," he said. "It wasn't our money, so we didn't have to be constrained in our thinking. So we hired I. M. Pei, the world's greatest architect."

"It probably doubled the cost, once you have a celebrity architect," former Ohio governor Dick Celeste said. "It was worth the time and effort, but as he started drawing the building, the price went up."

Builder Albert Ratner, who would become close to the architect, said, "The New York people picked I. M. Pei because they thought he'd never do it, and he agreed to do it because he thought they'd never ask."

He was famed for work that included the East Wing of the National Gallery of Art in Washington, DC, the John F. Kennedy Presidential Library in Boston, and, most recently and maybe most significantly, the Louvre Pyramid, the glass-and-metal structure that is the main entrance to the Louvre Museum in Paris.

He had some history in Cleveland as well, though he downplayed the significance of his role. Twenty-five years earlier, he and his firm prepared the Erieview Plan for downtown urban renewal, with the slablike, 40-story Erieview Tower as its hub. Unfinished, the plan was mostly known for a legacy of wholesale bulldozing that left bleak streetscapes and parking lots.

And Pei, then 70, admitted he knew nothing about rock and belonged to a different generation. But his children encouraged him, and he was interested in learning.

"He said, 'Well, let me think about it,'" Suzan Evans recalled. "And he called me one day, and he said, 'You know what my daughter said to me: "Why do they want you to do this, you're an old man, you know nothing about rock and roll."' He said, 'Suzan—I'm doing it.' We had to teach him about rock and roll. We took him to Graceland, to New Orleans to see the roots, to concerts. We sent him books."

Jack Soden, the CEO of Graceland, well remembered Pei and his wife visiting with Evans, Ahmet Ertegun, Wenner, Seymour Stein, and others. They were stars, and Graceland was accustomed to that. "I stuck close to Pei," he said. "I was impressed with the questions he asked. They were smart. Pei remembered why he was there. He was asking about the pulse and the flow. I remember chalking him up as yet another truly unique person."

Mary Rose Oakar sat next to Pei at a dinner during that time. "He has a tape recorder and his little earplugs during the whole banquet. He said, 'I've got to listen to this.' He was listening to rock music because he didn't know it, and he wanted to know the feeling of rock and roll. That's what he did for two hours, eating a little bit and listening."

"He'd walk around with earphones, listening to the music so he could capture it," Al Ratner recalled with a smile. "I had a wonderful relationship with I. M. Pei, thoroughly enjoyed it. He became a very dear friend."

"Finally, after all that," said Wenner, who'd taken personal charge of the architect's tutelage, "he came to me and said, 'I think I've got it. I understand rock and roll.' I said, 'What is it?' He said, 'Energy.' With that insight he designed that building, which is meant to display all the form of energy."

Pei unveiled a paper model of his design privately to board members at his offices on Madison Avenue on December 3, 1987. The public got its first look six weeks later, on January 20, 1988, the day of the Rock and Roll Hall of Fame's third induction ceremony. There, a larger model was

I. M. PEI ADMITTED HE KNEW NOTHING ABOUT ROCK.

Scale model of I. M. Pei's design for the Hall of Fame that was first shown to the public at the third annual induction in January 1988. The view from Tower City overlooks the Cuyahoga River and the Flats, with the river's Collision Bend at left and the Scranton Peninsula at top. (Courtesy of the Ohio History Connection, SA4144_Cleveland_B05)

shown to a group that included New York board members with Celeste, Mayor Voinovich, Cleveland congressional representatives Mary Rose Oakar and Louis Stokes, and Ohio representative Pat Sweeney.

The design, rising from the east bank of the Cuyahoga River to Huron Road and Tower City, included an 18-story tower, a pyramid of glass and matte-finish metal that was compared to a glass tent, four theaters, and a total of more than 95,000 square feet of space. The top of the tower, up a ceremonial flight of stairs, would hold the Hall of Fame itself, "a pantheon of the greats of rock and roll," Pei said.

Its most playfully bespoke feature was a drum-like wing jutting off from the glass pyramid and perched atop a thin column that called to mind a vintage record player, with a stack of 45-rpm singles ready to drop down the spindle to a turntable.

"It's not an 'establishment' building," Pei said. "It's my interpretation of what rock and roll is. What is rock and roll? It's tremendous energy, openness, and youth."

He called it a "tiny little building" that he hoped would spur development along the riverfront in the Flats. "It doesn't have to be big to pack a wallop," he said. "If we capture the spirit of rock and roll, it will be a powerful building."

Slides of the design were shown at the Hall of Fame inductions that night at the Waldorf Astoria. Ertegun said, "We believe it's going to be a work of great art and beauty."

The cost of the building was estimated at $29 million, bringing the total project cost close to $50 million. But Dick Kelso, the new chairman of the Rock and Roll Hall of Fame and Museum, Inc., sounded a note of caution. Pei's design could change and costs could rise, he said, depending on the plans for the interior. Those were still being developed separately by Barry Howard, an exhibition planner based near Los Angeles.

"There's no timetable, and frankly we're not in a rush," Ertegun said. "We want to make sure we don't make any mistakes."

Maybe there wasn't a timetable, but there was no question that the clock was running. Some members of the New York foundation remained skeptical that Cleveland could come up with enough money to turn Pei's design into reality. Ertegun and Wenner were committed, but a few board members still had thoughts of putting the hall elsewhere. Headed by Kelso as chair, the Cleveland group formed a new executive steering committee, including BP America chairman Robert Horton, Nestlé Enterprises chairman James Biggar, Higbee's chief executive Robert Broadbent, Malrite chairman Milton Maltz, and attorney Richard Pogue. Horton loaned a planner from BP to the effort to develop an operating strategy.

Committee member Broadbent, a dedicated civic booster, became head of the fundraising drive in April 1988. Understanding as well as anyone the Rock Hall's significance and potential impact on the city, he brought in a professional fundraising consultant from Chicago, Don Campbell & Associates, and began drawing on his many relationships. Not easy. "When you ask someone for $350,000 to $500,000, you don't get an answer overnight," he said.

Milt Maltz donated $250,000 from Malrite, just to prime the pump. "I threw a few bucks on the fire and got a few of our friends to do the same," he said. "They needed money to make something happen—tangible support.

"It was not easy," Maltz said. "We were at some social affair, and—I won't mention his name—one of our leaders came up to me and said, 'How dare you try to put rock and roll on a pedestal here in Cleveland; you have no right to do that.' I lost my temper, almost. My wife knows me too well, she gave me a big pinch in the thigh before I teed off verbally."

By September, Broadbent said the Hall of Fame development group had raised $13 million, mostly from local companies and foundations. He also disclosed the effort's urgency. Without that money, he said,

Robert R. Broadbent's business career included three storied names in American retailing. The Ohio native started at Halle Brothers in Cleveland, served as president and CEO of Gimbel's in New York, and in 1984 became chairman and chief executive of the Higbee Company, founded in Cleveland in 1860. All three companies are gone, but Bob Broadbent's legacy is secure. Without him, said former Ohio governor Richard Celeste, Cleveland would not have the Rock and Roll Hall of Fame.

Besides serving on the boards of Kent State University, the Cleveland Play House, and the Cleveland Ballet, Broadbent served as chairman of the Rock and Roll Hall of Fame and Museum, Inc., during the critical six years before it opened. Most significantly, he led the campaign that raised as much as $60 million, more than half of what was needed for construction, when members of the Hall of Fame Foundation in New York doubted Cleveland could come up with the money. He died at age 94 on July 13, 2015.

Cleveland had been in danger of losing the Rock Hall because of the doubts within the New York foundation. With the money—largely from Higbee's, BP America, Nestlé, East Ohio Gas, and Forest City—New York was satisfied. "For the first time in this entire project," Mayor Voinovich said, "I feel comfortable that we indeed will build the Rock and Roll Hall of Fame in Cleveland."

The bids to bankroll the building came in a wild array. They even included a bake sale: The local Orlando Baking Company introduced Cleveland Rockin' Rolls, donating a nickel for every package of buns sold.

Singer-songwriter Marc Cohn, a Cleveland native and Oberlin graduate, expanded a song he'd recorded as a *Plain Dealer* commercial into the single "The Heart of the City." With the paper's support, it became the Rock Hall's first official fundraiser. Proceeds of Eric Carmen's single "The Rock Stops Here" and then Joan Jett's Cleveland version of "Roadrunner" went to the cause. Higbee's sold "The Rock Stops Here" T-shirts along with Carmen's record.

Local real estate developer Bruce Felder, Hank LoConti, and I staged the first benefit show officially sanctioned by the New York governing board, a Rock On Revue at Stouffer's Tower City Plaza, with Johnny Maestro and the Brooklyn Bridge, the Jive Five, the Cadillacs, and Vito Balsamo of the Salutations. I pledged 50 percent of the royalties from my *Rock On Almanac* to the Rock Hall.

In November 1989, Ian Hunter, the British singer-songwriter who wrote the anthemic "Cleveland Rocks," and Mick Ronson, his bandmate from Mott the Hoople, played a benefit at the Music Hall for the Rock Hall.

Shows, movie screenings, and parties were staged as fundraisers at venues including the Hanna Theater, Stouffer's Tower City Plaza, Shooters on the Water, and Cleaveland Crate & Truckin'.

There were benefit auctions of Continental Airlines tickets and a dealer-donated 1988 Oldsmobile Cutlass Supreme.

But what really mattered, Broadbent showed, was the lead gifts of big donors. He understood the significance of the Rock Hall, carried the message to the business community, and helped boost private contributions from $650,000 to $12 million between 1988 and 1989.

As chairman of the local board, Broadbent announced the hiring of Larry R. Thompson as the Rock Hall's director in October 1988. Thompson, 41, was a lawyer who had spent seven years as special assistant to the president of the Ohio State University, overseeing administration and negotiating contracts. Broadbent hailed his understanding of budgeting and fundraising and said Thompson's chief job would be raising another $35 million for a building whose cost was then estimated at $48 million.

Five months later, the Cleveland board added a full-time fundraising director, 34-year-old John Zoilo, who was credited for leading the $30 million campaign for restoration of the Statue of Liberty.

But three years had passed since Cleveland "won" the Hall of Fame. Clevelanders had nothing to show for it. Impatience was giving way to doubt. News stories began referring to the "proposed" Rock and Roll Hall of Fame and Museum. Not "coming" or even "planned." Proposed.

There was plenty of frustration to go around. The cost of the project had doubled from early projections, in large part because of the involvement of I. M. Pei. Cleveland had to raise most of the money—almost twice what was originally pledged—before the New York foundation and music industry would contribute anything. After the Founders Club fell disastrously short of its goal, New York's attitude to contributing had hardened and its confidence had weakened.

Besides, Ertegun said, "If the record industry paid for it, chances are it would be put in New York or Los Angeles, because that's where the record companies are."

Remarkably, Cleveland and New York still lacked a formal agreement and answers to the questions it would settle. Who would own the Hall of Fame? Who would operate it? What sponsorships would be permitted? Would the capital drive to build it get any money from television rights to the induction ceremonies, which had yet to be televised?

There was a complication: the Black Tie Network.

Black Tie had incorporated under the name Rock and Roll Hall of Fame after conceiving it as a pay-per-view television event, and it had a five-year contract with the foundation led by Ertegun and Wenner for television rights to the inductions. Unknown to the public, Black Tie's licensing rights presented an obstacle to Cleveland. An internal memorandum of the Hall of Fame and Museum in Cleveland from 1986 noted that "relations with the New York Foundation [were] strained" and that fundraising and merchandising efforts were "on hold until resolution of the contract with Black Tie Network, Inc."

When Black Tie's contract ran out in 1988, without resolution and without any of the inductions having been televised, producer Bruce Brandwen and Black Tie sued the Rock and Roll Hall of Fame Foundation in the New York Supreme Court, the state's general jurisdiction trial court, claiming breach of contract.

The New York foundation, meanwhile, was again throwing down the gauntlet to Cleveland.

"The New York people said, 'Things have changed. You've got to raise another $20 million by November 1 [1989],'" Dick Pogue recalled.

NEWS STORIES BEGAN REFERRING TO THE "PROPOSED" ROCK AND ROLL HALL OF FAME AND MUSEUM.

"They sent us a letter saying we had to raise these additional funds or they're going to pull the plug on Cleveland."

In a March 3, 1989, letter, Ahmet Ertegun told Broadbent that Cleveland needed to raise $40 million, up from an earlier goal of $28 million, in cash or in immediately collectible pledges. He said the foundation board had "no obligation to take any lead in assisting Cleveland to raise these funds." While the foundation would help where it was able, he wrote, "such efforts will not be full scale and will only occur after the $40 million is in hand."

Ertegun also rejected Barry Howard's interior design plan, which included moving sidewalks and settings like a 1950s diner meant to re-create different eras in rock music.

"We reaffirm our original intent that the purposes of the Rock and Roll Hall of Fame facility are to be a museum, library, archive, and hall of fame," Ertegun wrote. "With the scholarly purposes in mind, the facility should be designed as such, and not as an amusement/entertainment center designed to be supported by tourism revenues."

Mayor Voinovich was out of patience and enraged. He demanded a legal operating agreement between the New York and Cleveland boards.

Judge Ethel Danzig of the New York Supreme Court may have brought matters to a head by deciding against the New York foundation in the Black Tie lawsuit (*Black Tie Network, Inc., v. Rock & Roll Hall of Fame Foundation, Inc.,* 1989). The decision was unanimously affirmed by a panel of five justices of the Appellate Division of the Supreme Court in March 1990 after the foundation appealed it (*Black Tie Network, Inc., v. Rock & Roll Hall of Fame Foundation, Inc.,* App. Div. 1990). The suit was settled quietly, without publicity. Terms were not made public, and details of the suit and court order remained unavailable for this book; in response to a request for the documents, the New York county clerk said the file "was in storage offsite" and "is missing from storage."

Years later, Suzan Evans said, "It was settled. They were paid off for their idea." Allen Grubman said he "didn't think it was difficult. I did not think it was very adversarial." Jann Wenner recalled, "That's all they [Black Tie] were interested in doing, was a TV show. They had certain rights, they came up with it, we went our separate ways, and we could go about creating a hall of fame." Members of the Cleveland board remember the settlement less dismissively.

"New York screwed it up," Mike Benz said. "Cleveland had to come up with the money as part of the overall deal."

Cleveland was blindsided but had to come up with about $1 million to pay the settlement, as participants remember. Three days after the May 17 verdict in favor of Black Tie, the ruling joined Ertegun's ultimatum on the agenda for a somber meeting in Cleveland. The room

MAYOR VOINOVICH
WAS OUT OF
PATIENCE AND
ENRAGED.

included Voinovich, Celeste, city council president George Forbes, and other political and business leaders.

"We were all pretty desperate," Dick Pogue said. "So we had a series of meetings on Saturday mornings, several of them down at Jones, Day [law firm]. We said, 'What are we going to do, this is serious. We've already raised all this money. How can we possibly raise another 20 million?'

"We went around the room, and we had all the big funders there, the corporate heads," Pogue said, "and as I recall, the first guy to speak up was Jim Biggar," the civic-minded CEO of locally based Nestlé USA. "He said, 'I'll put in a million.' And then somebody else. And they went around the room, and we had most of it raised in an hour. Biggar stepped forward. It was pretty dramatic. It just seemed like every couple of months there'd be another big issue threatening the whole project."

On May 23, the New York and Cleveland boards finally signed a joint operating agreement. New York committed to putting the Hall of Fame in Cleveland and sharing control of it with the local board, ending threats to relocate. Cleveland won rights to the Hall of Fame name—no longer tied to the Black Tie Network—to market to national corporate sponsors. And Cleveland agreed to raise the $40 million by a November 15 deadline.

Cleveland made that date, thanks to a combination of financing by the state, the city, Cuyahoga County, corporate donors, and foundations. And developer Jeffrey Jacobs, owner of the Nautica Stage in the Flats, and his father and uncle, developers Richard and David Jacobs, committed to cover any shortfall.

Would missing the deadline have cost Cleveland the Hall of Fame? The question is moot.

Decades later, Jann Wenner said that at least early on, the Cleveland group had "low-level people who didn't have the wherewithal not really getting the job done. There was some real stalling going on. Several times I had to give them the threat. 'You have one year left to raise the money or we are going to leave.' Two or three times, just to get them to focus. I was doing come-to-Jesus time with them, 'or we are walking, I'm not kidding,' and each time it worked.

"Bit by bit, Cleveland just kept stepping up to the challenge and were flexible about going through this creative process of discovery of what we wanted to do. This was going to be special."

At one point, Wenner said, "one of our members started a little revolt" to reconsider Cleveland, and he batted it down because "you pull out of Cleveland and it will never be built anywhere."

"They were never going to lose it," Peggy Mathna said flatly. "I used to spend a lot of time with Ahmet. He used to come to Washington a lot. Anytime he'd come, he'd call me and we'd go to dinner. He said that he was getting frustrated because Cleveland said they would raise all this money, but they didn't raise any money. Ahmet was getting frustrated, and he'd say, 'You know, I'll just buy a townhouse and put a plaque up because it's really the inductions that matter.'

"I don't think he would have ever pulled it because, remember, his reputation was on the line. Because nobody else wanted Cleveland, and Ahmet stuck his neck out."

Wenner's assessment was almost certainly correct. Other cities coveted the Hall of Fame, but it's questionable how willing they would have been to chase it, especially if Cleveland could lose it after raising and spending millions, after the site had been selected and plans had been drawn.

After delay upon delay, the Rock Hall was rolling.

Then New York sent Cleveland back to the drawing board.

CHAPTER 9

"We Built This City"

—STARSHIP

A lot of people didn't buy the story in 1990, and some board members denied it. Decades later, you could still find some who suspected it was the cover for some sort of land grab. The idea that the Rock and Roll Hall of Fame and Museum, a likely cultural and architectural icon, would relocate because a record store was nearby seemed preposterous.

But it was true. Handwritten notes and confidential memoranda in the archives of the Celeste administration in Columbus bear out the unlikely story and document the recollections of people involved.

When Tower City Center opened in 1990, one of the first tenants was Record Town, a 14,000-square-foot store owned by Trans World Music of New York.

"When the New York people found out" about Record Town, recalled Cleveland group member Dick Pogue, "they became very upset and started shouting. They thought this was kind of a treasonous act."

"We actually had a meeting in which one of their guys almost hit one of our guys in the course of the meeting," said Albert Ratner. "There are guys in New York hollering, 'We should have nothing to do with them; they put the record store there.'"

"Vinyl was still a profit center in their world back then," said Joe Marinucci, economic development director in the administration of Cleveland's new mayor, Michael White. "The ability of the museum to sell records was one of the keys." Graceland CEO Jack Soden estimated that a crucial 30 to 40 percent of that attraction's revenue came from the gift shop.

"Mike White was trying to act like a pacifier, but it wasn't to be," Pogue said, and a meeting of the New York and Cleveland boards climaxed when one of the New York people pounded his fist and demanded a caucus. "And so they all left the room. It was pretty dramatic. They came back and agreed to appoint a task force to determine what the new location would be."

Michael Leon, a vice president of the foundation and senior vice president at A&M Records, led the committee's review with Jann Wenner lawyer Ben Needell and Pogue, while I. M. Pei returned to Cleveland with Wenner and other board members to look at eight potential locations with the real estate group Grubb & Ellis. This was May 1990, and it felt like 1987 all over again.

Needell reported to a meeting of New York and Cleveland trustees that while the record store was the catalyst for reconsidering the site, it was no longer the primary reason. Problems not foreseen in 1987 included limits at Tower City on the Hall of Fame's space and ability to expand, he said. And trustees originally thought Tower City's visitor traffic would provide support for the Hall of Fame. Now they believed the hall already had enough of a name that it wouldn't need to depend on surrounding development for its success, and it might even spur development of its own.

"We looked at the triangle at Ontario Street and Huron Road"—close to Tower City and adjacent to the Gateway area earmarked for a new stadium and arena—"but it was too small," Marinucci said. "We looked at the Scranton Road peninsula in the Flats. A number of people really liked that. The New York folks came and looked at all these sites.

When we took them down to the lakefront, the Great Lakes Science Center was just about to break ground. I. M. Pei walked to the edge of the site, looked up at the city, and said, 'This is where we should build the museum.' Jann and Ahmet immediately concurred."

"I didn't want to be part of a retail shopping center," Wenner said later, discussing the move. "They said, 'You can't go by the lake, it's so cold.' I said, 'That's where I want to go, that's where we can really build something. We're not going to get a lot of traffic in the winter months anyway.'"

Ratner didn't mind. "I wasn't anxious to have it in Tower City because I had my hands full with what I was doing," he said. "We put a record store in Tower City, and the Rock and Roll Hall of Fame people said, 'You can't have a record store; we don't want to be where there's a record store.' But I put it in."

"Mike White came to me and said, 'I want to develop the lakefront. Would you be willing to have it moved?' I said, 'I would be thrilled. I have my hands full with what I'm doing.' 'Would you be willing to let them take the tax increment from Tower City and use it for the Rock Hall?' I said if that's what it takes, that's fine, I would do that."

Giving up the tax increment meant giving up a substantial tax benefit. Tax increment financing, simply put, is an economic development mechanism that allows the increased tax revenue from an increase in property values to be diverted to a specific use, such as reimbursing a developer for public improvements and infrastructure. Cleveland's tax increment financing from Tower City was estimated at as much as $18 million over 20 years.

The relocation, to a city-owned property off East Ninth Street at North Coast Harbor, was announced to the public in December 1990. The groundbreaking, endlessly delayed already, was scheduled for late 1991.

Pei had already reworked his design, keeping its signature "glass tent" and tower. Space beneath the large pedestrian plaza doubled the original exhibition area, which had been a mere 27,000 square feet.

"It was really designed to be behind the Terminal Tower," Peggy Mathna said. "That's why it's missing a garage and other amenities" that would have been part of the complex at Tower City. "What was interesting about Cleveland for Pei was the industrial look of the river and all the bridges. He loved the bridges."

And he loved the water as a vital part of feng shui, literally translated as *wind water*, the Chinese tradition of understanding and relating the elements to design.

"I. M. Pei said it's got to be in the water," Dick Pogue said. "Not near the water, in the water"—a directive that added a raft of new problems.

"If it's in the water," Pogue said, "that means the Army Corps of Engineers will have jurisdiction over it, and that'll add five years to the

THE GROUNDBREAKING WAS SCHEDULED FOR LATE 1991.

process. So we were really fortunate because one of our team was Mary Rose Oakar. She said not to worry, 'I'll write a rider on some appropriations bill to take it out of the jurisdiction of the Corps.' And it worked. She did it and it worked."

As Oakar remembered, "I'm not on the Public Works Committee, but I knew the chairman real well. I go to him and say, 'I need you. We have to get part of the Rock Hall in water or I. M. Pei doesn't want it there.' He says, 'It's a transportation route, even though you don't use it for that, but I'll tell you what, if you bring I. M. Pei to Washington, I'll listen to what he wants to do, because he's my favorite architect.' I said, 'You're kidding.' He said, 'No.' Pei did something in Texas that this guy loved. So I took him, we took the train, he has his model, and he meets my chairman. He just wowed 'em. The chairman was a real fan of I. M. Pei. So he does the legislation, puts it in for me." And if the Corps of Engineers objected, "He said, 'I won't fund them.'"

If that took care of the *shui* in *feng shui,* however, there was still the matter of *feng*—wind. The new Hall of Fame site sat less than half a mile west of Burke Lakefront Airport, whose approach zones made the building subject to height restrictions set by the Federal Aviation Administration. The FAA gave its approval to Pei's design, but not until his tower was reduced to 162 feet from the original height of 200.

I. M. Pei's 1992 Rock Hall model (Janet Macoska photo)

CHAPTER 10

"Shop Around"

—THE MIRACLES

Five years after the first induction ceremony, five years after Cleveland officially became its home, the Rock and Roll Hall of Fame and Museum truly qualified as music's Valhalla: it was the honored home of heroes, the hall of fame of the gods, and it existed only in myth.

Two years had passed since Mick Jagger, at the 1989 inductions, had referred to it as "the phantom temple of rock," a title better suited to an *Indiana Jones* cliff-hanger than a cultural institution. One year had gone by since Jann Wenner announced, "The shovel

will hit the dirt this year." By January 1991, *Spin* magazine was referring to "the Rock and Roll Hall of Shame."

Wenner dismissed the impatience. "We could have stayed at Tower
City and gotten up the project a year earlier," he told the *New York Times*.
"But all this has been necessary to ensure the longevity and character
of the museum."

In an interview years later, Wenner said his apparent lack of worry
was real, that Jackie Onassis had told him the JFK Presidential Library
and Museum took 10 years to build. In fact, it took 15.

Even so, there was enough impatience that Bill Hulett, new head
of the Cleveland trustees, needed to assure the group in a confidential
memo: "The New York group does not have sinister motives at the basis
of their foot-dragging but are still committed to the Rock and Roll Hall
of Fame and Museum being built in Cleveland."

He also told members, after a board meeting in New York, "It is
still extremely unclear as to just how the Rock and Roll Museum is
to be supported by any New York efforts" and "the New York group's
position is that it is 'Cleveland's responsibility to build this facility.'

"It was also quite clear," he added, "that we really do not know *what*
we are building and that an agreed-upon program for construction is
not being utilized."

The New York group was "very disorganized," he said. "We, on the
other hand, at this point don't seem substantially better.

"My gut feeling is that if we are going to get this accomplished, it is
not going to be easy, and we are going to have to substantially crank
up our time spent on the job to accomplish it."

Bill Hulett, who replaced the retiring Bob Broadbent as chairman,
was a smart and reassuring choice. A confident and hard-driving ex-
Marine, he was president of the Stouffer Hotel Company, part of mul-
tinational Nestlé Enterprises, and was credited for building the small
chain into a rising force in the industry. He and Albert Ratner were
the only members of the of the Rock Hall board who had experience
overseeing large-scale construction projects. He said Broadbent's job
had been to raise money. His was to get the ground broken and start
pouring concrete. He was determined to make it happen.

Designers Bruce and Susan Burdick came to town from San Francisco in May to unveil the new interior plans for Pei's building, replacing the early scheme that came to be called the "Happy Days Hall of
Fame" for its depiction of the rock world as sock hops and malt shops.

A few weeks later, the Cleveland board hired a curator, Bruce Conforth, to build the museum's collection of artifacts and memorabilia.
Conforth, 40, was director of the Indiana University Archives, taught
courses on rock music at the school, and enjoyed being "doctor of rock";

he'd written his doctoral dissertation on the folk-rock community of San Francisco's Haight-Ashbury district. He was a blues fan who would go on to coauthor an authoritative biography of Robert Johnson. He'd played in bands around New York, and he had also studied visual arts and "altered states of consciousness."

I. M. Pei discussed his plans for the lakefront Rock Hall in public for the first time in a presentation to the Cleveland City Council in June and then, for the second, in August with the Planning Commission.

In August, the board hired Peter Arendt, a former projects director for Tower City, as director of design and construction. A 44-year-old architect with bachelor's and master's degrees from Columbia University and a master's degree in architecture from Harvard, Arendt had worked with Pei and became familiar with the Rock Hall during the years it was planned for Tower City. He was a builder.

Robert P. Madison International, a Cleveland firm, was hired in October to plan the hall's underground major exhibition area, produce construction blueprints, and serve as on-site local architect.

The year ended on a high note in December when the Rock Hall finally signed a $5.3 million contract with Pei, an event that officials said marked the start of construction and Pei called "one of the happiest days of my life." So impatient was the local board to break ground and show progress that it staged the signing outdoors, on-site at North Coast Harbor, with a backhoe engine revving in the background. Financing also seemed to be revving up. Hulett said that the Coca-Cola Company, PepsiCo, and Eastman Kodak had submitted proposals for corporate sponsorships, and others were expected from Sony and Anheuser-Busch. The plan would have two companies getting the right to use the Rock Hall's name in advertising and promotion, for $20 million each, and giving others smaller deals.

Then came another cliff-hanger, this one worthy of the last reel in an *Indiana Jones* adventure, though the drama played out largely behind the scenes.

Late in February 1992, board chairman Hulett announced that groundbreaking had been delayed a year, until summer 1993. The price tag on the project had risen to $75 million, $10 million more than had been estimated just a month earlier. Fundraising, especially with potential corporate sponsors, had been hurt by the recession; going forward, that job would be handled in Cleveland, without the complicated and sometimes counterproductive involvement of New York. And Larry Thompson had resigned after three years as director. He was being replaced immediately by Mike Benz, the executive vice president of the Cleveland Growth Association, who had led the early effort to bring the Rock Hall to Cleveland. Thompson, it was said, was frustrated

The Hall of Fame construction site, April 1993 (Janet Macoska photo)

that construction was again being delayed and by the slow pace of fundraising.

"I really need all the help I can get," Benz told reporters at a news conference where the announcements were made. "If any of you have money, we'd be happy to accept it."

Privately, he said that there is nothing like the threat of hanging to focus attention. Cleveland was facing the gallows.

What had happened was that the boards of the New York foundation and the Cleveland Rock Hall had met in New York, and the Cleveland trustees had been given an ultimatum: fund the project or lose it. Yes, the costs had risen—skyrocketed, really—but Cleveland had had six years, from 1986 to 1992, to get the funding and break ground and hadn't done it. Time was up.

Mayor Mike White stepped up and brought the matter, and the meeting, to a close.

"Give us until the end of the year," he said. "We'll make this happen."

By all accounts, he didn't know how they'd do it. He had not even consulted or warned other members of the Cleveland board that he was going to accept the challenge. But he knew there was no alternative.

On the somber flight back to Cleveland, the board floated and discussed ideas and names. When the plane landed, Dick Pogue, chairman of the Growth Association, called its executive director, Bill Bryant, and asked where Mike Benz was.

Benz, still the association's vice president, was at a conference in Texas, which was where Bryant reached him—and told him he needed to come back for a 6:30 breakfast meeting with Pogue at the Union Club. A command performance. Benz made the meeting, and Pogue told him about the ultimatum and said the Rock Hall needed him to come back, as executive director.

"It didn't seem like an opportunity," Benz said. "I was out doing my career. I didn't want to do it." He was even angry about it. But they wanted him full-time, using the connections and skills he'd used leading the campaign that "won" the Hall of Fame in the first place. And his bosses were telling him to do it. He took the job, and the job was finding more money.

By the way, Pogue told him, he shouldn't get too hung up on the higher new cost estimate of $85 million, shocking though it might have been, because the real figure would be closer to $93 million.

Publicly, progress continued. In April, Turner Construction Company was named as general contractor and construction manager, chosen from among seven companies that bid on the project.

View of the Rock Hall construction site, April 1993 (Janet Macoska photo)

Dennis Barrie (*right*) at the construction site, April 1993 (Janet Macoska photo)

In June, more than a hundred items of memorabilia from the Hall of Fame and Museum went on display for three months at the Western Reserve Historical Society in Cleveland's University Circle. The exhibit titled "Are You Experienced?" was anchored by items from Howard Krantz, a Cleveland lawyer who had donated 22 pieces from his personal Elvis Presley collection, out of "civic obligation" to Cleveland. Among the notable items were Presley's blue suede coat, for which Krantz said he'd paid $25,000; his karate jacket; and a large replica of Nipper, the RCA Victor mascot dog.

Featuring dozens of photographs, posters, concert tickets, and programs, the exhibit also included a leather jacket worn by Jimi Hendrix, an autographed Beatles album, and items from a collection of Janis Joplin memorabilia donated by Jann Wenner and *Rolling Stone* magazine.

The question remained as to whether the display at the historical society would be a taste of what would be seen one day in a glittering hall on the lakefront or whether it would become a mothballed memory.

The peril was underlined as summer turned to fall and the Cleveland Rock Hall planned to announce 1993's Hall of Fame inductees. After the list was leaked in advance to *USA Today* by someone in New York, the announcement ceremony was canceled by Cleveland and replaced by a news release. It was also announced by Cleveland that the induction dinner would be held outside of New York for the first time—in Los Angeles.

Benz told reporters that the leak and moving the dinner shouldn't be taken as a slight to Cleveland, but of course these actions were widely seen that way. Rather than a slight, however, I think the leak was a reminder of the New York board's ultimatum and a way of asserting that

Dennis Barrie and on-site architect Peter Arendt at the Hall of Fame construction site, April 1993 (Janet Macoska photo)

the New York board administered the inductions that were the Hall of Fame's original purpose. Cleveland had the physical Hall of Fame and Museum, but still only prospectively. Ground had not yet been broken.

The financial clock was ticking, time was running out, and corporate sponsorships were not putting points on the scoreboard. The recession hurt, hitting corporate profits and cutting into advertising and promotion budgets. The lack of an actual Rock Hall to show some potential return on investment also impeded efforts to court sponsors.

Bill Hulett and Mike Benz gathered a group, as Dick Pogue had done a few years earlier, but now adding financial experts from outside the Hall of Fame board for what became a series of meetings. They knew that promises and simple progress would not suffice. They needed a new idea—and a big one.

Participants in the meetings said credit for the big idea belongs to investment banker Paul Komlosi, a director at McDonald & Co. Securities. A specialist in public finance and municipal projects, he proposed a bond issue. Dennis Lafferty, in the room as executive advisor to Dick Pogue at Jones Day and a former vice president of the Growth Association, also happened to be a mayoral appointee to the Cleveland-Cuyahoga County Port Authority. He suggested that it could issue bonds.

A bond issue would be a first for the Port Authority, putting it solidly in the economic development business, but it made sense. The Port Authority's core job is to maintain and operate port authority facilities and waterways. But the Port Authority, formed in 1968, also billed itself as the only local government agency whose sole mission was to spur job creation and economic vitality in the county.

The plan that emerged would have the authority issue $39 million in bonds, guaranteed by the State of Ohio and targeted at large institutional investors. A bit like a mortgage, the money from the bond issue would become a construction loan to the Rock Hall, and the Port Authority would become the Rock Hall's landlord. The bond money would be repaid by an increase in the county's bed tax, or occupancy tax on hotels and motels, and a surcharge on admissions to the Hall of Fame.

The plan would require approval from not only the Port Authority but the Cuyahoga County commissioners and the Ohio General Assembly. Working out the approval and the details would take months.

But the Cleveland board, which already had raised an estimated $44 million in city, county, state, and private money, had answered the ultimatum. The trustees of the New York foundation accepted the plan.

Construction could go forward. Ground could be broken at last.

CHAPTER 11

"Having a Party"

—SAM COOKE

The long-anticipated groundbreaking was a big deal. Trying to make it a bigger deal turned into an embarrassment.

The event was scheduled for June 7, 1993. Two months in advance, local officials of the Rock Hall said a major concert would be staged that night in celebration. Paul McCartney, on a break in the middle of a US tour, would be the headliner, and Bruce Springsteen and Billy Joel were reported as other artists who might perform in the benefit show at the 13,000-seat Cleveland

State University Convocation Center. Jules Belkin of Belkin Productions and Milt Maltz were working to put it together.

The announcement naturally stirred popular excitement and speculation. A lot of people saw a concert like this as what the Hall of Fame was all about. The groundbreaking seemed like little more than an excuse to put on a show.

A month later, however, the show was off. McCartney, it was said, might make a cameo appearance instead of performing. Belkin and Bill Hulett, chairman of the local trustees, said two months was simply not enough time to work out all the details. Performers had scheduling conflicts. Popular reaction ranged from disappointment to bitterness at what was called an embarrassment or even a fiasco.

Disappointment was understandable, but it was easier to understand the reaction of Hulett, who labored so long to make the day happen. His disappointment, he told the *Plain Dealer,* was that so much attention focused on "peripheral issues" and not the Hall of Fame itself.

"We just sold $62 million in bonds," he said. "We've heard for years about how it couldn't be done, how this thing was never going to be built. Well, it's done. It's a reality. But that doesn't seem to be worth a news story. I think we should feel good about ourselves."

The New York board might have been able make the concert happen, if it had wanted. But a concert was not a priority. Milt Maltz went so far as to say Suzan Evans, the executive director, had let him down.

"She said, 'Let me handle this. We will have a top-flight talent open up the Rock Hall; you don't need to put that burden on yourself. I'm working on it.'" After weeks passed, "she called me and said, 'I'm sorry to tell you my talent has backed out. It's up to you.' I was stuck."

Joe Dabila, a painter with Soundsation Entertainment Services, puts the final touches of paint on the guitar-shaped stage for the Rock and Roll Hall of Fame groundbreaking. The stage was 88 feet long and 36 feet wide. (Mike Levy photo. Courtesy *Cleveland Plain Dealer*)

Above left: Billy Joel, Chuck Berry, Pete Townshend, and Soul Asylum vocalist Dave Pirner on the dais at the Rock Hall groundbreaking, June 7, 1993 (Janet Macoska photo)

Above: Pete Townshend is interviewed at the Hall of Fame groundbreaking, June 7, 1993. (Janet Macoska photo)

Left: Ohio governor George Voinovich speaks at the Rock Hall groundbreaking, June 7, 1993. (Janet Macoska photo)

Jann Wenner, increasingly acting as CEO to Ahmet Ertegun's chairman, was impressed with what the Cleveland board had accomplished, but he didn't share its concern about media coverage. "They were always trying to come up with ideas to show there was progress going on, but they were all public relations ideas," he said. "I didn't feel the pressure, so I didn't care."

He, and Evans, did care about the groundbreaking, however. They and Ertegun attended it with other members of the New York board, plus I. M. Pei and the expected lineup of officials headed by elated Governor Voinovich and Mayor White.

About 5,000 fans also showed up at the construction site at the foot of East Ninth Street, greeted by a bright sun and the Goodyear blimp overhead. They were given commemorative painter's caps and an event worth watching. Unannounced in advance, a constellation of stars personified different eras and styles of rock and roll.

Billy Joel represented contemporary music, along with Dave Pirner of the alternative-rock band Soul Asylum. Chuck Berry, a charter Hall of Fame inductee, embodied the roots. The presence of Sam Phillips, an undisputed father of rock and roll, the man who discovered Elvis Presley, and a proudly outspoken Memphis booster, gave Cleveland a sort of benediction. There were Ruth Brown, the Tony Award–winning Queen of R & B, whose 1950s hits for Ertegun's Atlantic made it "the house that Ruth built"; Carl Gardner, founder and lead singer of the Coasters; Bill Pinkney of the original Drifters; and Sam Moore, of Sam & Dave, who helped define and name soul music in the 1960s.

An exuberant Pete Townshend of the Who flew in for the noontime Monday festivities the morning after winning a Tony for his score of *The Who's Tommy*, the Broadway adaptation of the rock opera. On the plane, he gave Suzan Evans the guitar he wrote "Tommy, Can You Hear Me?" on, for the museum.

He arrived with a flourish at North Coast Harbor, loudly and comically demanding to know, in mock grand imperiousness, "IS THERE LIQUOR? IS THERE LIQUOR HERE?"

As a matter of fact, there was not, much to the embarrassment of some of the local organizers. A business lunch was planned on the site, post-groundbreaking, with iced tea as the properly sober libation.

Rocker Pete Townshend addresses the crown as VIPs look on at the Rock and Roll Hall of Fame groundbreaking, June 7, 1993. (Janet Macoska photo)

Facing page, top: Rock-and-roll legend Chuck Berry at the podium at the Hall of Fame groundbreaking, June 7, 1993 (Janet Macoska photo)

Facing page, bottom: Rock and Roll Hall of Fame groundbreaking, June 7, 1993. *From left:* Dave Pirner, lead singer of Soul Asylum; I. M. Pei; Governor George Voinovich; Mayor Mike White; vocalist Ruth Brown; Rock Hall CEO Bill Hulett; Billy Joel; and Ahmet Ertegun. (Janet Macoska photo)

Above: Chuck Berry and Pete Townshend hold shovel guitars as I. M. Pei looks on at the Rock Hall groundbreaking, June 7, 1993. (Janet Macoska photo)

Right: Chuck Berry duckwalks and Pete Townshend plays shovel guitar while Ahmet Ertegun looks on at the Rock Hall groundbreaking, June 7, 1993. (Janet Macoska photo)

Tim LaRose, the stalwart Cleveland board member who, as liquor distributor, uniquely straddled the worlds of business and rock, heard Townshend and quietly saved the day. He drove to the restaurant Sammy's in the Flats and—knowing the crowd—loaded cases of Stoli and Budweiser into his car.

The ceremony lasted an hour. Celebrity guests and speakers sat on a guitar-shaped, 88-foot long stage, best appreciated from the Goodyear blimp, with go-go dancers performing on platforms above it. The next level of VIPs sat in chairs arrayed in front, and fans stood behind a low fence. Two skydivers clutching American and Ohio flags drifted to earth, presenting the colors, and Jimi Hendrix's taped version of the national anthem set a shattering tone.

Ahmet Ertegun said, "Many people have asked us over the years why we chose Cleveland to be the site of the Rock and Roll Hall of Fame and Museum. My answer to them is that we chose Cleveland because Cleveland chose us. The quality of the people who represented the city when they came to see us was so far superior to everyone else we met that there was no doubt in our mind that this was where we wanted to be. This is a great moment for the music industry, for the city of Cleveland, and the state of Ohio."

Jann Wenner, Pete Townshend, and Sam Moore at the Rock Hall groundbreaking, June 7, 1993 (Janet Macoska photo)

Mayor Mike White said, "The Rock Hall of Fame isn't just a Cleveland project. It's a one-of-a-kind project for the world to see, for the world to experience, and for the world to visit."

Pete Townshend said rock and roll originally "was music that came from people that were in trouble, and spoke deeply and hugely and heroically from deep down in their soul. That's what we inherit here today. It's a real, living, breathing religion. Let's hope it doesn't become a monolith to a bunch of dinosaurs. Then the cynics would have their way with us."

On this day, the cynics were silent. Jann Wenner handed out 66 gleaming ceremonial blue-and-white shovels. The Rolling Stones' "Satisfaction" blared in the background, the crowd counted down, and a conga line of celebrities and officials in ceremonial hard hats turned and tossed shovels of earth. Townshend and Chuck Berry played air guitar on their shovels and kicked up dirt doing Berry's signature duckwalk.

Fireworks burst overhead. It had happened. It was done.

For Mike Benz, it was a last hurrah. His job, the one he had been so reluctant to take, was done. He had already announced he was resigning as the Rock Hall's executive director. His background was in development and administration, he said, and it was time for a "trained museum director" to step in.

"We've delivered the baby," he said. "I don't want to be a museum director. I'm not a museum guy."

Two months after the groundbreaking, after a national search, Dennis Barrie was named as his successor. Barrie, 46, was a Cleveland native with a master's degree from Oberlin College in American cultural history.

And he was a museum guy.

CHAPTER 12

"It Don't Come Easy"

—RINGO STARR

Crisis was a regular occurrence on the road to building the Rock and Roll Hall of Fame and Museum. Dennis Barrie was only weeks into the job when he faced his. He was not someone who scared easily, and it left him terrified.

Barrie, who had started his career at the Smithsonian Institution's Archives of American Art, where he spent 11 years as director, had come to international prominence for his principled stand in the face of prosecution as director of the

Contemporary Arts Center in Cincinnati in 1990. He and the center were charged with obscenity for presenting "The Perfect Moment," a traveling exhibition of photographs by the late artist Robert Mapplethorpe. In what was believed to have been the first criminal trial of an art museum over the contents of an exhibition, Barrie and the museum were acquitted by a jury on all counts after five days of testimony.

He left the arts center in 1992 and started a consulting firm that developed traveling art exhibitions.

After Cincinnati, he recalled, "I vowed quietly to myself that I would never take another museum job, because it's too fraught with controversy. Then I was being interviewed by a reporter, and I said the same thing. And laughingly I said, 'Unless it's the Rock and Roll Hall of Fame.'

"Then I got a call a couple weeks later saying, 'We're looking for people for the Rock Hall job.' I said sure. I interviewed so many times, 13 interviews, mostly with the East Coast members of the board and a couple with the Cleveland side of the board. Art museum people were other candidates.

"Jann [Wenner] told me I had the job and told me I had 51 percent of the vote," he added, laughing. "That's classic Jann.

"When I came on, some of my colleagues said, Why do you want to do that, it's a dead art form? It's not going to have any value. Who cares about rock and roll? And how would you even do it in a museum? I don't think anyone really knew how to do a rock and roll hall of fame or any music museum. It was interesting to figure out how you were going to do this more than anything else."

He met with key people, including Al Ratner, Dick Pogue, Tim LaRose, and Bob Broadbent. He noticed Ahmet Ertegun stepping back from his lead role as a "driving force and diplomat who could bring New York and Cleveland together" and Wenner moving to the forefront with construction under way. He toured the construction site and saw the building's footprint taking shape. But he was stunned by what he saw next.

"The state of things was actually pretty grim," Barrie said. "To the credit of the Cleveland board, they had done a great job in getting enough money to break ground. But they had nothing to go in it.

"I was told that we had something like 30,000 artifacts. OK! Thirty thousand! All right! They were all in a warehouse at Berea Moving & Storage. The curator at that time was Bruce Conforth. I said, 'We have to go see the collection and think about how we're going to use it.' We went to Berea. Inside the hulking building was another structure that looked like maybe a two-car garage.

"We walked in, and I saw six cardboard boxes, a keyboard, and four- or five-headed mics that I think belonged to the Temptations. I said to Bruce, 'Where's the collection?' He said, 'This is it.' I said, 'What do you mean this is it? How do you account for the thousands of artifacts?' He said, 'We catalog every CD or tape that comes to us as an artifact, and we catalog every clipping on rock and roll as an artifact.' They'd put that in a scrapbook and count that as an artifact. They had done almost no collecting. I don't want to condemn anybody, but they did not collect.

"I went back to Jann and said, 'We're in great trouble. We don't have anything.' It was terrifying."

Wenner, who'd donated *Rolling Stone*'s collection of Janis Joplin memorabilia two years earlier, was stunned. "Nothing had been done to collect anything," he said. "We were building a building and had nothing to put in it."

Barrie knew something about rock, but his experience was in museums and exhibitions. So Wenner took the lead as they assembled a team of collectors.

Jim Henke was hired by Wenner and Barrie in December 1993 to replace Bruce Conforth as chief curator. Henke, 39, was vice president of product development at Elektra Entertainment, and he had become well acquainted with Wenner and the Rock Hall as music editor of *Rolling Stone* and as an editor of *The Rolling Stone Illustrated History of Rock and Roll.* He was also a Cleveland native who'd played in a rock band in high school and started in journalism as a copy editor at the *Plain Dealer* after graduation from Ohio Wesleyan University.

Hired to work with him was a core group of consultants who essentially became assistant curators: Bob Santelli, who eventually became head of the Rock Hall's education programs, was a writer widely published in national music publications who was teaching courses on American studies at Rutgers University and working on *The Big Book of Blues.* He focused on the blues and rock's roots. Michael Goldberg, the West Coast editor of *Rolling Stone,* was enlisted to focus on the West Coast. David McGee, an author and rock journalist who wrote for magazines including *Rolling Stone,* was recruited to concentrate on Nashville, Memphis, and the rest of the South.

To manage the collections and exhibitions, the Rock Hall hired Ileen Sheppard Gallagher, who had been running the Library of Congress Traveling Exhibit Program.

The challenge, Barrie said, was that the interior designers, Bruce and Susan Burdick's group from San Francisco, "had designed an encyclopedic museum. I think they had been told that the Rock Hall would have everything from Little Richard to the Beatles to whatever, so the designs were such that you would go through, to 1948 or whenever, and have something. And the truth is, we had nothing. It caused a kind of internal crisis. So we embarked on a plan.

"We knew we could not do an encyclopedic museum. So we decided we would do a thematic museum, and we would look at what areas and key genres we really wanted to focus on or that we could focus on. We

James "Jim" Henke was the right person at the right time. Maybe the perfect person. The Cleveland native had spent 15 years as an editor and writer at *Rolling Stone,* then a year working with talent as an executive with Elektra Records, when friend Jann Wenner called for help late in 1993. "We were building a building and had nothing to put in it," Wenner said.

Henke, who would serve as chief curator from 1994 to 2012, led the team that collected close to 3,500 artifacts of significance before the opening in September 1995, drawing on his own connections and friendships that included Yoko Ono, U2, and Bruce Springsteen. Known as a keen judge of talent, soft-spoken, and immensely knowledgeable, he continued collecting and oversaw numerous exhibits after the museum opened, and he wrote several books, including *The Jim Morrison Scrapbook, Lennon Legend,* and *Marley Legend.*

He died at age 65 in July 2019 of complications related to dementia.

came up with the roots of rock and roll that preceded what we know as rock, influences, censorship, fashion, and key cities of the rock world.

"We got together writers, because there really weren't any museum curators. We had a roundtable and said, 'What can we do in the two years we have to open this place?' It was like sending the knights out for the Holy Grail."

"Most of the collecting stuff was up to me," Henke said. "I started making out outlines of the history of rock and roll, thinking of exhibits we might have.

ONE OF THE FIRST PEOPLE APPROACHED WAS YOKO ONO

"I started reaching out to some people I knew. One of the first people I reached out to was Yoko Ono, since I'd known her from *Rolling Stone*. I went over to her house, at the Dakota, and she had all this stuff of John Lennon's. She had handwritten lyrics, guitars. She agreed to loan us some of the stuff for the museum.

"Then I'd go to other artists and say, 'Here's what we've got from John Lennon. What are you going to give us?' That was really helpful," Henke said, smiling at the understatement. "It was amazing. That was the first great collection we got." The collection, acquired in October 1994, included the uniform and wire-rimmed glasses Lennon wore on the *Sgt. Pepper's Lonely Hearts Club Band* album, one of the collarless jackets he wore with the Beatles in the mid-1960s, and the black leather jacket he wore earlier, when the group was playing clubs in Hamburg. There were items ranging from Lennon's report cards from the Quarry Bank School in Liverpool through the guitar he played during the Beatles' 1965 tour to the handwritten lyrics to "In My Life," "Lucy in the Sky with Diamonds," and "Starting Over."

Barrie called the acquisition "one of the tipping points. We had a press conference in the AT&T Building in New York when Yoko gave us John's stuff. John is for many people a great hero. I give Jann a lot of credit on that; he was very close to Yoko. And I give Yoko credit, too, for doing it."

Les Paul was another of Henke's first visits. "It turned out he was one of those guys who had saved everything and had everything in his house. He was another good one; he ended up loaning us a lot of stuff."

David McGee was writing his biography of Carl Perkins when Henke recruited him to join the effort. In an interview with RockCritics.com, McGee remembered spending 1994 to 1995 traveling to meet artists and their families, "hoping to convince them to loan some memorabilia to the museum so that we could honor their work with an exhibit. Some of these were fairly easy to accomplish."

"I had met and became friends with Johnny Cash while doing the Perkins book," McGee said, "and he wound up loaning us some great stuff. Carl loaned us one of his guitars that he had used at Sun, and one of his stage outfits. I drove over to Macon and met three times with

Zelma Redding, Otis's widow, and she wound up loaning one of Otis's suits and some concert posters."

He recalled how on a cross-country car trip with his sons, he had left Nashville with one of Buddy Holly's amplifiers in the backseat, dropped it off in Cleveland, then drove to California. "We spent an afternoon in Watsonville with Ritchie Valens's sisters and brother, laying the groundwork for a loan of Ritchie's memorabilia, then drove down to Pacoima and met Ritchie's aunt Ernestine Reyes, the wonderful woman who raised him, and she opened her house to us, showed us the family scrapbooks, some of Ritchie's stage outfits, his first pair of roller skates, and his first electric guitar. Later, she made a loan of some of those items to the museum. In between these visits," McGee said, "we also spent an afternoon visiting Donna Fox, of Ritchie's song 'Donna,' at her office in Sacramento."

"The interesting thing," Henke said, "was that it was the first major rock-and-roll museum. Now people keep their artifacts. Then, there was no Hard Rock Cafe to sell it to. I'd go to people's houses, see what they had. It didn't have to be a donation, it could be a long-term loan— they got their name on artifacts. Initially we thought artifacts should be donated, so we wouldn't have to buy them, but the loan idea ended up working out so we didn't need a lot of money."

"People just gave and gave," Barrie said. "Mostly loans, but they're never going to take them back. A lot of them just became gifts or will be gifts.

"There was initially a great deal of skepticism about the project from the artists themselves. Was it real? Was it a scheme? Was their stuff going to be exploited? They'd been there before. But this was a museum, it was a nonprofit with real museum people. It was nobody's get-rich scheme."

The museum's collectors, Barrie said, "are people the artists knew in a legitimate way, as opposed to the music management. There's always been an antagonistic relationship between performers and management. We would have been less successful if we didn't have people who were respected by these artists and believed to be legitimate.

"I have a generalist background. These guys knew them personally. I think that was really key."

Construction went on through the winter and spring, literally capped by the traditional topping-off ceremony, when the last I beam of the building's steel skeleton was lowered into place. With buildings of any significance and size, the event is a celebration, and the beam is signed by all the workers. For the Rock and Roll Hall of Fame and Museum, the topping-off, on July 28, 1994, was an event that rivaled or, appropriately, topped the groundbreaking.

A giant "honky-tonk woman" from the Rolling Stones' tour presides as construction workers watch the final steel beam swing into place at the topping-off ceremony for the Rock and Roll Hall of Fame on July 28, 1994. (Robin Layton Kinsley photo. Courtesy Cleveland *Plain Dealer*)

In the days before, the final beam had been displayed on Public Square, allowing more than 25,000 regular people to sign it. Then about 5,000 of them turned out in the rain, with lightning flashing in a dark sky over the lake, for what was billed as a "Top the Rock" party.

Bobby Womack headlined a "house band" of Cleveland-born and Cleveland-connected musicians: Sonny Geraci of the Outsiders and Climax; Wally Bryson, Jim Bonfanti, Jeff Hutton, and Opie O'Brien from the Raspberries; Michael Calhoun of the Dazz Band; Michael Stanley; bassist Dale Peters of the James Gang; Ken Margolis of the Choir; David Green of Forecast; Rich Spina of Love Affair; drummer Joe Vitale of the Eagles and Crosby, Stills & Nash; singer Sasha McCrone of the Ghost Poets; and Gary Lewis, who fronted the Playboys.

Surprise guest Jerry Lee Lewis joined them, performed three songs, and said, "It's a great honor to play here. Cleveland is my favorite city in the rock and roll industry." Breathless, ah.

The weather could have been scripted. After cursing the darkness, Wally Bryson, music coordinator for the event, decided to light a candle, or at least chase the clouds away. He led the band in the Beatles' "Rain," the showers stopped, and the sun burst out over a scene that included a 50-foot inflatable "honky-tonk woman" from the Rolling Stones' 1989 *Steel Wheels* tour, perched on a scaffold in a pink and green outfit.

If the sun hadn't arrived, Governor George Voinovich's smile would have done the job. Voinovich thanked and congratulated everyone, starting with his predecessor, Dick Celeste. Ahmet Ertegun and Jann Wenner proclaimed their love for Cleveland. I. M. Pei, modestly, or superstitiously reticent, said an architect should say less as a project nears completion—maybe he was suggesting the work should do the speaking.

Amid cheers and applause, a towering crane lowered the final beam into place. The band played until 3:00 P.M.

The work went on, and the tempo quickened. Suzan Evans, executive director of the New York board, remembers flying to Cleveland every Wednesday for inspections and construction meetings in a trailer with Albert Ratner. "We were very hands-on," she said. "It was very important to us, and a very exciting process. In my eyes, we were true partners."

"It was quite a preoccupation," Wenner said. "There was a lot of travel to and from Cleveland. A lot of phone calls. Albert was doing what I'm sure he's done a hundred times. He was somebody who could put the project together, and we got to be terrific friends."

"A lot of the artists came though while we were building," Barrie said, "and that was an influence. They were performing in town, and you'd see this pretty massive building coming out of the ground, we'd take them through, and even the doubters were impressed. I remember the Eagles coming through, and REM, and being really impressed."

The challenge and opportunity facing him and his staff became more apparent as the structure took shape.

The vision became clearer, he said, as they considered "how you could build a collection kind of out of thin air. We weren't going to censor language or content. It's 'sex, drugs, and rock and roll.' It's the soundtrack of the Vietnam War. It's the music of protest. It's the music of your teenager being bad. It was all to everybody's credit that we said, 'We're not going to censor.'

"The other key thing was, you were taking an art form that was about performance. You have to see and hear performance. That led to it being heavily AV-driven, interactive-driven. We did so many films, two-thirds of which are still there. We did a lot of film so you could see the artist in concert or onstage to give some context to the work.

"For many of the true believers, you've got to have pieces of the true cross, as I say—the guitar, the handwritten lyrics, the jacket, or whatever. But I think they're kind of meaningless without the context, especially as time goes on, of what it was like to see the real Elvis, the early Elvis, and understand why he was such a phenomenon. Those kinds of things are critically important."

"It's about the history of rock and roll," Henke said, "not just about the inductees. We managed to incorporate things like listening stations for the 500 songs that shaped rock and roll, and video theaters showing induction ceremonies."

"It was one of the most interactive museums of its kind when it opened," Barrie said, even though "the idea of interactivity was pretty much nonexistent." He cited the question that comes up about the list of influential songs that Henke curated: "Why'd you do 500 songs?"

"The reason that we made it the 500 songs that shaped rock and roll, and not more, was that that was all our programmers could do in the time we had to get the museum open," Barrie said. "It was like a superhuman effort, to get 500 songs in an interactive exhibit. Now you can get 50,000 songs on your phone. This was all they could do, the tech people and Burdick. They were pretty good songs, don't get me wrong, but it was the limits of technology at that time."

Barrie and his staff also found it "interesting with people who are still going strong," unlike sports halls of fame, whose honorees are inducted after their careers are over.

In fact, Barrie said, "I think the museum part is the strongest part of the Rock and Roll Hall of Fame and Museum. I didn't think the Hall of Fame ever worked as an experience, but I don't think halls of fame ever work as an experience. Go to Cooperstown, it's pretty boring to see those plaques on the wall. But the rest of Cooperstown I like a lot—those exhibits are pretty good."

The curators added sound and video to the original Hall of Fame, at the top of the seven-story tower, "just to have something not a tomb. It was too reverential. It's not the Nobel Prize, it's rock and roll."

As the building neared completion, the designers also encountered its realities, and sometimes its limitations.

"It's an iconic, beautiful building," Barrie said. "But the design is very limited. It's amazing to me they even thought about building it behind Tower City. The original design had almost no exhibit space. Once they moved it to the lakefront, the Erie side down to the water gave you the 35,000 square feet of exhibit space, which is the main exhibit space. If that building did not have the lower floor you would not have much exhibit space.

"I. M. Pei was a fascinating choice because you wouldn't associate him with rock and roll. He's a true gentleman. When I went to meet him as the building was going up, he said, 'You have a great building with many problems.' That's a quote, and I said, 'What do you mean?' He said, 'Well, the limits of the building, the way it goes up, precludes you from doing certain things.' I found out later—no freight elevator, limited access to getting things in and out. Staff space is underground, with no windows. . . . Not a lot of storage. The plaza in January. No kitchen—it was a great mistake. It cost a lot of money, ultimately, not having a kitchen," because all events had to be catered from outside.

"I. M. and I had a discussion about putting sound in the lobby. He did not want sound, and I said, 'It's a rock hall, we're putting sound in.'

"The other discussion we had was, we got these wonderful Trabants from U2"—the plastic-bodied shells of four homely, East German–made cars that U2 used in their Zoo TV concert tour in support of their 1991 album *Achtung Baby*.

Trabants from U2's Zoo TV concert tour of 1992 and 1993 hang in the Rock Hall atrium. (Courtesy Rock and Roll Hall of Fame)

Barrie smiled recalling the exchange. "He was not happy. I literally said to him, 'They're like where you have the Calder [mobile] hanging in the east wing of the National Gallery of Art.' And he grew to like them. I still think they're the best thing in there. They kind of say rock and roll.

"The building says nothing about rock and roll. It is gorgeous. Oftentimes there are buildings that don't say anything about what their topic is, and I don't think it did. We really had to make it about rock and roll as soon as you came in."

Such disagreements caused some tension with the New York board, where "there were certain people who were such I. M. Pei supporters that you couldn't question anything he wanted to do," Barrie said. He thought some of the tension also came because the board did not yet know "how big, how important the museum was going to be, that it was actually going to be bigger than anyone expected in terms of its impact. Some of us always knew it was going to be pretty significant, and thought once everyone saw how significant it was, the gates would open up.

"When you haven't done it, you don't know what it's going to be. Everyone's seen a stadium. Everyone knows how a stadium is supposed to act. No one had built anything like a Rock and Roll Hall of Fame. I think that was one of the reasons for the tension. You literally needed

The entrance to the main hall (Courtesy Rock and Roll Hall of Fame)

to let us run with it. We had to run with it to make it work. I don't think anybody was unhappy with it once it opened. They realized that the Rock and Roll Hall of Fame was going to be bigger than the awards ceremony, that it was going to become one of the ionic museums.

"It's truly a complex story. It's an evolutionary story. I don't think people knew what they had from the very beginning, from the awards dinner at the Waldorf. The original budget was $25 million and it became 92. It grew and grew, and along with that the need for certain people.

"There's a core of people I relied on and whom the staff relied on for decision-making, a small group of people who were key in its development artistically and politically. Jann Wenner, Albert Ratner, Suzan Evans, Milt Maltz, Tim LaRose, Dick Pogue.

"The guys at WMMS doing the campaign were key at one point. Mary Rose Oakar was key at one time. The guys behind the bond issue. They all had a role. And there are a lot of people who continue to make it happen.

"George Voinovich embraced that project—Mister Non Rock and Roll, and I say that with love and affection. That was not his world, yet he knew it was good for Cleveland, and he worked really, really hard to make it happen. Without George, without Dick Celeste, without

Pat Sweeney, it would not. People that rise at a certain moment to the occasion.

"Tower City would have been a great place for it—it's the heart of the city more than the lakefront. It would have been a great benefit for Tower City and Albert Ratner, developing the Avenue. He put civic concern over private concern. That's why I admire people like Albert, George Voinovich, Tim LaRose, Dick Pogue, Mary Rose Oakar. Tim's a rocker, the other guys aren't. It was about what they were doing for the city. You've got to give them a lot of credit."

As the opening drew closer, Henke announced a major coup he called "the most important collection we have put together." Sam Phillips gave the Hall of Fame and Museum the long-term loan of the original studio equipment he used to produce the Sun Records singles of Elvis Presley, Jerry Lee Lewis, Carl Perkins, Johnny Cash, and others, which are often considered the first rock-and-roll records. With the addition of a large collection of other Sun Records material and artifacts, the equipment enabled the Rock Hall to build one of its stellar attractions, an authentic re-creation of the Memphis Recording Service control room on its second floor.

"The John Lennon collection and the Elvis Presley collection may be sexier," Henke told the *Plain Dealer,* "but this is much more historically

A group of visitors pose with Elvis memorabilia on display in the Rock Hall. (Courtesy Rock and Roll Hall of Fame)

significant. If you were going to single out one person as being most responsible for the development of rock and roll, that person would be Sam Phillips."

"I have a lot of trust and respect in the Hall of Fame," Phillips told the paper. "I wanted to make any contribution I could—emotionally and literally." He hoped that the exhibit would make an emotional connection with visitors too. "People are going to wonder how we got the sound we did out of the equipment we had. But you can overcome a lot of things with just a little pioneering spirit. I hope that the exhibit inspires some young person to go for broke, to do something. I hope they look at it and say, 'Man, it started from this? There's hope for me!'"

CHAPTER 13

"Let the Good Times Roll"

—RAY CHARLES

Right on schedule. Ten years after I pitched Ahmet Ertegun the idea of putting his Hall of Fame in Cleveland, nine years after the Hall of Fame Foundation agreed to do it, eight years after the site was chosen, five years after it moved, four years after an ultimatum to fund it or lose it, two years after ground was broken and after the cost of building soared from $26 million to $92 million—the opening of the Rock and Roll Hall of Fame and Museum was set for Labor Day weekend 1995.

Labor Day was appropriate, because workers worked wonders building the Rock Hall. More than 2,500 of them had put in 359,000 hours getting the job done, from the laborers who dug and poured the foundation to the ironworkers and cleaners who climbed what they called Mount Pei in scorching sun and freezing wind. The labor would total close to 9,000 40-hour weeks, but in the rush to get it done, workweeks had stretched to 80 hours for some of the builders.

The celebration was as much of a mash-up as rock and roll, combining a festival with a political convention with Mardi Gras.

The opening day, Friday, started with CNN and the three network morning shows—NBC's *Today,* ABC's *Good Morning America,* and *CBS This Morning*—broadcasting from the Rock Hall, each on a different floor, the first time they'd all covered the same event since the 25th anniversary of Woodstock a year earlier. Little Richard, at a grand piano on the lobby level, played off *GMA* with "Good Golly, Miss Molly" and declared, "I am the architect of rock and roll!"

The "Rockin' in the Streets" parade stepped off a few blocks south at 11:30 A.M., with more than a thousand participants and thousands more watching them, standing five and six deep along the route down East Ninth Street. There were parade-standard marching bands, dancers, and antique cars, of course, but also the Flying Elvises parachuting down over floats, costumes, and props that had been built, sewn, and assembled over the previous three months. Among them were 15-foot puppets of Elvis accompanied by an 8-foot hound dog on wheels; of Madonna, sporting tasseled pasties; and of skeletons festooned in tie-dye, representing the Grateful Dead. There were a Janis Joplin look-alike riding in—what else?—a Mercedes-Benz; a Pinball Wizard; a costumed Sgt. Pepper's Lonely Hearts Club Band; and a Yellow Submarine with a crew of Blue Meanies. There were legs representing Tina Turner, doors for the Doors, and rolling stones for, well, what else?

The logistics were daunting, even beyond dealing with the crowd of 10,000 in and around the plaza.

Ed Miller, the chief engineer of Cleveland's ABC affiliate, WEWS-TV, served as the volunteer broadcast engineering consultant. For the month leading up to the opening, it was more than a full-time job as he coordinated coverage involving dozens of camera crews, 140 news vehicles, 400 phone lines, and 1,400 credentialed members of the media.

The route ended after an hour in front of the Rock Hall at Key Plaza, named for its sponsoring bank, where seated rows of invited and paying VIP guests were waiting. Jimi Hendrix's performance of the national anthem from Woodstock in 1969 opened the ceremony, capped by a flyover of Marine Corps jets from the Cleveland National Air Show—a bit of pizzazz cooked up by Milt Maltz, who'd looked in the direction of Burke Lakefront Airport while standing on the plaza during planning for the event.

Elvis and hound dog puppets joined the revelers at the Rock Hall opening parade on September 1, 1995. (Janet Macoska photo)

"I thought, 'There's going to be an air show. What a way to open up this thing!'" Maltz met with air show officials and the officers in charge to ask for a flyby. "We could do that," he remembered one of them saying, "but there's one condition. I understand you're going to have an event," meaning the opening concert. "I want tickets for all my men."

"I said, 'You got it!'" Maltz said. "We shook hands and had a deal."

Hendrix's national anthem, however, was an accidental addition that bookended its playing at the groundbreaking.

"We were supposed to have Aretha do 'The Star-Spangled Banner,'" Dennis Barrie recalled. "The night before, Suzan Evans said she's not going to make it. Somebody came up with Hendrix. I laughed because it goes on and on with that guitar riff," which left some dignitaries looking around a bit uncomfortably—*What is this? What's going on here?*—as they stood holding hands to hearts.

Seated behind the podium on the plaza stage were the speakers, names from the performing and, especially, business side of the music industry, and some of the key leaders and officials who'd led the effort to build the hall.

Bill Hulett, chairman of the board of directors, justly proud of what he'd steered to completion, had the last laugh and his final answer for

The Grateful Dead was represented in the parade on East Ninth Street in front of the Rock and Roll Hall of Fame, September 1, 1995. (Scott Shaw photo. Courtesy Cleveland *Plain Dealer*)

naysayers when the speeches started. "It took 15 years to raise the money to build the John F. Kennedy Library in Boston," he said. "It took more than 80 years to finish the National Cathedral in Washington, DC. If it took a combined 100 years to build a monument to John Kennedy and God Almighty, 10 years for rock and roll has got to be some kind of record."

The brief speeches shared a common theme.

"We did it! We did it! We did it!" Mayor Mike White shouted ebulliently. "Tell the world we did it!"

Governor George Voinovich, bursting with elation, exclaimed, "We did it, Cleveland!"

"You did it, Cleveland!" echoed Yoko Ono, who was dazzling in a black-and-white checkered jacket and somehow recognizable a block away. "You are changing the map of America. You are changing the map of the world. Your gift to the world shall inspire for many years to come. Thank you, Cleveland."

Yoko also said that John Lennon "would have loved the fact that he's here and not anymore in my closet."

Jann Wenner told the crowd of more than 10,000 people to stay forever young. "This music crosses boundaries of race, religion, politics, nations, and generations," he said. "And no one can stop it. This building is a reminder of that energy and power."

I was touched and honored when Voinovich recognized me from the stage, saying we wouldn't be there if I hadn't made the case to Ahmet Ertegun to give Cleveland a chance. After so much work by so many people over so many years, it was a special moment.

Ahmet, in turn, singled out Voinovich, who, he said, "stuck by us through thick and thin, putting himself on the line by authorizing the principal financing. He had a vision of what this project could be for his city and state."

There was another countdown. Nearly in the spot where a line of VIPs had turned the dirt to break ground, many of the same people stood with scissors and ceremonially cut the foot-wide red ribbon around the stage. The air show next door and the packed crowd in and around Key Plaza meant there could be no fireworks this time, but Mark Cheplowitz and Wizard of Ahs, his event production company, creatively had confetti cannons shoot ribbons and streamers overhead.

Said Mike Benz: "I remember Sam Phillips coming across the stage and giving me a big hug and saying, 'You guys worked harder than any of the rest of us, you deserve it, congratulations.'

"That was a big deal. The other one I got a hug from was Yoko Ono, on the stage. And that was a big deal."

I had been surprised earlier not to see Pat Sweeney onstage; he was the state legislator who'd delivered the education funding that was the Rock Hall's essential seed money and who had seen the project to completion. But I was fairly certain he would make it up there, remembering how he managed that feat during the jam session capping the first Hall of Fame induction ceremony in New York. That night, in black tie, Sweeney had draped a napkin over his arm, grabbed a tray, and headed for the stage. The act was so convincing he was stopped en route to take an order from Bruce Springsteen. Years later, Sweeney chortled, "He's still waiting for his drink!" He didn't need to resort to such measures for the ribbon cutting. Ahmet spotted him, greeted him in delight, and said, "Pat, gimme a cigarette!"

"It was a great day. A collective sigh of relief," said Dick Pogue, the lawyer who'd been central to shepherding the project through legal tangles and financial woes. Then came lunch, a casual gala for 3,200 people. Four hundred were inside at the mayor's luncheon, in the third-floor cafe area, and 2,800—including I. M. Pei and former governor Dick Celeste—were outside on the promenade overlooking Lake Erie. Serving as emcee was *American Top 40* disc jockey Casey Kasem, who'd been "Casey at the Mike" 35 years earlier on Cleveland's WJW, the onetime home of Alan Freed. Not only coming without a fee, as a favor to Cleveland lawyer Avery Friedman, Kasem hired a Learjet for $16,000 to make it after missing a commercial flight from Los Angeles because of a TV taping.

The bigger event was the evening gala, for which they all returned, a black-tie dinner on the promenade with champagne and caviar and a red carpet entrance where donors, sponsors, directors, and officials mingled with stars. The original ticket cost for this event was $1,000, and it kept rising. The entertainment—going for something different, said Mark Cheplowitz—was the Rock Bottom Remainders, a wryly

A huge crowd filters down to the Rock and Roll Hall of Fame as the morning parade finishes in front of the new structure for the grand opening ceremonies, September 1, 1995. This photo was taken from the 19th floor of the North Point Tower Building at the corner of East Ninth Street and Lakeside Avenue from the offices of The P. I. E. Mutual Insurance Company. (Chuck Crow photo. Courtesy *Cleveland Plain Dealer*)

Streamers fly at the Rock Hall's opening celebration, September 1, 1995. (Janet Macoska photo)

rocking band of writers fronted by Stephen King, Dave Barry, and Amy Tan. E Street Band guitarist Nils Lofgren, hurling himself into the spirit of the occasion, insisted on joining them. Maybe taking advantage of the distraction, Bruce Springsteen arrived unnoticed and took a tour of the museum in a small group led by curator Jim Henke.

One lingering tragedy marred the opening weekend, though it was beyond the control of the Rock Hall and the view of most visitors. Dr. John T. Carey, a beloved and nationally known AIDS researcher who founded and directed University Hospitals' Special Immunology Unit, was watching the gala from a private party on the deck of the steamship *William G. Mather,* a retired ore freighter restored as a maritime museum and anchored at the end of the East 9th Street Pier. He died after he lost his balance, flipped over a cable railing that later was cited for being too low and unstable, hit the pier, and fell into the water. He would be cremated and interred at Lake View Cemetery.

☢ ☢ ☢

The public got its first look inside the museum on Saturday, the day after the gala, starting at 10 o'clock. People who had paid for membership had time-coded tickets, but others came without tickets and swelled the first-day crowd to 10,000. It made for a chaotic crush outside on Key Plaza, but the beleaguered staff coped. Inside, the crowding seemed to melt away, and visitors' impatience turned into enthusiasm.

To the public and to the Boss, the hall was a hit. To director Dennis Barrie, the success was a relief.

"It was a bit of a roll of the dice when it opened whether we were going to have money to operate," he said. "Without that concert being a success and that fundraiser before, with 3,500 people in the tent, we were out of money. Then we saw people lined up down the street."

The concert had been a serious worry, partly because of its scale and even more because of lagging ticket sales.

The Concert for the Rock and Roll Hall of Fame, as it was officially billed, was being staged almost next door, in 64-year-old Cleveland Stadium, a cavernous lakefront facility with a surprising music history. In their second visit to Cleveland, in August 1966, the Beatles played the venue's first show. In the 1970s, it was the home of the famed World Series of Rock shows, staged by WMMS and Belkin Productions, which featured acts including the Rolling Stones, the Beach Boys, Pink Floyd, and Fleetwood Mac, among many others. Bruce Springsteen, U2, the Who, the Jacksons, Paul McCartney, the Eagles, and others played there later.

About 60,000 tickets went on sale for the Rock Hall opening, ranging in price from $30 to $540, with about two-thirds around $80 and 1,000 at the top level. The show was also televised live by HBO, whose

Yoko Ono and Jann Wenner climb the dais for the Rock Hall ribbon cutting, September 1, 1995. (Janet Macoska photo)

subscriptions in northeast Ohio spiked as the date approached. (Selling the television rights to HBO underwrote some of the show's costs.) Artists were paid only expenses for the benefit.

"Tickets were not selling for the opening," Barrie said. "We thought we had a product that would just sell itself. Quite honestly, there were some mistakes made about promoting the concert and making the community feel like it was theirs—and it [building the hall] was a community effort."

Barrie gave radio some of the credit for boosting promotion.

"We had left them out of the process in terms of promoting this project," he said. "But I remember vividly Milt Maltz and John Chaffee from Malrite literally got all the broadcasters in the building and said, 'This is our civic moment. You need to support this.' It really changed the dynamic."

The other vital element, Barrie said, was "the Belkins, Jules and Mike and their organizational skills to put that concert together. I wasn't a concert producer. Suzan [Evans] wasn't. Getting the coordination of all those artists for that concert. . . . People rise at certain moments, and it's really kind of remarkable when they do. There are lots of people who deserve credit. It was a logistical miracle."

Belkin Productions worked without pay as a consultant in marketing and producing the concert. Los Angeles–based Joel Gallen, whose Tenth Planet Productions had produced the induction ceremonies the previous three years, was primary producer. Suzan Evans served as executive producer for the Rock Hall.

"We had this seven-hour concert, which was like nothing else anybody had ever produced with all these moving parts and all these bodies to move around," she said. "More than 200 bodies to move around the stage. Can you imagine? It was a massive undertaking."

Naturally, it had unexpected aspects. "Little Richard was to open," Evans said. "He arrived in Cleveland, didn't say anything. The day of the concert comes, Saturday, he says, 'I can't open the show.' 'You came to rehearsal.' 'I'm an Orthodox Jew. I can't perform before sundown, it's Shabbos.' All of a sudden he's an Orthodox Jew! I said, 'Walk to the museum. By the time you get there it'll be sundown. You can go on.'"

At least he made it. Advertised but absent were Dr. Dre and Snoop Dogg, Brian Wilson, and Prince. Bob Dylan was an unbilled surprise guest performer.

Chuck Berry opened the show at 7:30 P.M., wearing a white tuxedo and playing "Johnny B. Goode," with Springsteen and a reunited E Street Band backing him and staying determinedly in the background. Maybe the night's busiest act, Springsteen and E Street returned for their own set, then played another with Jerry Lee Lewis and one with Dylan.

With 36 acts performing mostly three-song sets, often in unusual combinations, the all-star concert offered both the pleasures and drawbacks of a major-league all-star game. There were, noted *Los Angeles Times* music critic Robert Hilburn, "some classic pairings"— Aretha Franklin and Al Green, John Fogerty with Booker T. and the MG's—and "captivating individual performances," among them Green, Franklin, Johnny Cash, Chrissie Hynde and the Pretenders, the Kinks, James Brown, and the Allman Brothers.

Inevitably, in a show scheduled to last six hours, there were less than magical moments. And inevitably, in a show with 36 acts, it ran long. "For a while Saturday night," Hilburn wrote, "it looked like the Rock and Roll Hall of Fame celebration concert at Cleveland Stadium wasn't just going to salute four decades of rock music but make us relive every minute of them."

"By 1 AM," opined the entertainment paper *Variety,* "the concert was feeling less Jerry Lee Lewis and more Jerry Lewis Telethon."

It was close to 2:00 A.M. when Chuck Berry, who had opened, returned to close with Springsteen and Melissa Etheridge on "Rock and Roll Music." It did not go well. "The marathon ended on a bizarrely abrupt note," *Variety* noted, "with Berry returning for a ragged, Springsteen-backed 'Rock 'n' Roll Music.' After struggling through the number, Berry beat a hasty retreat and the lights came up. No goodbyes or thank-yous, much less the rumored all-star jam finale."

"There was chaos on stage," producer Joel Gallen told critic Michael Norman of the *Plain Dealer*. "But we got it back on track. The idea was to let them play the song and say their goodbyes and then roll the credits and do the logos. But my assistant director misunderstood me when I radioed him to start rolling the credits. He rolled the credits and signed off right during the middle of the song. But it's live and it's rock and roll, and these things happen."

In a 2015 oral history interview with the Rock Hall, E Street guitarist Nils Lofgren recounted his experience. "At the end," he said, "Chuck comes out, we're backing up Chuck Berry; I think you have G. E. Smith, with his great band; you've got Steve Van Zandt, Chrissie Hynde, Bruce Springsteen, myself, two or three other amazing guitarists, and Chuck's out there. I got an acoustic guitar; I'm just trying to get something going; it's real free form, and again, we're just going to do something off the cuff. Chuck, again, not too communicative; he's standing there, and he starts playing. Well, we're all pros, so we start following along.

"Somehow, a minute or two in, he like shifts the song in gears and a key without talking to us. Now, we all . . . OK, we're pros, right? So, we're all like . . . trying not to make a train wreck, and it's tricky. OK, what key is he in? Let's start playing there. He shifts keys again. He shifts keys four or five times; I can only imagine to mess with us. I can't imagine why else this happened.

"We're all looking around at each other, the cast of characters and the backup band; these are pros, decades in. We are making these horrible sounds, collectively, in front of a stadium, sold out. We're looking at each other like, 'This can't be happening, right? We're not creating this thing we're listening to. Yes, we are.' At the height of it, when no one has any idea how to fix this, Chuck looks at us all and starts, looking at us, duckwalking off the stage, away from us. He leaves the stage, leaves us all out there playing in six different keys with no band leader, gets in the car and drives away. Now if that's not rock and roll . . . "

Backstage, in fact, Berry was being urged to return to end the show. He smiled mischievously, picked up his guitar case, held out his arm, and wagged a finger reproachfully.

"Uh-uh-uh," he said. "Not in the contract." And he walked off.

Now if that's not rock and roll, it's vintage Chuck Berry.

"Then on the ride back," Lofgren went on, "we kind of started talking, and I was in a van . . . and there's a lot of other stuff going on that day, but Bruce and I started talking about that, because I don't think the two of us . . . we've been in a lot of clubs together, jams separate from the E Street Band, and I don't think the two of us have ever participated in something that godawful musically since we were probably 13 or 14. I didn't even start playing until I was 14. The fact that we did that in a stadium, in an event like the Rock and Roll Hall of Fame opening—it was just so insane and absurd and bad, that we got into one of those laughing jags where you can't stop laughing; we were howling. When we could barely talk, we would explain another awful thing that happened with Chuck as our leader. We just couldn't . . . It was just hilarious and awful all at once."

Unruly, unexpected, and weirdly memorable.

The ragged finale doesn't get credit for bringing the house down, but the old stadium was razed the following year. The concert for the Rock and Roll Hall of Fame became the last one ever staged there.

Just as well. If the ghosts of rock and roll needed a place to roam, a place for their bootheels to be wandering, they'd find it next door, among the living and breathing and rocking on, in the house that Freed built. With a little help from his friends.

Overleaf: Letter from *Rolling Stone*'s Jann Wenner to Norm N. Nite (Author's collection)

1290 Avenue of the Americas, New York, NY 10104 (212)484-1616

October 2, 1995

Norm N. Nite
WCBS-FM
51 West 52nd Street
New York, NY 10019

Dear Norm:

The Rock & Roll Hall of Fame is a great triumph, far
greater than any of us had reason to expect. With all the
hoopla past us, I just want to take a moment to go on
record and thank you for linking Cleveland to the Hall of
Fame Foundation in the first place.

Without your being there and doing the right thing at
the right time -- when nobody else saw it -- it may
never have happened. So my hat is off to you, an
unsung hero of the Rock & Roll Hall of Fame.

Best personal regards,

Jann S. Wenner
Editor & Publisher

JSW/mm

EPILOGUE

"Everybody knew it would work," Dennis Barrie said. "The music is important to people."

More than a million visitors came through the doors in the Rock Hall's first year alone, more than half of them from outside of Ohio.

But those early visitors would scarcely recognize what the place became, because it is in a constant state of becoming. Through all the ch-ch-changes, it's getting better all the time.

One early change started literally at the top, in 1998, with the dismantling of the original Hall of Fame, a silent sanctum on the sixth floor, in the building's peak. Replacing it, the building's larger third level was converted into the Hall of Fame floor featuring the Power of Rock Experience—an immersive theater dominated by a video installation, 80 feet wide and 20 feet tall, designed by Dreamchaser Productions, the Irish company that created the staging for U2's Zoo TV concert tour. Its feature production is the final film of Academy Award–winning director Jonathan Demme; he used great moments from more than 30 years of induction ceremonies to create an emotional, seat-shaking experience that *Plain Dealer* critic Michael Norman called "as loud and flashy as the old Hall of Fame chamber was somber and dull." In the plaque gallery outside, visitors can hear and watch artists' induction speeches and performances and read their essential stories—and then go into a memory booth to leave their own favorite stories.

The idea, said Greg Harris, the hall's president and chief executive, is to "tell the inductee's story in a grand way" and to make a more direct connection with visitors.

Visitors see evidence of change before entering the Rock Hall's iconic glass pyramid. On the stark, circular open plaza that originally was supposed to call to mind an LP record, bright scarlet letters standing eight feet high spell out "Long Live Rock" in a sign 80 feet wide.

"We want people to climb on them," Harris said of the letters, which were installed in 2016 as part of a multi-million-dollar makeover. The redesign of the plaza also included the seasonal installation of a sheltered stage where a curated selection of local artists perform almost daily all summer, "Rock Box" loudspeaker and art installations, food

At the Rock Hall's entrance, large red letters spell out the message "Long Live Rock." (Courtesy Rock and Roll Hall of Fame)

trucks, and a beer garden—plus JC Unit 1, Johnny Cash's tricked-out, 40-foot tour bus, which is stored during winter months in a secret suburban garage.

"It's intended to be a living, breathing space that has the DNA of rock and roll, not a blank space," Harris said. "We love the iconic I. M. Pei design. It's world class. One of our approaches to the space in this new era is to venerate that, really appreciate it, but also not treat it as if it's too pristine and precious. This is a shrine to rock and roll, not to an architect. Our new era is about energy and excitement and not being restricted."

Greg Harris joined the Rock Hall in 2008 to oversee development, after 14 years as a senior executive at the National Baseball Hall of Fame and Museum. In 2013, he became the Rock Hall's sixth director since its opening, building on Terry Stewart's strong legacy.

Dennis Barrie had resigned from what he called "the best job and the worst job" six months after the opening, later citing politics and meddling from some members of the New York board. He started his own consulting business and, often teaming with Malrite Communications' Milt Maltz, worked on building the International Spy Museum in Washington, DC; the Maltz Museum of Jewish Heritage in Beachwood, Ohio; the Woodstock museum in Bethel, New York; the Mob Museum in Las Vegas; and the US Olympic Museum in Colorado Springs, Colorado.

Bill Hulett, six months into the job of CEO and unafraid of butting heads, added the director's job to his duties, preceding David Abbott and Janis Purdy through what became a director-of-the-year revolving door.

Then came Stewart. He arrived as president and CEO in January 1999 at age 52 and seemed to have been born for the job, able to move easily in any of the worlds the position touched. A soft-spoken native of Alabama, he held bachelor's degrees in engineering and education from Rutgers, had earned an MBA and a law degree from Cornell University, and had worked in corporate mergers and acquisitions before becoming president of the giant Marvel Entertainment Group in New York.

He was also an intensely devoted music fan with a collection of more than 200,000 records. He'd attended the opening of the Rock Hall in 1995, because a Marvel subsidiary printed the weekend's program, and sat next to music director Paul Shaffer on the plane ride to town. He knew Ahmet Ertegun because they both sat on the board of directors of the Rhythm and Blues Foundation.

In 14 years at the helm, he built relationships, smoothed the workings between Cleveland and New York, put the museum on solid financial footing, and gave it stability as both a cultural institution and a tourist attraction.

Obstacles were considerable. An example Alan Freed would have

The Rock Hall entrance features giant painted guitars. (Janet Macoska photo)

133

recognized came with one of the Rock Hall's first corporate sponsorships; the executive who signed it was fired by his conservative employer as soon as he returned home. Stewart and the Cleveland board also had to lobby the Ohio legislature to change the agreement enabling the bond sale that financed the Rock Hall's construction, because the original language required sponsor money be used to pay off debt. Sponsors want to see their names on something more than a thank-you note.

Money grew so tight as sponsorships fell off, despite rising attendance, that it became a serious worry early in 2000 when Yoko Ono called Jim Henke, wanting to mount an exhibit for John Lennon's 60th birthday. The staff thought the exhibit would conservatively cost half a million dollars. "We didn't have the money," Stewart said. But fortune intervened when he met someone who introduced him to someone who said he would contribute $1 million for a Lennon exhibit. "Nobody in my entire life has given me way more than what I asked for," Stewart said—though he would subsequently take a pay cut and lay off staff to steer through the recession that started in 2001.

Stewart established an endowment, giving the institution a financial safety net. He gave the Rock Hall its first major interior redesign, adding bold colors and graphics to blank white walls and giving visitors

A young man and woman view the Cleveland Rocks exhibit at the Rock and Roll Hall of Fame. (Courtesy Rock and Roll Hall of Fame)

In the Rock Hall's Connor Theater, patrons watch the Power of Rock Experience. (Courtesy Rock and Roll Hall of Fame)

a clearer path to navigate rock and roll's evolution. And he oversaw funding and building of the long-planned Library and Archives.

The original plan for the archive would have put it in a laughably small space in the Rock Hall that had to be taken for offices when the building opened. After looking at other options, Stewart signed an agreement to put the repository two miles away, on the Metropolitan Campus of Cuyahoga Community College, whose state funding had served as the hall's critical seed money two decades earlier.

At its opening in 2012, music writer John Soeder greeted it as "the attic of rock 'n' roll heaven." Greg Harris sees it as "a presidential library for rock 'n' roll." And director Andy Leach aimed to make it "the world's pre-eminent research center for rock 'n' roll." Filling about a third of Tri-C's 75,000-square-foot Center for Creative Arts, the climate-controlled facility houses books, recordings, photographs, personal papers and correspondence, contracts and other business documents, dissertations, posters, and periodicals. The hundreds of archival collections include dozens of boxes of papers from Ahmet Ertegun and dozens more from other music executives and artists. There are Ertegun's personal LP collection; court documents from the payola case against Alan Freed; Jimi Hendrix's original, handwritten lyrics to "Purple Haze"; a concert set list handwritten by Elvis Presley;

Above: The growing list of inductees is displayed in the Rock and Roll Hall of Fame. (Courtesy Rock and Roll Hall of Fame)

Right: A family poses with a word sculpture outside the Rock Hall. (Courtesy Rock and Roll Hall of Fame)

Art Garfunkel's high school notebook (inscribed with "Please return if found!"); Buddy Holly's high school diploma; pages from LL Cool J's notebook; Jim Morrison's death certificate; and perpetual Mass cards noting that the Ramones will be remembered in daily Masses and prayers at the Holy Apostles Seminary in Connecticut.

The pace of change did not slow under the leadership of Harris, a 47-year-old native Philadelphian with a youthful outlook and rock-and-roll sensibilities. He had owned and operated the Legendary Philadelphia Record Exchange, a store still flourishing after 35 years,

The Rock and Roll Hall of Fame's plaza at night (Courtesy Rock and Roll Hall of Fame)

and road-managed a band before earning a master's degree in museum studies. Harris came to the top job with the advantages of long experience at the nation's original hall of fame, the baseball shrine in Cooperstown, and five years working alongside Stewart. He brought passion, an eagerness to innovate, and the convictions that museums are magical places and that the Rock Hall "is the greatest museum in the world."

It had been evolving since it opened. As it approached its 20th anniversary, Harris decided it was time to "pause and look deep at what our mission was and what it should be for the future, not to be content with maintenance mode. We wanted to grow and be as much as we could possibly be.

"The old mission was to be the foremost authority on the music that changed the world. It was an important mission to legitimize that rock and roll belonged in a museum. Now we were legitimate. Our new mission is to engage, teach, and inspire through the power of rock and roll. That happens in everything we do," including exhibits, traveling exhibits, performance programs, and outreach.

The makeover that started in 2016 included a slight change of name, from "Rock and Roll Hall of Fame and Museum" to simply "Rock & Roll Hall of Fame." It recognized what the institution was almost universally called, and it subtly underlined that this museum would be a place to be experienced, not merely seen or visited.

Nothing exemplifies that more than the Interactive Garage, which occupies the museum's entire second floor. The hands-on exhibit is an actual studio where visitors can play instruments including keyboards, drums, and guitars—real Les Pauls and Fender Telecasters—and digitally record what they play.

Renovations also addressed the hall's inefficient layout ("You had to buy a ticket just to go upstairs to get a bottle of water in the cafe," Harris said) and problems like the lack of ventilation ducts needed for a kitchen and restaurant because Pei had believed they would mar his design.

"We were not going to go 20 more years without a kitchen," Harris said. "We hired terrific architects and designers, and we're no longer trucking in pre-cooked meals from miles away."

The most ambitious alteration is the 50,000-square-foot expansion connecting the Rock Hall with the Great Lakes Science Center. Increasing the size of the hall by a third, it has room for indoor performance spaces, exhibits, and classrooms, plus a glass-covered, waterfront walkway linking the Rock Hall and Science Center. By enabling visitors to

A crowd gathers outside the Rock Hall at APMA's Fan Day in 2017. (Courtesy Rock and Roll Hall of Fame)

park in the Science Center's garage and reach the Rock Hall without going outside, the walkway is a critical improvement, especially in cold-weather months.

Even before that enhancement, however, visitors were coming in ever-increasing numbers, from all over the world. More than 80 percent of them come from outside the northeast Ohio region, and the majority say the Rock Hall is their reason for coming to Cleveland. Female and male, they represent all ages and ethnicities.

The hall tries to engage with each of them. Judging from surveys and observations, it usually succeeds. Because rock and roll is the soundtrack of their lives, the Rock Hall is about visitors as well as the inductees. The stories it tells are their stories, and telling stories is what makes the Rock Hall more than a mere repository. The items it exhibits are part of history. Instead of an "off-the-shelf guitar that's been signed by an artist," Harris said, "we want the actual instrument that played that specific song on that specific record or performance. It allows us to tell a story, to tell a story of what came before. We can tell a story about the actual guitar that plays the lead run for 'Rock Around the Clock,' which was used as the soundtrack in the movie *Blackboard Jungle*. When the film was distributed, teenagers responded. In London there were riots in movie houses when they showed that film. That became the clarion call for rock and roll."

When artists visit, "they want to see the people they loved, the people who influenced them. It's a common link they have with other fans. When Simon comes in he wants to see the Everly brothers stuff. Springsteen went to the letters of John Lennon. The original lyrics to 'A Day in the Life.' That's powerful stuff. That's what makes this place so special. These stories have meaning. People care. It's important to tell the story. We believe this is the most powerful art form ever created."

Mirroring the power of the music, the Rock Hall has become the signature of Cleveland. It is a face of the city that means something to the world. It will remain significant long after all of us who had any role in creating it are gone.

Also gone will be those who opposed it and questioned its value. But history has already given its verdict for those who measure achievement and the public good only in dollars and cents. A study published in 2018 by the economic and policy analysis firm Oxford Economics found that visitors to the Rock and Roll Hall of Fame were directly responsible for more than $127 million in business sales in Cuyahoga County in 2017, which alone is almost double the public investment of $65 million in the $92 million structure.

They've paid it back with interest.

To the Rock and Roll Hall of Fame—ROCK ON!

LIST OF INTERVIEWEES

THE NEW YORK GROUP

Jann S. Wenner—chairman of the Hall of Fame Foundation
Seymour Stein—President Emeritus of the Hall of Fame Foundation
Joel Peresman—president and CEO of the Hall of Fame Foundation
Allen Grubman—secretary treasurer of the Hall of Fame Foundation
Suzan Evans Hochberg—former assistant to Ahmet Ertegun

THE CLEVELAND GROUP

K. Michael Benz—former chairman of the Cleveland Civic Committee and
    executive vice president of the Greater Cleveland Growth Association
George Voinovich—former mayor, governor, and senator
Richard Celeste—former Ohio governor, 1983–91
Mary Rose Oakar—former congresswoman
Peggy Mathna—former assistant to Mary Rose Oakar
Pat Sweeney—former state representative
Dennis Barrie—executive director of the Hall of Fame, 1993–96
Terry Stewart—former CEO and president of the Hall of Fame, 1999–2013
Greg Harris—current president and CEO of the Hall of Fame, 2013–present
Jim Henke—former curator of the Hall of Fame
Tim LaRose—chairman of the House of LaRose and board vice chairman
    of the Cleveland Civic Committee
Milt Maltz—former chairman of Malrite Communications
Albert Ratner—former chairman of Tower City Enterprises
Dick Pogue—former managing partner Jones, Day law firm
Joe Marinucci—president of Downtown Cleveland Alliance
Jack Soden—CEO and president of Elvis Presley Enterprises
Lance Freed—son of Alan Freed

COMMUNITY AND ECONOMIC IMPACT OF THE ROCK AND ROLL HALL OF FAME

- Nearly 12 million visitors, and 80 percent have come from out of town

- $349,000: visitors spend daily at northeast Ohio businesses

- $2 billion: generated for the Cleveland–Cuyahoga County economy

- 570,000: visitors in 2018

- $127 million: annual spending by Rock Hall visitors

- 1,800: jobs generated

- $59.9 million: total wages generated

- $36.5 million: economic impact of induction ceremonies

- $199 million: annual economic impact on northeast Ohio, from a structure that cost $92 million

NOTES

PROLOGUE

Interviews: Stewart, Harris, Freed.

Tom Feran, "The Mintz behind Rock 'n' Roll Myth," *Plain Dealer,* Mar. 22, 2002.

Tom Feran, "Alan Freed Gets His Final Home: Rock DJ to Be Interred at Lake View," *Plain Dealer,* May 1, 2016.

Tom Feran, "Music-Inspired Memorial to Freed Unveiled: Jukebox Tribute Depicts Father of Rock 'n' Roll," *Plain Dealer,* May 8, 2016.

John Soeder, "Alan Freed Urns Spotlight in Rock Hall," *Plain Dealer,* June 25, 2002.

John A. Jackson, *Big Beat Heat: Alan Freed and the Early Years of Rock and Roll* (New York: Macmillan, 1991).

1. "WOULDN'T IT BE NICE"

Interviews: Evans, Wenner, Stein, Grubman, Mathna.

Greenfield, Robert. *The Last Sultan: The Life and Times of Ahmet Ertegun* (New York: Simon & Schuster, 2011).

Skip Moskey, Caroline Mesrobian Hickman, and John Edward Hasse, *The Turkish Ambassador's Residence and the Cultural History of Washington, D.C.* (Istanbul: Istanbul Kultur Univ., 2013).

George W. S. Trow Jr., "Ahmet Ertegun: Eclectic, Reminiscent, Amused, Fickle, Perverse," *New Yorker,* May 29, June 5, 1978.

"Noreen Woods Appointed V.P. of Atlantic Records," *Jet,* Dec. 26, 1974.

2. "THIS MAGIC MOMENT"

Interviews: Soden, Celeste, Benz, LaRose.

Motown Museum, www.motownmuseum.org/about-the -museum.

Deanna R. Adams, *Rock 'n' Roll and the Cleveland Connection* (Kent, OH: Kent State Univ. Press, 2002).

John Gorman and Tom Feran, *The Buzzard: Inside the Glory Days of WMMS and Cleveland Rock Radio* (Cleveland: Gray, 2007).

William Hickey, "Commercials Made Here," *Plain Dealer,* Dec. 6, 1968.

Tony Mastroianni, "'Shakin' Location'—Promoter Seeks Rock-n-Roll ID for City," *Crain's Cleveland Business,* Apr. 29, 1985.

Jane Scott, "Cleveland to Get Rock Museum?," *Plain Dealer,* May 5, 1985.

Tom Feran, "The Mintz behind Rock 'n' Roll Myth," *Plain Dealer,* Mar. 22, 2001.

Ahmet Ertegun, Warner/Chappell Music, www.warner chappell.com/artist-details/74.

3. "SEARCHIN'"

Interviews: Benz, Evans, Wenner, Oakar, Mathna, Celeste, Sweeney, Larose, Gorman.

"Rock Hall of Fame Tallying Votes for First Inductees," *Billboard,* Aug. 17, 1985.

John DeWitt, "Rock Hall of Fame Honchos Coming for a Look-See," *Plain Dealer,* Sept. 28, 1985.

"Rock Museum Panel 'Impressed' with City Tour," *Plain Dealer,* Oct. 5, 1985.

4. "MONEY"

Interviews: Oakar, Mathna, Wenner, Evans, Stein, Benz, Sweeney.

Peter Guralnick, *Sam Phillips: The Man Who Invented Rock 'n' Roll* (New York: Little, Brown, 2015).

"Music City 'Fame' Push," *Billboard,* Jan. 18, 1986.

Robert Hilburn, "Misplacing Rock's Hall of Fame?," *Los Angeles Times,* Mar. 2, 1986.

Justin Mitchell, "Rock Hall of Fame Pick Could Come on Jan. 23," Scripps Howard News Service via *Plain Dealer,* Dec. 24, 1985.

Eric Zorn, "City Drums Up Bid for Rock Museum," *Chicago Tribune,* Feb. 3, 1986.

A Joint Resolution to Designate April 24, 1985, as "National Day of Remembrance of Man's Inhumanity to Man," H.J. Res. 192, 99th Cong. (1985–86).

5. "CELEBRATION DAY"

Interviews: Benz, Sweeney, Stein, Evans.

Deanna R. Adams, *Rock 'n' Roll and the Cleveland Connection* (Kent, OH: Kent State Univ. Press, 2001).

John Gorman and Tom Feran. *The Buzzard: Inside the Glory Days of WMMS and Cleveland Rock Radio* (Cleveland: Gray, 2007).

Laurie Shafer Rokakis, "Dinner Standby Gains Entry into the Nicest Places," *Plain Dealer,* Feb. 20, 1991.

John DeWitt, "Even the Governor Was Rockin'," *Plain Dealer,* Mar. 22, 1986.

Alfred Lubrano, "City's Rockers Howl," *Plain Dealer,* Mar. 22, 1986.

6. "(WE'RE GONNA) ROCK AROUND THE CLOCK"

Interviews: Oakar, Mathna, Benz, Evans, Maltz, Wenner.

John DeWitt, "The Hall Rolls In," *Plain Dealer,* May 6, 1986.

"Hall of Fame Selects Site," *Billboard,* May 17, 1986.

7. "WE CAN WORK IT OUT"

Interviews: Soden, Benz, Mathna, Wenner, Pogue, Ratner, Maltz.

John DeWitt, "Big 'Thank You' Goes to Workers for Rock Hall," *Plain Dealer,* July 29, 1986.

Mary Strassmeyer, "Mary, Mary," *Plain Dealer,* July 29, 30, 1986.

"Trustees Selected for Rock Hall Board," *Plain Dealer,* Sept. 20, 1986.

Mary Strassmeyer, "Tower City Site Favored for Rock Hall of Fame," *Plain Dealer,* Jan. 16, 1987.

8. "IT'S NOW OR NEVER"

Interviews: Wenner, Ratner, Evans, Soden, Oakar, Celeste, Maltz, Benz, Pogue, Grubman, Mathna.

Joe Hagan. *Sticky Fingers: The Life and Times of Jann Wenner and* Rolling Stone *Magazine* (New York: Knopf, 2017).

Deanna R. Adams. *Rock 'n' Roll and the Cleveland Connection* (Kent, OH: Kent State Univ. Press, 2001).

Black Tie Network, Inc., v. Rock & Roll Hall of Fame Foundation, Inc., 159 A.D. 2d 240 (1990).

Christopher Johnson, Fundraising memorandum to Gov. Celeste. Celeste Administration, 1986, Rock & Roll Hall of Fame collection, Ohio Historic Archives and Library, Columbus.

Catherine L. Kissling, "The Beat Grows On," *Plain Dealer,* June 27, 1987.

Catherine L. Kissling, "Hall of Fame Hits Rocky Road as It Seeks Donations," *Plain Dealer,* July 19, 1987.

Catherine L. Kissling. "Leadership a Changin' at Rock Hall of Fame," *Plain Dealer,* Aug. 30, 1987.

Jane Scott, "'Heart of the City' Record Kicks off Fund Drive for Rock Hall of Fame," *Plain Dealer,* Nov. 6, 1986.

Jane Scott, "Benefit Gives Rock Hall a Life," *Plain Dealer,* Oct. 13, 1989.

Wilma Salisbury, "Rock Hall Design 'Explosive,'" *Plain Dealer,* Jan. 21, 1988.

Wilma Salisbury, "Pei Wanted Design to Express Energy of the Music," *Plain Dealer,* Jan. 31, 1988.

Catherine L. Kissling, "Rock Hall Strategy to Be Laid Out Tuesday," *Plain Dealer,* Sept. 18, 1988.

Catherine L. Kissling, "Rock Hall Survives Danger," *Plain Dealer,* Sept. 27, 1988.

William F. Miller, "New Director Sets the Tone for Rock 'n' Roll Museum," *Plain Dealer,* Oct. 13, 1988.

Debbi Snook, "Rock Hall of Fame Names New Fund-Raising Director," *Plain Dealer,* Mar. 3, 1989.

Stephen Phillips, "Many Heads Must Share the Crown," *Plain Dealer,* Apr. 2, 1991.

Debbi Snook, "Tempo Picks Up on Shrine to Rock," *Plain Dealer,* June 11, 1989.

Debbi Snook, "Interior of Rock Hall Is Still in Embryonic Stage," *Plain Dealer,* June 11, 1989.

9. "WE BUILT THIS CITY"

Interviews: Wenner, Mathna, Pogue, Marinucci, Ratner, Oakar.

William H. Roj, May 30, 1990, Minutes of Board of Trustees of the Rock and Roll Hall of Fame and Museum, Inc., Celeste Administration Rock and Roll Hall of Fame collection, Ohio Historic Archives and Library, Columbus.

Catherine L. Kissling, "Tower Re-Emerges as City Centerpiece," *Plain Dealer,* Mar. 25, 1990.

Debbi Snook, "N.Y. Board Might Try to Move Rock Hall," *Plain Dealer,* May 7, 1990.

Debbi Snook, "Lakefront Site Sets Rock Museum Board to Humming," *Plain Dealer,* May 31, 1990.

Debbi Snook, "Oakar Says Rock Hall Will Rise from Harbor," *Plain Dealer,* Oct. 30, 1990.

Debbi Snook, "Rock Hall to Anchor at Harbor," *Plain Dealer,* Dec. 19, 1990.

Steven Litt, "Pei Wants a Prime Corner of Harbor for Rock Hall of Fame," *Plain Dealer,* June 15, 1991.

Steven Litt, "FAA Clears Rock Hall Plans for Harbor Tower Near Burke," *Plain Dealer,* Feb. 21, 1992.

10. "SHOP AROUND"

Interviews: Pogue, Benz, Mathna, Wenner, LaRose.

Deanna R. Adams, *Rock 'n' Roll and the Cleveland Connection* (Kent, OH: Kent State Univ. Press, 2001).

Karen Schoemer, "Building a Music Museum: The Long and Winding Road," *New York Times,* Jan. 6, 1991.

Debbi Snook, "Stouffer Chief Takes Reins at Rock Hall," Plain Dealer, Jan. 14, 1991.

Debbi Snook, "Design Tunes In to Rock History," *Plain Dealer,* May 3, 1991.

Debbi Snook, "Dedicated Doctor of Rock," *Plain Dealer,* May 11, 1991.

Catherine L. Kissling, "Former Tower City Official to Oversee Rock Hall Work," *Plain Dealer,* Aug. 6, 1991.

Debbi Snook, "Rock Hall and Architect Sign Contract," *Plain Dealer,* Dec. 11, 1991.

Dan Kening, "Construction on Rock's Hall to Roll Soon," *Chicago Tribune,* Jan. 15, 1992.

Steve Luttner and John Funk. "Recession Blues Delay Hall," *Plain Dealer,* Feb. 29, 1992.

Debbi Snook, "'Perfect Guy' on Rock Job," *Plain Dealer,* Mar. 5, 1992.

Catherine L. Kissling, "Turner Construction Gets Rock and Roll Hall Jobs," *Plain Dealer,* Apr. 3, 1992.

Michael Norman, "Rock Hall Will Seek Coca Cola's Backing," *Plain Dealer,* Apr. 22, 1992.

Stephen Phillips, "Setting Sites on the Harbor," *Plain Dealer,* May 17, 1992.

Karen Sandstrom, "Relics of Rock's Giants Revive the Experience," *Plain Dealer,* June 25, 1992.

Michael Norman, "Rock Hall Inductees Leak Cancels Event," *Plain Dealer,* Sept. 12, 1992.

Stephen Phillips, "Rock Hall of Fame Backers Plan $38 Million Bond Issue," *Plain Dealer,* Nov. 11, 1992.

Stephen Phillips, "Rock Hall Outlines Plans for Construction Bonds," *Plain Dealer,* May 1, 1993.

11. "HAVING A PARTY"

Interviews: Wenner, Evans, Maltz, LaRose, Mathna, Benz.

Deanna R. Adams, *Rock 'n' Roll and the Cleveland Connection* (Kent, OH: Kent State Univ. Press, 2001).

Michael Norman and Stephen Phillips, "McCartney to Headline as Rock Hall Gets Rolling," *Plain Dealer,* Apr. 28, 1993.

Michael Norman, "Rock Hall Events on—But Concert's Off," *Plain Dealer,* May 14, 1993.

Michael Norman, "Stars Won't Come out for Rock Hall Show," *Plain Dealer,* May 13, 1993.

Rich Harris, "Ground Being Broken on Rock Hall of Fame," Associated Press, June 7, 1993.

Michael Norman, "Rock Hall Gets Rolling," *Plain Dealer,* June 8, 1993.

Fran Henry, "Billy Joel Cheers 'Lovers of Rock 'n' Roll,'" *Plain Dealer,* June 8, 1993.

12. "IT DON'T COME EASY"

Interviews: Wenner, Barrie, Henke, Evans, Benz.

Sheila Rule, "Rock Hall of Fame Names Its Director," *New York Times,* Aug. 12, 1993.

"Barrie Named Director of Cleveland Museum for Rock and Roll," *Wall Street Journal,* Aug. 12, 1993.

Michael Norman, "Barrie Ain't Nothing but a Great Choice for Rock Hall," *Plain Dealer,* Aug. 14, 1993.

Steven Litt, "Looking Back at Trial over Mapplethorpe Exhibition," *Plain Dealer,* Oct. 9, 2010.

Steven Ward, "From the Archives: David McGee (2001)," RockCritics.com, Feb. 27, 2013, https://rockcritics.com/2013/02/27/from-the-archives-david-mcgee-2001/.

"Rockers Top the Rock with Party Tomorrow," *Plain Dealer,* July 27, 1994.

Drexler, Michael. "Beaming with Pride City Has Thunderous Celebration as Framers Top Off the Rock and Roll Hall of Fame," *Plain Dealer,* July 29, 1994.

David Yonke, "Rock Artifacts Await Museum Space in Cleveland," *Toledo Blade,* Mar. 19, 1995.

Michael Norman, "Legend Lends Rock Hall Sun Equipment," *Plain Dealer,* June 3, 1995.

Michael Norman, "It's No Fantasy: Lennon on Loan 'Most Appropriate Place for John's Work,'" *Plain Dealer,* Oct. 14, 1994.

13. "LET THE GOOD TIMES ROLL"

Interviews Barrie, Maltz, Evans, Benz, Pogue, Sweeney, Larose, Klein.

Michael Norman, "Fans Not Knocking Down Rock Hall Doors for Tickets to Opener," *Plain Dealer,* July 23, 1995.

Mary Strassmeyer, "Celeste Sets Date for 2nd Knot Tying," *Plain Dealer,* Aug. 31, 1995.

Brian Albrecht, "Last-Minute Tuneups Aplenty at Rock Hall," *Plain Dealer,* Sept. 1, 1995.

Tom Feran, "TV Crews Jump at Chance to Cover Cleveland's Story," *Plain Dealer*, Sept. 2, 1995.

James F. McCarty, "Dancing in the Streets," *Plain Dealer*, Sept. 2, 1995.

Michael Norman, "Hail, Hail, Rock 'n' Roll . . . Rites Launch Hall of Fame," *Plain Dealer*, Sept. 2, 1995.

Fran Henry and Mary Strassmeyer, "3,200 for Lunch? The Schmoozing Was the Best," *Plain Dealer*, Sept. 2, 1995.

Tom Feran, "Rock 'n' Roll Heaven Visitors' Impatience Dissolves in Museum's Superstar Galaxy," *Plain Dealer*, Sept. 3, 1995.

Joanna Connors and Steven Litt, "House That Rock Built Has Visitors Drop By," *Plain Dealer*, Sept. 3, 1995.

Bill Lubinger, "Officials Pay Tribute to Rock Hall's Builders," *Plain Dealer*, Sept. 5, 1995.

Michael Norman, "Rock Concert's Abrupt End Explained," *Plain Dealer*, Sept. 9, 1995.

Michael Norman, "Summit of the Stars Rockin' the World Live from Cleveland, Show Rolls Out Greats," *Plain Dealer*, Sept. 3, 1995.

Robert Hilburn, "Rock Almost Didn't Go Away: The Beat Goes On and On at Celebratory Rock and Roll Hall of Fame Concert," *Los Angeles Times*, Sept. 4, 1995.

Greg Evans, "Rock and Roll Hall of Fame Concert," *Variety*, Sept. 5, 1995.

Rock Hall, "The E Street Band's Nils Lofgren: 'What Chuck Berry Was to Keith Richards, Keith Richards Is to Me,'" Rock and Roll Hall of Fame website, Aug. 4, 2015, https://www.rockhall.com/e-street-bands -nils-lofgren-what-chuck-berry-was-keith-richards -keith-richards-me.

Dave Barry, "Who's Nervous? We Came, We Saw, and We Rocked!," Dave Barry.com: The Official Dave Barry Website, Sept. 4, 1995, www.davebarry.com/misccol/ halloffame.html.

Christopher Evans, "Irreparable Loss: How the Death of Dr. John T. Carey Touched the Poorest and the Wealthiest," *Plain Dealer*, Dec. 10, 1995.

EPILOGUE

Interviews: Harris, Stewart, Barrie, Benz, Mesek.

Michael Norman, "Firing Up the Rock Hall," *Plain Dealer*, Apr. 3, 1998.

John Soeder, "Stewart Is Ready to Rock," *Plain Dealer*, Dec. 6, 1998.

John Soeder, "Rock Hall Plans New Library, Archives," *Plain Dealer*, Jan. 23, 2001.

Donald Rosenberg, "Dennis Barrie, Cleveland Arts Prize," *Plain Dealer*, June 24, 2012.

Michael Norman, "Rock Hall Loses Another Director," *Plain Dealer*, July 21, 1998.

John Soeder, "Rock Hall Archives Taking Shape at New Tri-C Center," *Plain Dealer*, Feb. 28, 2010.

John Soeder, "Rock Hall's New Library Opens Tuesday," *Plain Dealer*, Jan. 16, 2012.

Emmet Smith, "A Long and Winding Road Led New President to Rock Hall," *Plain Dealer*, Jan. 6, 2013.

Steven Litt, "Concert Stage and Outdoor Cafe Part of 'Museum 2.0' Redesign," *Plain Dealer*, Mar. 2, 2016.

Steven Litt, "Rock Hall Looks to Future," *Plain Dealer*, Apr. 13, 2019.

INDEX

Page references in **bold** refer to illustrations.

About Norm N. Nite

Norm N. Nite is a legendary broadcaster, disc jockey, and impresario known by many as "Mr. Music" for his extensive knowledge of music history and popular culture. Nite worked for over half a dozen radio shows in New York and Cleveland during his six-decade-long career, including a SiriusXM radio show broadcast live from the Rock and Roll Hall of Fame. He has also chronicled the history of rock and roll music in his *Rock On* encyclopedia series.

In 1984 Nite became an original member of the Rules and Nominating Committee of the Rock and Roll Hall of Fame and went on to play a pivotal role in the decision to locate the institution in Cleveland. His *Heart of Rock 'n' Roll* show on WCBS-FM was the first regularly scheduled program to originate from the Rock and Roll Hall of Fame and Museum from 2003 to 2005 and his SiriusXM radio show was live from the Alan Freed studios in the Rock Hall from 2005 to 2014. Nite now resides in Cleveland.

Norm N. Nite photo taken by Janet Macoska. *Clockwise from above:* Norm with Rock Hall inductees John Lennon, Stevie Wonder, Bill Haley, Billy Joel, Chuck Berry, Little Richard, the Righteous Brothers, and the Bee Gees. All photos from the author's collection.

ORIENTAL GARDENS

ORIENTAL GARDENS

An Illustrated History

Norah Titley & Frances Wood

CHRONICLE BOOKS · SAN FRANCISCO

HALF-TITLE PAGE
Detail from *Chikuzan teizoden* (How to make mountains and gardens)
Japanese woodblock print, 1795

TITLE PAGE
Winter-flowering narcissus, camellia and prunus, from *Jie zi yuan hua juan*
(Color prints from the Mustard Seed Garden painting manual)
Chinese colored woodblock print, *c.*1679–1791

THIS PAGE
From Akisato Rito's *Ishugumi sono yaekiden* (Eight Methods of piling rocks
to create a garden); [*see* 107].

CONTENTS PAGE
Flowering trees; [*see* 70].

First published in the United States in 1992 by Chronicle Books

First published 1991

Copyright © The British Library Board 1991

Library of Congress Cataloging– in – Publication Data available

Printed in Singapore

ISBN 0–8118–0132–2

10 9 8 7 6 5 4 3 2 1

Chronicle Books
275 Fifth Street
San Francisco, CA 94103

Contents

Introduction

Gardens have played a part in most of the world's great civilizations. For the inhabitants of Asia, they have long represented a refuge, whether from the stark landscape and baking heat of Persia or the bureaucratic cares of office in China. The landmass of Asia, repository of many of the plants that are now cultivated in the back gardens of the West, has, despite its natural barriers, served as a highway along which plants and ideas of garden design travelled to and fro. Europeans travelled to China in search of plants as early as the 16th century when the Portuguese first discovered rhubarb and camphor. Yet the movement of plants across Asia began far earlier: exotic edibles including grapes, pomegranates, walnuts, sesame and cucumber were imported to China from Central Asia and beyond as early as the Han dynasty (206 BC–AD 220). Of these, grapes and pomegranates, at least, were later grown as much for their attractive foliage and flowers as their economic significance. Later, the depiction of the early flowering prunus in the Chinese style occurs in Ottoman ceramics and Mughal miniatures, suggesting that the plant itself had been brought to the gardens of those areas. And though China is credited as the native home of some 80 per cent of European garden flowers, plants such as the tulip, introduced to Europe from Turkey in the 16th century, have made an indelible impression on European planting.

Links between the great civilizations of Asia are complex. The landmass is physically divided yet the Mongol empire stretched right across it in the 13th to 15th centuries, allowing the free movement of goods and ideas. The Mughal emperor Babur who reigned from 1526–30 was a descendant of the great Turkish conqueror Timur and of the second son of Ghenghis Khan who had begun the Mongol conquests. Mughal miniatures, which frequently depict gardens, illustrate the mixed heritage. Gardens are divided by waterways in the Persian style yet some of the flowers depicted, such as the prunus, are of Chinese origin and the style of painting owes much to both West and East Asia. The elevation of the art of garden design in Ottoman Turkey, Persia, Mughal India, China and Japan, forms another link; for the elite of all these, gardens were an essential aspect of private life. Whilst a Mughal emperor might spend his youth in conquest, the gardens that he saw as he swept across national

OPPOSITE
A delicate Deccani plan for an orchard, Indian, c.1685.

barriers helped to form the gardens he created for himself. In China, government officials would complain of the sound of the bugle, calling them to work, for they would prefer to linger in the rustic seclusion of a tiny garden.

If the gardens of Asia can be thus linked in inspiration, their styles are vastly different. Climate determined the differences to a great extent though the differing local cultures also created different ideals. The fundamental contrast is between the geometric designs of Persia and India and the rugged 'natural' mountains and pools of the Far East. As the illustrations in this book reveal, the geometry of Persian and Mughal gardens allows a complete view of the garden from raised pavilions. Gardens were the settings for feasts, gatherings and clandestine meetings, flowered carpets spread on the ground and silken tents erected for the event, the whole scene laid out for the viewer in magical detail. Gardens were used similarly in the Far East but, when depicted in illustrated books and albums, the whole is rarely revealed; instead, a corner of the garden is shown, the rest hidden. A visitor to a Chinese or Japanese garden was similarly presented with a series of views, one hidden from the next. The Chinese and Japanese themselves compared their gardens to handscroll paintings which were gradually unfurled for visitors, revealing one scene after another. Later Japanese gardens, constricted by the fast growth of towns and cities, began to use the fixed viewpoint that characterizes many Near Eastern gardens. Their contents, however, were markedly different. Instead of the profusion of flowers between the regular water channels, a sombre grey and silver scene created from raked sand and irregularly disposed rocks, with only a hint of greenery, is laid out for the contemplation of visitors.

Illustrated books and albums from all corners of Asia are well represented in The British Library's collections. Many of them depict gardens, as the setting for the great epic poems of Turkey and Persia or the rambling novels of Japan and China. In their attention to detail, they represent an ideal source of information on garden design. Even in the Far East, where often it is only a corner of a garden that is glimpsed, these details convey the care with which corners of gardens or areas adjacent to houses were landscaped to provide a refreshing view from a verandah or pavilion. The depiction of landscaped gardens in Far Eastern books is supplemented by the number of garden design manuals that survive from the 13th century. Chinese manuals, such as Ji Cheng's 17th century *Yuan Ye* (The Craft of Gardens), not only lay out the details of construction of pavilions, rockeries, pools, paths and beds, but also convey the poetic ideal of the gentleman's rustic retreat. Later Japanese manuals concentrate on layout. Illustrations of tea-house gardens show each rock in a stepping-stone series carefully numbered, sometimes with measurements of the exact distance desired between each stone. Works such as these can still enable us to construct our own tea-house garden, with grass, stepping-stones and lanterns placed according to traditional principles, whilst the jewel-like colours of Near Eastern miniatures provide inspiration for planting, mixing brilliant blues and reds and shading the ground with dark trees.

GLOSSARY

Bonsai: the Japanese form of *pen cai* (*see* below), popular since the 17th century, producing smaller, spikier miniatures than the Chinese version.

Chahar Bagh: the 'four gardens' system of garden design which originated in Iran. Four water channels flow at right angles between flower-beds into a central pool.

Kiosks: Turkish garden pavilions.

Pen cai: a Chinese term literally meaning 'reared in pots' where the roots of plants are cut and their stems twisted to form miniatures.

Pen jing: a technique related to *pen cai*, literally 'pot scene'. Rocks and pebbles are set in water in earthenware dishes to form decorative 'mountain and lake' scenes.

Qanat: An Iranian system of irrigation dating back to the sixth century BC. Underground tunnels on different levels divert the water supply to where it is needed.

Yalis: Turkish summer dwellings.

Ottoman Turkey

In Turkey, the interest in flowers and gardens is evident from contemporary accounts of the earliest period of Ottoman rule up to the present day. Whether palace or private gardens or public parks, Turkish gardens have always been of a more haphazard design than the geometric layout of those in Iran and Mughal India, which serve as a refuge from the heat of summer. The *chahar bagh* or four gardens system of water channels at right angles to each other enclosing flower beds was not often employed in Ottoman gardens, the preference being for fountains and pools. In particular fountains were a feature not only of Ottoman gardens but of city and village streets. In different sizes and designs, they are to be met with everywhere and were used in garden kiosks (pavilions) in preference to water channels.

The Ottoman Sultan, Mehmed II, who conquered Constantinople (renamed Istanbul) in 1453, first made his capital at Adrianople (modern Edirne) and built a palace there surrounded by gardens and parkland. He moved his capital to Istanbul in 1457 and built the Topkapi Saraye (or palace) on its magnificent site. As at Edirne, he planned pleasure gardens round the palace which are still in evidence today although succeeding sultans altered them and added more kiosks and other buildings. Mehmed II was a practical gardener who delighted not only in planning gardens wherever he built palaces or mosques, but, according to contemporary accounts, actually working in them whenever he could spare time between his various campaigns. He founded the imperial cemetery at Bursa, where his own tomb dating back to 1451, together with ten others, is set in a rambling garden where roses are now grown.

The Topkapi Saraye had very extensive gardens in the 15th century, laid out with flower beds and trees of all kinds – cypress, planes, pines, willows and box amongst them – the whole area being surrounded by a high wall. The gardens originally covered a far larger area than they do today, extending to what is now the modern coast road running by the Sea of Marmara and including the Gülhâne Park on one side and extending to the Golden Horn on the other.

Istanbul, in contrast to the desert conditions suffered by Iran and India, has the advantage of its position on the shores of the Bosphorus,

2 Decorative paper cut-outs of flowers in vases, an Ottoman speciality. [Or. 13763D]

OPPOSITE
1 Festivities and entertainments at the Sweet Waters of Europe (Kağithâne) in its heyday, depicted in a late 18th-century manuscript painting. [Or. 7094, f. 7a]

the Sea of Marmara and the Golden Horn which provide relief from the worst of the summer heat. Sultans, nobles and eminent citizens built palaces and summer dwellings (*yalis*) at the water's edge, each with a garden that stretched up the slopes behind it. Evliya Çelebi in his *Narrative of Travels*[1] compiled in the 17th century, commented that if he were to describe minutely all the pleasure palaces, gardens, *yalis*, kiosks and walks in Istanbul, it would be a long work. Some of the old *yalis*, carefully restored, still stand on the shores, together with more modern buildings. These are best seen from the ferry boats which ply up and down the Bosphorus between the fishing villages, and to the Princes' Islands on the Sea of Marmara. Terraced gardens are laid out on the slopes behind the houses, reaching up to the natural area of trees and shrubs where paths ramble among umbrella pines, Judas trees, cypresses, and other indigenous trees.

Evliya Çelebi, writing of the gardens and houses at the village of Beşiktaş down the Bosphorus, noted that 'there were no less than a hundred and sixty gardens, every one like a paradise, fragrant of roses, narcissus and oderiferous [*sic*] herbs'. A tulip festival is held every April above Emirğan while Büyükada, the largest of the Princes' Islands, still has beautiful 19th-century wooden houses with their original gardens. These gardens, with their shady paths, terraced borders, fountains and kiosks provided colour, coolness and privacy.

Charles White,[2] writing in the mid-19th century, described private gardens in the vicinity of the Bosphorus and the variety of plants grown in them. Vegetables were planted among the flowering plants in the borders, and vines, roses and other climbers were trained on walls, fences and trellises. Parterres, edged by clipped box-hedges, were filled with lemon and orange trees as well as standard pomegranate, bay and lilac bushes. Lilies, irises, sunflowers, larkspurs, mignonette, lupins, convolvulus and sweet peas were some of the flowers planted round the bushes, and flowerpots full of geraniums, carnations, lychnis, stocks, anemones, fuchsias and heliotrope stood on the terrace steps and walls. The secluded areas on the hillside were shaded by trees such as chestnut, ilex, fig, walnut, pine and cedar. The walks of the terraces were sheltered by the vine trellises and each parterre would have a central pool or a fountain. Most private gardens, like the palace and public gardens, had at least one kiosk, either situated in a tiled courtyard, or at the water's edge, or placed high up amongst the shade of trees to afford the best views. These pavilions had flat or domed roofs and the walls would be constructed with open spaces or grilles to take advantage of cool breezes, with a pool and fountain let into the tiled floor. Some kiosks would have an inner room with latticed walls for entertaining while others would simply be a shelter from the sun open at the front and with a door or

1 Evliya Çelebi, *Narrative of Travels*, translated by J. Von Hammer (London, 1834).

2 C. White, *Three Years in Constantinople*, 3 vols, (London, 1844).

window at the back for through breezes [*see* 4]. Garden kiosks of various periods and designs can be seen today in palace gardens such as the Topkapi Saraye or the Yildiz Palace in Istanbul. There was Persian influence in kiosks built by Mehmed II in the 15th century and, in turn, small Ottoman-designed pavilions became a feature of gardens in Egypt during the Ottoman rule there.

Tools and equipment used by gardeners were simple and changed very little over the centuries. Baskets carried on asses or on the backs of gardeners were a substitute for wheelbarrows. A century before White described the tools used by gardeners, Evliya Çelebi mentions those carried in one of the Processions of the Guilds in Istanbul as hoes, spades, rakes and pruning or grafting knives.

Shortly after his conquest of Istanbul in 1453, Mehmed II laid out a garden on what is now the site of the Dolmabahçe Palace. In the 17th century Ahmed I and his son, Osman II, extended the garden by filling in the small harbour there. All ships using Istanbul were ordered to load up with stones and to drop them into the sea at that point. 'Dolmabahçe' literally means 'filled-in garden'.

Creation and upkeep of gardens was carried out by successive Ottoman sultans and, to a lesser degree, by their courtiers and palace officials. Hundreds of gardeners, including specialist grafters, were employed and plants were ordered from far and wide. It is recorded that plants were brought to the palace gardens from throughout Turkey, particularly bulbs from Anatolia and thousands of trees of all kinds from Izmet. Bulbs were also imported from outside Turkey for there is a record of half a million hyacinth bulbs having been ordered from Aleppo in 1595. Works were written on flowers in general and also on single species such as tulips and hyacinths. Textiles, Iznik pottery, architecture, tiles, bookbindings and miniatures featured flowers from the early 16th century, while the language is full of the imagery of the garden paradise. Exquisite designs incorporating flowers and trees cut out of paper and formed into tiny collages are an Ottoman speciality which reached its peak in the late 18th century [*see* 2].

The obsession with tulips culminated in the so-called Tulip Era (*Lala Devre*) of the early 18th century when 'tulipomania' led to economic ruin and the deposition of the sultan, Ahmed III, in 1730. His reign became notorious for the fanatical love of gardens and flowers, particularly tulips, which eventually led to his downfall. The craze was shared by his son-in-law and Grand Vizier, Ibrahim Paşa, and, to a lesser degree, by his courtiers and nobles who vied with each other in the acquisition of rare tulip bulbs and in the splendour of their gardens. Bulbs were used by officials as a means to obtain favours from the Sultan, including high rank. Aided and abetted by Ibrahim Paşa, Ahmed III spent a fortune on buying rare varieties and creating tulip gardens in the grounds of his various palaces.

Besides his passion for tulips, Ahmed III was a lover of all flowers and gardens; he not only created gardens but decorated the interiors of his new buildings in the Topkapi Saraye complex with flowers. The dining room in the Fourth Court is known as the Orchard Room from its wallpaintings of flowers and bowls of fruit, and the ceiling of the Library, built in 1719 in the Third Court, is decorated with paintings of flowers. He laid out a tulip garden in the Fourth Court [3], the part of the Topkapi Saraye grounds furthest from the main entrance. It leads up from the building now used as the restaurant, to a terrace with fountains and a pool.

3 An album photograph of the former tulip garden established by Ahmed III in the Fourth Court of the Topkapi Saraye. One of a series of photographs commissioned c.1880 by Abdul Hamid II. [Album 4 (10)]

بنام خداوند جان آفرین حکیم سخن در زبان آفرین

4 *Entertainment in a garden*
pavilion, sheltered from the
sun, c.1580. *[Or. 7084, f. la]*

Beyond the terrace is the Circumcision Room with ceramic tiles bearing designs that include flowers growing in the garden – tulips, carnations, prunus and others [*see* 6]. The Tulip Garden was the setting for the Tulip Festival held by Ahmed III at the time of the full moon each April. The gardens were decorated with cages of singing birds and coloured lights. Vases of flowers interspersed with lamps were put on shelves made for the purpose and other small lamps were fastened to the shells of the tortoises that trundled about the flower beds and paths. When the ladies of the Harem visited the gardens, all men, except the eunuch guards, were banished. A gate leads out of these gardens to the road that slopes down to the Gülhâne Park, once the outer garden of the Fifth Court of the Topkapi Saraye, but now a public park. A week-long Tulip Festival is held every year in Gülhâne Park at the beginning of April when the beds of tulips are at their best.

Ahmed III created other gardens round his palace at the lower end of the Golden Horn on the shore opposite Eyup. He built a series of kiosks in the meadows at Kağithâne where two streams flow into the Golden Horn. Known as the Sweet Waters of Europe [5], it became polluted by industrialization. Now, however, steps are being taken to clean up the environment and to restore the pavilions. In its heyday people flocked

5 A late 19th-century view of the Sweet Waters of Europe (Kağithâne) [see also 1]. [Album 6, (26)]

6 Ceramic tiles in the Topkapi Saraye bearing a variety of flower designs, photograph c.1880. [Album 7 (37)]

7 Houses and gardens along the Bosphorus, 1738–39. [Or. 13882, ff. 68b–69a].

there on foot, by oxcart or by boat and were entertained by buskers, musicians, acrobats and fortune-tellers, and the vendors of fruit, sweets and nuts who hawked their wares [*see* 1]. A similar valley near the Anadolu Hisar on the Bosphorus was known as the Sweet Waters of Asia, a notable feature there being a handsome fountain.

It was during the reign of Ahmed III that the courtiers and wealthy of Istanbul, following his example, built their mansions and wooden *yalis* at the water's edge down the Bosphorus, with tulip gardens laid out behind them [7, 8]. Archival material in the Topkapi Saraye Museum in Istanbul gives details of bulbs imported from Europe and also of an Act of 1727–28 which increased the amount of tax payable on tulip bulbs. Manuscripts of the 18th and 19th centuries list the names and descriptions of many tulips which are mainly of the highly-prized lily species with sharp-pointed petals. The ideal tulip, which was almond-shaped with petal points as sharp as needles, is the variety that appears on textiles and

8

9

tiles. Tulips given exotic names such as Petals of Love or Rose Arrow, were of every colour or combination of colours known at the time. Although the excesses of this period led to the downfall of Ahmed III there was no lessening in the popularity of tulips which remain a favourite flower, still grown in quantities in public and private gardens. Ogier Ghiselin de Busbecq, the Habsburg Ambassador to Turkey from 1554–62, during the reign of Sultan Suleyman I (the Magnificent) is usually credited with taking tulips back to Vienna and thus introducing them into Europe.[3]

Tulips featured in textile and Iznik pottery designs from the early 16th century and also in Ottoman book illustrations or miniatures. A miniature of *circa* 1520 [9] of a young prince on his way to visit his beloved, portrays him as carrying a bouquet of tulips to present to her. There are no tulips represented amongst the wild flowers in the miniature which may imply that even as early as this, they were particularly special and highly prized.

8 A late 19th-century album photograph of houses and gardens along the Bosphorus. [Album 4 (2)]

9 Designs in textiles, Iznik pottery and book illustrations from the early 16th century onwards reveal the Ottoman love of tulips; in this miniature (c.1520) a young prince prepares to present a bouquet of tulips to his beloved. [Or. 13948, f. 101b]

3 E. S. Forster, *The Turkish Letters of Ogier Ghiselin de Busbecq, Imperial Ambassador at Constantinople, 1554–62*, translated by E. S. Forster (Oxford, 1927).

10 The garden of the Military
School of Medicine, Istanbul,
c.1886. [Album 15 (23)]

Illustrated records and contemporary accounts of festivals and processions held by the sultans during celebrations are also witness to the importance of gardens and to the enormous number of men employed in horticulture. Amongst the floats in a procession during a festival held by Suleyman the Magnificent in 1530 were those of miniature gardens complete with orchards, pavilions, beds of flowers and pools. Evliya Çelebi (died 1679, see note 1), during his travels in Europe and Asia, was in Istanbul in 1638 when Murad IV reviewed the Guilds which passed in procession before him at the Alay Kiosk (Procession Pavilion) with emblems of their respective trades. Çelebi relates that the guilds numbered a thousand and one and goes on to describe their floats, portable workshops, studios, shops, equipment and tools. They passed in front of the Sultan and his entourage demonstrating the skills of every imaginable trade. The gardeners formed a body of men carrying hoes, spades, saws and all the implements of gardening. Watering machines were drawn by oxen, and the gardeners, who wore floral creations on their heads, tossed flowers to the spectators. The Guild of Grafters, some 500 strong, carried plates of fruit on their heads and branches in their hands together with knives, saws and other grafting tools. They were reputedly skilled in grafting vines and mulberries to obtain new varieties.

Palaces on the Bosphorus with formal gardens included Dolmabahçe,

built 1843–56, and Beylerbeyi Palace situated near the Bosphorus Bridge, built in 1861–65. When Abdul Hamid II succeeded in 1876, he preferred to live in the Yildiz Palace high up overlooking the Bosphorus. There he created ten acres of rambling gardens and parkland which contained several buildings including a small palace, as well as several pavilions, arbours and ponds, in addition to flower borders, shrubs and trees. He had a miniature canal constructed with small landing stages equivalent to those situated at villages up and down the Bosphorus. These gardens, which have been restored, demonstrate the difference between Ottoman Turkish gardens and those of Iran and India, with the emphasis on winding paths, fountains and pools. Small pavilions at the water's edge echo the *yalis* on the shore of the Bosphorus.

Abdul Hamid II had a series of photographs taken for the Yildiz Palace library to provide a record of every aspect of life in Istanbul and elsewhere in Turkey. He was anxious that his country's achievements should be more widely known and recognised. With that end in view, he sent handsomely-bound volumes of a large selection of photographs to the Library of Congress in Washington in 1893 and a further 51 albums to the British Museum in London in 1894 and 1895.[4] Mostly dating from the 1880s, these albums include photographs of palaces, academies and schools with their respective gardens [10, 11] and views of the Golden

11 The garden of the Imperial Ottoman School, Istanbul, c.1880. [Album 47, (3)]

4 Carney E. S. Gavin and the Harvard Semitic Museum (eds), 'Imperial Self-Portrait: the Ottoman Empire as revealed in the Sultan Abdul Hamid II's photographic albums. A pictorial selection with catalogue, concordance, indices and brief essays', *Journal of Turkish Studies* (Turkluk Bilgisi Arastirmalari), vol. 12 (Harvard, 1988).

Horn and the Bosphorus. Among several photographs of the Yildiz Palace gardens is one of a small boat on a stretch of water [12], possibly a miniature boat for the canal. A late 16th-century Ottoman miniature [13], one of several illustrations to a collection of fables and stories, is of a king, some 300 years earlier, sailing a small boat on a garden pool.

The Turkish people's love of flowers and gardens is as much in evidence today as it ever was. The tulip festivals in the parks and gardens are occasions for great rejoicing and enjoyment by the crowds who flock to them in April, and flower markets do a roaring trade. Gardens surrounding tombs and graves in cemeteries such as those in Eyup and Bursa are carefully tended as are those of the mosques and museums. Museum gardens in Istanbul range from the extensive grounds of the Topkapi Saraye Museum to the delightful fig orchards of the Museum of Mosaics and to the tiny courtyard with its pool and fountain enclosed in baytrees and box hedges at the old Museum of Turkish and Islamic Art near the Suleymaniye Mosque.

12 The Yildiz Palace garden, Istanbul, c.1880.
[Album 7 (20)]

Garden entertainments: in an illustration to a late 16th-century manuscript, a king sails a miniature boat in a garden pool.
dd. 15153, f. 382a]

چه را رنگ پر آب واو دید
منزل کرد بر شاه و دید

14 A walled garden, fr[...]
illustration to a collecti[...]
poems, c.1396 [see 16[...]

15 A 16th-century min[...]
depicting Timur in the[...]
Garden of Heart's Deli[...]
Samarkand.
[IOL MS 137, f. 254b]

Iran

The love of flowers and interest in gardens have been features of life in Iran down the centuries. Archaeological surveys have produced plans for palaces with extensive gardens dating back to the pre-Islamic Sassanian dynasty (AD 224–641). In addition, travellers to Iran from that period right down to the present day give descriptions of gardens in their diaries and journals. Several accounts, particularly from the early 15th century

onwards, were recorded in diaries kept by envoys sent on diplomatic missions to the courts of Iran, and included descriptions of the royal gardens where they would be received and entertained on a lavish scale. Only the ruins of such grand gardens, which delighted and surprised those early travellers, still exist, but present-day visitors to Iran who are given hospitality in private homes know how the smallest garden or courtyard can provide coolness and shade as relief from the searing heat and arid landscape. To go through a door in a high wall off a dusty road or off one of the teeming noisy alleyways of a bazaar, is to enter another world of peace, coolness and tranquillity.

Whether on a grand scale or in the simplest garden, the layout usually consists of a central pool with a fountain and four channels at right angles to each other enclosing flower beds, while shrubs, shady trees and fruit trees line the paths to provide essential shade. This scheme, known as the *chahar bagh* (literally 'four gardens'), has been used in large or small gardens in Iran for centuries and was introduced to India by the first Mughal emperor, Babur, after 1526. Gardens retained the original plan under successive Mughal emperors but with increasing emphasis on the use of water. Narrow channels developed into terraced canals with waterfalls, chutes and series of fountains providing a remarkable vista.

The *chahar bagh* was the ideal garden, the earthly paradise, providing coolness and shade to offset the heat of an Iranian summer in which six to ten inches of rainfall is the annual average over much of the country, apart from the semi-tropical Caspian region. In a country with such low rainfall, plants of any kind could not be grown without irrigation and a regular supply of water has been provided for centuries by the remarkable *qanat* system which dates back to about the sixth century BC. Water tables form at the base of mountains from the melting snow which seeps through the porous sandstone and gravel and a tunnel on different levels is constructed to divert the water to where it is needed. Additional shafts are constructed, at intervals of fifty yards or so, from the tunnel to the surface to provide exit holes and these are used to dispose of soil being dug out and to provide air ducts and inspection pits. From the air these holes resemble a series of small bomb craters strung across the desert. The work is very highly skilled and the *qanat* men are considered to be the elite of the Iranian workforce. The water supply, which is strictly controlled, is available all the year round and is used for the irrigation of crops, orchards and gardens.

From the 14th century gardens have been a feature of Persian* miniatures and are often the setting or background of incidents related in romantic epic poems and tales, whilst the language of Iran (Farsi) is full of the imagery of flowers and of Paradise in the guise of a garden. These

*The word 'Persian', so long used in the context of the miniature painting of Iran, has been retained in this chapter to avoid confusion with pre-Islamic Iranian art.

miniatures are a valuable source of information concerning the layout of gardens and of the details of water courses, various kinds of pavilions and summer houses and of plants and trees included in them. In contrast to Ottoman Turkish gardens with their rambling paths and somewhat haphazard layout, Persian gardens were geometric in design. The cross channels ran at right angles to the central reservoir or pool which might be round, square or rectangular, hexagonal or octagonal, with scalloped or shamrock edges, often with a central fountain. In larger gardens, further channels would cross the central one at right angles forming several *chahar baghs* in one garden. This scheme or plan is very clearly demonstrated in the designs of the so-called garden carpets, which include fish in the channels, ducks in the pools, flower beds between the channels and shrubs and fruit trees in the outlying ground, the whole pattern enclosed in avenues of shady trees.

The concept of the Persian garden, like other Iranian traditions, was adopted by the ruling descendants of the Mongols who had swept over Iran in the 13th century. Gardens are mentioned by Marco Polo who spent nine months at Tabriz in north-west Iran in the late 13th century. Just over a hundred years later, Clavijo,[1] the Spanish envoy sent by Henry III of Castile, gave detailed descriptions of his arrival at Samarkand in 1404 and the events that took place.

Timur (Tamerlane), who died in 1405, made Samarkand his capital and created several gardens there. These gardens and life at the court of Timur were vividly described by Clavijo. He writes of a walled garden full of fruit trees and adjacent to a vineyard, also enclosed by a wall, which had a central stream with water channels flowing amongst the trees. The Garden of Heart's Delight (*Dilkusha*), [15] where Timur first received Clavijo and which contained many trees, had been constructed in 1397 in the meadows outside Samarkand, known as Kani Gil, where Timur periodically used to hold celebrations for immense gatherings of his people. Other gardens created at Samarkand by Timur and his successors included the Garden of the Plane Trees, the New Garden, the Paradise Garden and the Northern Garden. Altogether some 15 or 16 Samarkand gardens are mentioned in contemporary accounts of the 15th century. They were also visited by Babur as a young man and described in his memoirs, and his own abiding interest in gardens may well have been inspired by them.

Clavijo also writes of tents, awnings and palaces located in the gardens. The awnings were described as being long and high, secured above by cords attached to two poles so that they provided shade without excluding cooling breezes. These awnings were a regular feature of gardens for centuries and are illustrated in late 15th-century, mid 16th-century, and later miniatures [*see* 19, 20].

1 Ruy Gonzalez de Clavijo, *Clavijo, Embassy is Tamelane, 1403–1406*, translated by Guy le Strange (London, 1928).

Permanent garden pavilions, constructed in various styles, ranged from the simplest which provided a roof for shade, to a small palace with inner rooms, and these pavilions took the place of the tents of the earlier gardens. The small simple pavilions, the equivalent of permanent awnings, were open on three sides to allow cool air to circulate, while the larger buildings were constructed on two floors with balconies and inner rooms for receptions, recreation and entertainment and, light and airy with open views, were an extension of the garden. Contemporary miniatures portray these pavilions as places for entertainment of all kinds, music, feasting, painting, discussions and hospitality. The simplest designs included plain tiled floors but the grander the pavilion the more ambitious were the methods of cooling the building by incorporating pools, fountains and cross-channels.

A miniature illustrating a collection of poems dated 1396, and contemporary with the reign of Timur, is probably a true likeness of the kind of walled garden and small palace described by Clavijo and associated with Timur [14, 16]. It shows a garden house or small palace set in a walled garden in which the stream outside the wall in the foreground has been diverted to flow within the garden. Red waterlilies grow in the water and violets and pollarded willows line its banks. Daylilies and hollyhocks are growing in the garden as well as in the arid ground outside the walls while fruit trees, poplars and plane trees provide shade.

Over the centuries, wherever the centre of power was in Iran, whether Samarkand, Herat, Tabriz, Qazvin, Isfahan, Shiraz or Tehran, palaces, houses and pavilions were constructed with their accompanying gardens. They were built by the rulers themselves or by governors of provinces, courtiers and high officials. Herat, now in Afghanistan, was an important centre for hundreds of years. Timur's son, Shahrukh (died 1447), made Herat his capital, laying out new gardens and renovating existing ones. These gardens were designed on the *chahar bagh* geometric plan with the usual waterchannels, pools, flowerbeds, orchards, pavilions and avenues of shady trees, all surrounded by a wall. The ruler, Sultan Husayn Bayqara, a noted patron of the arts, was crowned in 1468 in the Garden of the Ravens and early in his reign ordered the construction of a *chahar bagh* which eventually covered a hundred acres outside the city. It is on record that the scribes and artists who copied and illustrated books for Sultan Husayn's extensive library worked in pavilions or under awnings in the White Garden at Herat. One of the fine manuscripts copied and illustrated for Sultan Husayn in 1494 includes a miniature of the interior of a garden pavilion [17]. A window at the back, providing a cross-draught, opens out onto the garden with its flowering and fruit trees, and vases of flowers are placed on the tiled floor either side of the pool. Water flows across the floor by way of a channel running from the central octagonal

16 *The stream in the foreground of this illustration, with red water lilies, violets and pollarded willows along its banks, has been diverted to flow inside the walled garden.* [Add. 18113, 18b]

17 *The interior of a garden pavilion, from a manuscript dated 1494. A cooling water channel flows through the building to a central pool, and flowering and fruit trees are visible through the doorway to the garden behind.* [Or. 6810, 62b]

pool. Another contemporary double-page miniature dating from the same period illustrates the kind of elaborate entertainment that took place in Persian gardens in the cool of the evening [*see* 19]. While waiting for the banquet to be prepared, the young prince, seated on a low throne under a superb awning, is being entertained by musicians. The peculiar angle of the awning is explained by the fact that Persian artists ignored perspective. Shadows, too, are non-existent, regardless of whether the scene takes place in brilliant sunshine or by moonlight.

Besides the gardens at Samarkand, the future Mughal emperor Babur was very impressed by those he saw in Herat in 1506 when he was in his early twenties.[2] Babur's interest in plants and gardens is evident from his memoirs, for he constantly wrote of gardens he had laid out or altered and of plants he had grown, whether in Kabul or, after 1526, when he was in India. Of the gardens he saw in Herat, he mentions several by name including the Garden of the Ravens and the White Garden. Others were the Town Garden and the Garden of Heart's Delight.

Tabriz in north-west Iran was an important centre for centuries and like Isfahan, Herat and other cities had famous gardens. Marco Polo wrote of the splendid gardens he saw during the months he spent there in 1300. At the end of the 15th century a magnificent garden known as the Eight Paradises (*Hasht Bihisht*) was constructed by the then Turkman rulers. In the 16th century when Shah Tahmasp made the city his capital, it became a famous centre of book production under his patronage. Two miniatures from a manuscript of the Five Poems (or *Khamsa*) of Nizami, which was copied and illustrated for Shah Tahmasp at Tabriz between 1539 and 1543, illustrate the coolness and tranquillity of Persian gardens. In one the small permanent pavilion is a simple structure of a roof supported by four poles, providing shade but still open to breezes [18]. A fountain is playing in the larger of the two pools set in the tiled floor with a channel of water running through both pools. A gate in the railings surrounding the courtyard opens out into the garden near a stream which meanders between banks of flowers and small rose bushes. Shade is provided by prunus, poplar, cypress and oriental plane (*chenar*) trees, and irises, poppies and hollyhocks grow in the bare ground beyond the garden.

The story which this scene illustrates centres round a rose, one of many poems and tales in Persian literature concerned with flowers. Two rival physicians quarrelled about the efficacy of poisons and eventually agreed to put their theories to the test. The wiser of the two swallowed an antidote with the deadly pill given to him by his rival. He then picked a spray of roses and breathed a spell on it, before handing it to his opponent who, greatly fearing the power of the spell, smelled the roses and fell dead from terror. The artist of this miniature has painted the roses lying on the tiles with particular care.

2 A. S. Beveridge (translator), *The Babur-nāma in English* (repr. London, 1969).

Flowers most often included in miniatures are roses, peonies, narcissus, pomegranate, prunus, irises of various colours, hollyhocks and daylilies. Strangely, crown imperials do not occur in Persian illustrations, although they appear regularly in Indian Mughal art. Sir John Chardin, when describing flowers he saw in Iran during his travels in the 17th century,[3] includes a rose bush of which he writes: '[it] bore upon one and the same branch, Roses of three Colours, some Yellow, others Yellow and White, and others Yellow and Red'. An illustration in the Houghton *Shahnama* (Book of Kings), a manuscript now dispersed, which is contemporary with The British Library's *Khamsa* of Nizami (*i.e.* mid-16th century), includes this particular rose. Illustrations by the most famous artists of the day for their royal patrons portray details of gardens with great care, including the layout, pavilions and plants and trees. This is also true of other aspects of contemporary life at court including costumes, weapons, furniture and

18 *This miniature from the story of two physicians and a rose, 1539–43, illustrates some characteristic, cooling features of Persian gardens: a permanent pavilion, with pools and water channels set in a tiled floor.* [Or. 2265, f. 26b]

3 Sir John Chardin, *Travels in Persia*, with an introduction by Sir Percy Sykes (London, 1927).

*19 Elaborate entertainments in a garden, 1493. A young prince shelters under a superb awning, while a banquet is being prepared.
[Add. 25900, ff. 3b–4a]*

20 A garden scene depicting gardeners at work, a central pool with fountain and channel and an awning providing protection from the sun, from a manuscript dated 1539–43. [Or. 2265, f. 48b]

musical instruments, making these miniatures an important source of historical information.

The second painting, also from Shah Tahmasp's *Khamsa* of Nizami includes an awning attached to two poles by cords and is similar to those described by Clavijo earlier [20]. Lack of perspective again shows the awning pitched at a peculiar angle. The small courtyard in this painting has one large central round pool with a fountain and channel. The stream flowing off the mountains in the background has been diverted round the garden to emerge in the foreground, flanked by willows, dark irises and hollyhocks. The water, originally painted silver, has been blackened by oxydization.

Shiraz, an oasis town in the south of Iran, has been famous for its gardens for centuries. Entering Shiraz by the desert road leading from Persepolis, the whole city appears to be one large garden, with an abundance of cypress, plane and fruit trees. Royal gardens created in the 19th century still exist and others surround the tombs of the famous poets Sa'di and Hafiz. The Garden of Heart's Delight (every city has one of that name) in Shiraz is very beautiful, with long flower beds full of roses and lilies, flanked by cypress, orange and pomegranate trees and bushes with a central channel and pool. Private gardens in Shiraz, as elsewhere, are cherished. One example is the small Pars Museum, an octagonal building, once a private house, set in a mulberry plantation and surrounded by its own garden. Both the setting and the garden are exquisite and on a par with the tiny courtyard with its fountains, flowers and baytrees at the old Museum of Turkish and Islamic Art near the Suleymaniye Mosque in Istanbul. It is well worth seeking out these small gardens for they retain the old traditions of garden layout and are quite delightful.

Shiraz, as elsewhere, was a centre of book production for hundreds of years. The academies were never on the grand scale of Tabriz or Isfahan, but their work was always interesting. An early 16th-century illustration (c.1505) includes a simple garden as a background. A young man returning home from his travels could hear women laughing and talking in his garden as he approached his home and discovered them bathing in his walled garden [21]. This charmingly naive illustration includes a stream flowing through a conduit under the wall into the pool. The young man, anxious about the identity of the intruders, but not wishing to be seen, is peering, upside-down, through the gap in the wall. Another unusual detail in a late 16th-century manuscript [22] is the carefully drawn vine, heavy with bunches of grapes, winding its way up a plane tree to burst out at the top of the page.

Sir Thomas Herbert[4] who travelled in Iran between 1627 and 1629 visited Shiraz and wrote that 'the gardens are many, and both large and beautiful. Most are enclosed in walls fourteen feet high and four feet thick'. Besides listing fruit trees, he noted that the gardens 'are spacious with plenty of trees, abound in cypresses, chenars, elm, ash, pines, oaks, myrtles and maples' and that ropes were attached to tree branches as swings. There were 'flowers rare to the eye, sweet to the smell and useful in physic'.

Herbert also spent some time in Isfahan and wrote that 'gardens here for grandeur and fragrance are such as no city in Asia outvies'. This was during the reign of Shah 'Abbas I (died 1629) who was the greatest creator of gardens in Iran, equal to the Mughal emperors in India. Shah 'Abbas had been brought up in Herat and no doubt gardens there influenced him, as they had Babur a century earlier. Shah 'Abbas moved

4 Thomas Herbert, *Travels in Persia, 1627–1629* (London, 1928).

his capital from Qazvin further south to Isfahan in 1598 where he set about creating splendid gardens. Previously Isfahan had been a simple oasis town which he had visited from time to time and no doubt he recognized its location as being favourable. Situated on a fertile plain below the Zagros mountains, in an otherwise arid desert, it was ideal for creating gardens. Most Iranian cities grew up near mountains so that the *qanat* system of water supply could be developed but Isfahan had the additional advantage of the Zayanda River that runs through the plain. The only part of the gardens laid out by Shah 'Abbas I in existence today is the Chahar Bagh, originally built as a promenade, but now a busy thoroughfare through Isfahan. It was constructed in the early 17th century as a promenade stretching some two miles to the gardens, Hazar Jarib (Thousand Acres), beyond the river, from the royal palace and gardens, Naqsh-i Jahan. A wide water channel with fountains and pools at intervals ran down its entire length, with smaller channels on either side. Pavilions and summer houses were built in the gardens each side of the promenade, including the Garden of the Nightingales, the Garden of the Vineyard and the Mulberry Garden. None of these original buildings constructed by Shah 'Abbas have survived. The mud walls were susceptible to extremes of climate and Sir John Chardin, who was in Isfahan in the late 17th century, vividly describes a destructive storm in which the mud walls were dissolved: '23rd December fell another Rain accompanied with such furious Storms that I never saw the like. It lasted four and twenty Hours and filled with Water not only the Streets, but also the Houses and Gardens'. The river overflowed and the Chahar Bagh was under four feet of water. 'The Gardens thereabouts were laid under Water and the Houses of Pleasure overthrown.'

Sir Thomas Herbert describes the Hazar Jarib gardens as having a series of terraces which led up to a large central 12-sided reservoir with fountains. Three gates led through the walls into the garden, the northern gate having a pavilion of six rooms, in which the ground floor had marble pools. Herbert mentions that water was brought 'by extraordinary charge and toil from the Elburz', probably by the *qanat* system. Ornate pavilions and small palaces were built in the gardens. At the opposite end of the Chahar Bagh was the palace and gardens, Naqsh-i Jahan, also laid out by Shah 'Abbas and much used by him. Iskandar Beg Munshi[5] describes the New Year (*Nuruz*) celebrations held by Shah 'Abbas each March when he was in Isfahan. These usually took place in the Naqsh-i Jahan gardens. The Iranian New Year has always been celebrated out-of-doors and Shah 'Abbas held royal garden parties, to which he invited vast numbers of his subjects. Each group of merchants, officials and ordinary citizens had their allotted spaces along the banks of the stream while courtiers, viziers and other officers of state were

5 Eskander Beg Monshi, *History of Shah 'Abbas the Great*, translated by R. M. Savory, Persian Heritage Series 28, 2 vols, (Boulder, Colorado, 1978).

21 *A simple walled garden with bathing pool and stream, c.1505.*
[IOL MS 387, f. 279a]

22 *A magnificent vine in a late 16th-century manuscript illustration.*
[Add. 27257, f. 44b]

allocated places by the huge pool 'as big as a small lake'. Extra pavilions
of various designs were decorated with lights, and silk brocade canopies
and gold tents were erected. Shah 'Abbas himself would go amongst his
guests who were entertained with feasting and music.

Other gardens constructed by Shah 'Abbas were described by Herbert
and Iskandar Beg Munshi. One, mentioned by Herbert, was situated in
the desert outside Isfahan and he describes it as full of fruit trees and
flowers, naming peaches, apricots, pomegranates, plums, cherries,
apples, pears, chestnuts, damask roses, tulips and other flowers. It had
streams, artificial grottoes, stone pools lined with marble and a summer-
house of 12 rooms. Herbert also mentions that gardens in the former
capital, Qazvin, are many and large but not to be compared with those in
Isfahan and Shiraz. Qazvin was irrigated by the *qanat* system and was
notable for the abundant fruit grown there including most of those
named above as well as grapes, figs, water and musk melons, citrus
fruits and various nuts including hazels, filberts, walnuts, almonds and
pistachios.

Shah 'Abbas I conquered the region of Mazandaran near the Caspian
Sea in 1596–97 and this area held as much delight for him as did Kashmir
for the Mughal emperors Jahangir and Shahjahan. In a country of
extremes of temperature, the fertile Caspian region is distinguished by a
semi-tropical climate with a relatively high annual rainfall of 40–60
inches, some five times the average for the country. Deciduous forests,
rice, tea, cotton, sugar-cane, tobacco and citrus fruits are included among
crops in an area where adequate irrigation is not a problem. Shah 'Abbas
made a highway through Mazandaran, with caravanserais (fortified
overnight stopping points) *en route*, leading to the Caspian. At Ashraf
(modern Behshahr), about five miles from the Caspian Sea, he built a
palace and laid out parks and gardens, the remains of which can still be
seen. He also built houses and palaces along the coast at Amol, Sari and
Barfarush. Sir John Chardin was in Mazandaran one February in the
1670s 'at which time I was in a manner charm'd and inchanted [*sic*] with
it; for the whole Country is nothing but one continued Garden, or a
perfect kind of Paradise, as the Persians call it. The Causeways and
Highways appear like so many Alleys of Orange-Trees, bordered on
either side with fine Parterrees [*sic*], and flowery Garden'.

Shah 'Abbas I died in 1629 aged 60 and was succeeded first by Shah
Safi' and then by Shah 'Abbas II (died 1666). The Chihil Sutun, a large
garden pavilion, was built by 'Abbas II in 1647 and survives, with its
garden, much as it was when first built. Just off the Chahar Bagh in
Isfahan, it was used by 'Abbas II for receptions and entertaining. One of
the grander garden pavilions, it resembles a small palace with open
sides, water channels, marble pools and tiled floors. Airy, yet protected

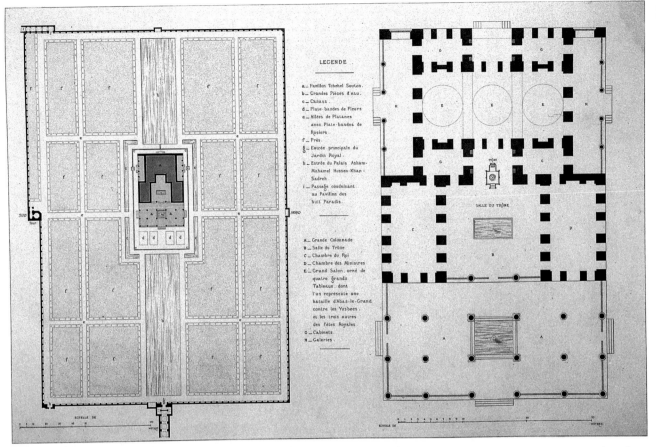

23 *A 19th-century plan of Chihil Sutun, a grand garden pavilion constructed in 1647. [N Tab 2000/2, Pl. XLI]*

from the fierce heat of the sun, with extensive views over the surrounding flower beds, it is an extension of the garden itself. The largest room, decorated with paintings, was used for receptions and there are two smaller rooms opening out on the garden. Twenty wooden pillars surrounding the large rectangular pool support the roof of the porch and the reflection of the pillars in the water is said to have inspired the name of the pavilion, Chihil Sutun or Forty Pillars. The plan published by Pascal Coste[6] in 1867 shows the pavilion situated in a garden much as it must have been in the 17th century [23]. Plane trees underplanted with rose bushes provided shade for the paths while the pavilion itself was surrounded by beds of flowers and shrubs divided by water channels in the usual *chahar bagh* plan.

The only surviving building along the Chahar Bagh, the Isfahan thoroughfare, is the Hasht Bihisht (Eight Paradises) pavilion. Situated near the Chihil Sutun, it was built during the reign of Shah Sulayman I (died 1694) in 1669 in what had been the Garden of the Nightingales in the time of Shah 'Abbas I. It is still an exquisite building but in its heyday, set in its own garden, it must have been particularly beautiful. Today it is situated, without its garden, on what has become a very busy road.

6 Pascal Coste, *Monuments modernes de la Perse, Mesures, dessines et decrits* (Paris, 1867).

24 An illustration of love-
lies-bleeding from a 19th-
century manuscript of the
poem, 'The secret language of
sweet-scented flowers'.
[Add. 22789, f. 324b]

Another extensive garden laid out in 17th-century Isfahan was called the Sa'atabad (Abode of Felicity) which was situated on the south bank of the river. Coste published several engravings of its palaces and pavilions in the 19th century before they were all destroyed. Another record of the Sa'atabad Garden is a poem 'The Secret Language of Sweet-scented Flowers' by Ramzi (*i.e.* Mirza Hadi). In his introduction, Ramzi relates how he had been summoned to the presence of Shah 'Abbas II in the garden and told to write a poem in praise of it. A manuscript of this poem in The British Library was copied and illustrated in 1835 and contains 29 paintings of flowers described in the poems. These include narcissus, violets, willow, hyacinths, irises, centaurea, larkspurs, tuberose, irises, tulips, poppies, the blossom of various fruit trees, lilies, Judas tree, white jasmine, Marvel of Peru, sweet basil, love-lies-bleeding [24] and several varieties of roses of different colours.

Besides being used as illustrations in manuscripts, flowers were painted on the borders of pages, book-bindings [25], page decorations

25 Rich floral illustrations on
a sumptuous early 19th-
century bookbinding.
[IOL Pers. MS 3558]

*26 A detailed study of violets
from a 16th-century
manuscript page decoration.
[Or. 2265, f. 396]*

[26], pen-boxes and mirror-cases, particularly in the 19th century during the Qajar dynasty. Some five hundred years earlier (1396) the artist of the walled garden [*see* 21] had provided an interesting study of specific flowers as the background to a celebration in a garden [27]. From the waterlilies growing in the stream in the foreground to the roses being gathered at the top of the page, the whole scene is full of flowers. They include daylilies, violets, hollyhocks, small rose bushes, willows, white lilies and narcissus with peonies, prunus, peach, pomegranate, cypress and other trees flanking the large rosebush. Courtyards of the simplest gardens and schools would often have a large shady poplar or plane tree and careful studies of single trees are sometimes included in illustrations dating back to the 14th or 15th century [28].

Tehran, the modern capital of Iran situated below the Elburz mountains, has many gardens particularly in the suburbs such as Gulhak, Tajrish, Shimran and Niavaran. Embassies, large houses and former palaces all had large gardens, some now in ruins, but, as in every city in Iran, cool, shady gardens are still hidden away behind high walls even in the smallest alleyway.

27 *A host of flowers provide the background to this late
14th-century illustration of celebrations in a garden.
[Add. 18113, f. 40b]*

28 *A careful study of a chenar tree in a school courtyard, 1493.
[Or. 6810, f. 106b]*

India

When considering the characteristic features of Indian gardens, those that spring to mind are the magnificent landscaped gardens designed on a grand scale by the Mughals at Agra, Delhi, Lucknow, Lahore, Kashmir and elsewhere. From the time of the first Mughal emperor, Babur (died 1530), who conquered India in 1526, until the decay of the empire early in the 18th century, the Mughal rulers, high officials and governors created them. But the Indian love of gardens in fact began centuries earlier. They are mentioned in Hindu epics, particularly in descriptions of temples which were built near springs and running water. Artificial water-courses, terraces and parterres were yet to come, but beautiful natural gardens of indigenous trees of the forests and river banks are described at the sites of temples and pilgrim shrines. Illustrations of such forest scenes are included in manuscripts produced for Hindu patrons who remained relatively independent of Mughal rule [see 50 and 51]. These illustrations are in Indian styles, almost untouched by Islamic and Mughal influences.

The spread of Islam extended to India from the 13th century, and the Ganges plain was dominated by Islamic rulers who, almost certainly, were the first to introduce the *chahar bagh* (four-gardens) system from Iran. In the 16th and 17th centuries this plan, reintroduced by Babur, was expanded in Mughal gardens. Early 16th-century illustrations produced at the studios of the so-called Sultanate rulers, who had introduced traditions of book production from Iran, exhibit strong Persian characteristics of style, while depicting plants, trees and flowers alien to Iran but abundant in India, such as the banyan, pipal, mango, plantain and lotus [30].

Throughout the Mughal period, following Babur's victory at Panipat in 1526, until the reign of Aurangzib (died 1707) and the decline of the Mughal empire, splendid gardens, palaces, pavilions and tombs were created. The great gardens range in date from the Rambagh at Agra, reputedly the first laid out by Babur, to that created by Fiday Khan, Aurangzib's foster-brother, at Pinjaur near Simla in the late 17th century. Originally inspired by the Persian *chahar bagh*, the garden design was geometric with a central water channel crossed at right angles by smaller channels, each section forming a flower bed. This geometric system was retained throughout the Mughal period but in succeeding years the emphasis was increasingly laid on the use of water to enhance the landscape. Each succeeding Mughal emperor designed gardens on a yet more ambitious scale, introducing wide canals, rows of fountains, waterfalls, cascades and chutes, together with small palaces and pavilions each with their own system of basement pools and channels. In terraced gardens the central channel would be so arranged that the water would fall gently from level to level or else race down cascades and waterfalls,

PAGES 44–45
29 The gardens of the Taj Mahal at Agra, painted by William Daniell in 1789 and published as an aquatint in 1801. [IOL p. 396]

activating a series of fountains on the way. Parterres divided by narrower channels were laid out at right-angles to the main canal while oriental planes (*chenars*), cypresses and other shady trees lined the paths.

Thanks to the diaries, journals and chronicles left by the Mughal emperors from Babur onwards, and to the few gardens which survive in their original form in Delhi and Kashmir, the origin, designs and development of Mughal gardens are well-documented. One of Babur's abiding interests was the creation of gardens wherever he went. A true gardener throughout his life, whether travelling or on campaign, he observed the local flowers, plants and trees, making entries about them, as well as reporting on the progress of his own gardens, in the diaries he kept so assiduously.[1]

Sixth in line of descent from Timur (Tamerlane), Babur was born in Ferghana near Samarkand in 1483. He was familiar with the gardens created by his ancestor at Samarkand and also with those at Herat which had been laid out by Timur's sons and grandsons. These gardens, designed in the *chahar bagh* system, were the main influence on those he himself created, particularly at Kabul (which, like Herat, is now in Afghanistan) and later in India. He writes of nine gardens at Samarkand, including the Dilkusha (Heart's Delight) with its avenue of white poplars leading to the Turquoise Gate. During a visit to Herat in 1506, Babur mentions, amongst others, the White Garden and describes its summer house ('Joy house') as 'a sweet little abode' built in two storeys.

Babur's favourite garden was the one that he created at Kabul, known as the *Bagh-i Vafa* (Garden of Fidelity) [31]. In an entry in his diary during October 1519 he writes: 'Those were the days of the garden's beauty: its lawns were one sheet of trefoil: its pomegranate trees yellowed to autumn splendour.' He laid the garden out in 1508–09 on rising ground facing south and when he went to India he sent back plantains and sugar-cane for the garden where 'they did very well'. He describes the garden as lying high, with running water close by, and a mild winter climate. A stream flowed past a small hill in the middle of the garden, on which there were four garden plots. Round the reservoir to the south-west there were orange and pomegranate trees, the whole encircled by trefoil lawns. 'Truly that garden is admirably situated.' The late 16th-century artist depicting the garden has followed Babur's description very carefully, illustrating the plants mentioned and the water flowing into the channels that form the *chahar bagh*.

Another garden created by Babur, also near Kabul, was at Istalif, one of the villages in the fertile fruit-growing area near the Paghman mountains. Babur describes planes, holm-oaks and Judas trees as growing in abundance round a spring nearby. He had a round seat placed on the hillside, diverted a stream to flow past it and put in cuttings of planes

1 A. S. Beveridge (translator), *The Barhur-nāma in English* (repr. London, 1969).

48

30 An early 16th-centu
(Indian Sultanate) gar
scene, showing the infl
of strong Persian
characteristics of style.
[Or. 4535, f. 83b]

 میان غرب و جنوب باغ حوض ده در دسی است اطراف انثام

درختهای نارنج است درختهای انارهم هست و کرد ا کرد حوض تمام

سبزه که زراست جای عین باغ همینست در وقت زردشدن

نارنجها بسیار خوب می نماید حسبی باغ خوبی طرح شده و طرف

and sycamores. In all, he created ten gardens in and around Kabul, in addition to the one he designed for his future burial ground. This tomb garden was restored and extended by his great-great-grandson, Shah-jahan (died 1666) who commented in his chronicles on the magnificence of some plane trees originally planted at Kabul by Babur.

It was the lack of rising ground, necessary to make terraces, and of natural streams for irrigation purposes that Babur found so daunting on the Indian plains, when he decided to create gardens at Agra after his conquest of India in 1526. Previous rulers had constructed canals and artificial lakes but water was generally raised from wells by the use of oxen yoked to a wheel or by a treadmill [32]. Babur used wells and invented improved methods for drawing water from them. 'One of the great defects of Hindustan being its lack of running waters, it kept coming to my mind that waters should be made to flow by means of wheels erected wherever I might settle down, also that grounds should be laid out in an orderly and symmetrical way ... then plots of garden were laid out with suitable borders and parterres in every corner and in every border, rose and narcissus in perfect arrangement.' As well as sending plants back to his gardens at Kabul, Babur imported plants into India, and a melon-grower from Balkh (then in Iran), a city renowned for melons. The lack of water channels and of gardens initially deterred Babur when he surveyed possible sites near Agra. He was so discouraged that he abandoned his original idea of making a *chahar bagh* there, only to change his mind when nothing better than the grounds 'so bad and unattractive we traversed them with a hundred disgusts and repulsions' could be found. Eventually he designed his first garden in India at Agra, reputedly the Rambagh, still there today but considerably altered.

What Babur began in India, his successors and their followers continued, and gardens, including tomb gardens, were created all over Central India and, later, in Kashmir. Wherever he went in India, Babur noted plants hitherto unfamiliar to him. He was so taken with red oleanders he saw in a garden in Gwalior, south of Agra, that he collected some for his own gardens. He listed and described trees and plants such as mango, banana ('out of its leaves rises heartlike, a bud which resembles a sheep's heart. The fruit has two pleasant qualities, one that it peels easily, the other that it has neither stone nor fibre'), mimusops, jack-fruit, monkeyjack, myrobalan, oranges of various kinds, limes [33], lemons, oleander, screwpine, hibiscus, banyan, pipal and many others.

In 1506 Babur held celebrations in the Chahar Bagh at Kabul for the birth of his first son, Humayun, and the miniature depicting this event is a good illustration of a royal Mughal garden [38]. Raised stone platforms were built under the shade of trees, covered with a carpet and given extra

xen used to draw up water for the irrigation of flower beds.
ail from 34]

33 Lime and bitter orange trees, depicted in an Imperial
Mughal manuscript, c.1590. [Or. 3714, f. 404a]

34 *A lively garden scene from an Imperial Mughal manuscript (1595), with characteristic water channels and pools and a range of garden activities and entertainments.* [Or. 12208, f. 65a]

35 *The Emperor Babur celebrates the birth of his first son, Humayun, in his garden, illustrated in the memoirs of Babur produced under the patronage of the Emperor Akbar, c.1590. As in Iran, Imperial Mughal gardens were often used for public celebrations and receptions.* [Or. 3714, f. 295a]

protection from the sun by an awning. Similar raised platforms situated so that the emperor could overlook the garden, are still in place in the Rambagh at Agra. Babur is being entertained by musicians and dancers while servants bearing gifts are approaching the garden gate in the foreground. Water channels flow into the square tank with its central fountain. As in Iran, gardens were used for celebrations, such as this, and for the reception of diplomats and deputations, for discussions and for entertainment, as well as for rest, coolness and tranquillity. On this occasion Babur wrote of the gifts brought to him, noting also 'it was a first-rate feast'.

Babur died at the end of 1530 and was buried in his garden tomb at Kabul. He was succeeded by Humayun who did not inherit his love of gardens. Humayun died in 1556 as the result of an accident before he had designed his own tomb or chosen a site for it. It was a tradition that the choice of a site, the tomb itself and the design of the gardens surrounding it, were usually begun by the future occupant in his own lifetime. Humayun's widow built the complex at Delhi and it was completed in 1573. The gardens surrounding it are one of the very few Mughal gardens to survive in the original Persian-inspired *chahar bagh* form and they are laid out in a series of *chahar bagh* plans. The parterres are divided by wide paths which have narrow water channels running down the centre. They are arranged on low terraces to provide gravity for a steady flow of water. Later Mughal garden landscape designers developed the water channels on a far larger scale until they resembled canals. They were also constructed on different levels but with deeper terracing, the water flowing from level to level down chutes, cascades and waterfalls.

Akbar, the greatest of the Mughal emperors, succeeded Humayun in 1556 when he was only 13, and reigned until his death in 1605. He was a man of wide interests, although garden landscaping was not such an outstanding passion as it had been for Babur. However, he appreciated Babur's skill and paid tribute to him, noting that he had enhanced India by landscape gardening, wide avenues and falling water. It is due to Akbar's patronage of the arts and of book production that manuscripts copied from the late 16th century at his atélier included the memoirs of Babur which were illustrated with miniatures of superb quality by the imperial artists. Miniatures that include Mughal gardens as subjects or as backgrounds provide invaluable insights, for, besides the layout, they also include details such as plants and trees, oxen working the water wheels to draw water from wells, gardeners' tools and the clay containers for keeping tree roots watered [36].

Chronicles[2] kept by Akbar's officials of the events of his daily life and of state affairs included numerous inventories as well as lists of indigenous trees, plants and flowers with descriptions of their characteristics.

2 Francis Gladwin (translator),
Ayeen Akbery; or the Institutes of the Emperor Akbar, vol. 1 (London, 1800).

36 *A magnificent tree in a clay irrigation container used to keep its roots watered, from the poems of Nizami.*
[Or. 12208, f. 52a]

Jahangir visited Babur's gardens at Kabul, 'seven in one day', and he was supported in his interest by his wife, Nur Jahan, and his brother-in-law, Asaf Khan, who both designed beautiful gardens. During the long periods they spent in Kashmir, the magnificent gardens Vernag [*see* 40, 41], Nishat [*see* 42, 43] and Shalimar were created. In addition, a series of palaces and buildings with gardens were built at the various stopping places, including Sialkot and Rajaur, on the road from Agra to Kashmir, as the emperors would be accompanied by a large entourage of courtiers, soldiers and servants, as well as members of their own families.

Jahangir's ideal garden, described by himself in his memoirs, was one laid out according to his directions in Sihrind which he visited on his way to Kashmir. He wrote that it afforded him the utmost delight: '. . . on entering the garden, I found myself immediately in a covered avenue, planted on each side with scarlet roses and, beyond them, arose groves of cypress, fir, plane and evergreens . . . Passing through these, we entered what was in reality the garden, which now exhibited a variegated parterre ornamented with flowers of the utmost brilliancy of colours and of the choicest kind'. He goes on to describe the reservoir of water in the centre of the green parterre, and the octagonal pavilion which was 'capable of accommodating two hundred persons with convenient room to sit and surrounded by a beautiful colonnade'. Similar to a Persian pavilion, it was two storeys high and decorated with murals.

The garden at Vernag, about 40 miles south of Kashmir, is notable for the large pool fed by springs of the purest water. It was full of fish when Jahangir saw it in the 17th century, as indeed it still is today. Water flows under the arches of the surrounding arcade and eventually into the river Jhelum by way of a 12-foot-wide canal. In Ottoman Turkey lamps and candles were used in gardens to enhance the beauty of the flowers, but in Mughal gardens in India they were placed behind water to create a sparkling effect as waterfalls flowed over them. Holders for lamps and candles were built into niches in the brickwork and can still be seen in the 16th-century Rambagh gardens at Agra. Succeeding Mughal emperors employed them in niches of cascades, waterfalls and pavilions. Buildings round the pool at Vernag were introduced by Jahangir in 1609. It was at Vernag that Jahangir and Nur Jahan spent much of their time and it was his unfulfilled wish to be buried there.

Nishat Bagh, situated on Lake Dal, was a far more ambitious scheme than Vernag. Entered from below, it provides a superb vista, its outstanding feature being a central canal constructed on a series of terraces down which water flows from one level to the next by means of cascades and waterfalls into the lake below. Rows of fountains are placed down the centre of each pool on every level. The central terraced pools are flanked by flower beds and the whole garden surrounded by shady plane trees. On some levels a dais or seat was constructed over the water just above the chute. An illustrated manuscript, produced in Lahore in 1663, of the poems of Zafar Khan, governor of Kashmir, includes miniatures of events taking place in Kashmir gardens. One is of Vernag with its fish pool and arcading [41] and another, with its pavilion, cascade and dais, is almost certainly Nishat Bagh [43]. Of the Shalimar gardens Jahangir wrote: 'Shalimar is near the lake. It has a pleasant stream which comes down from the hills and flows into the Dal Lake. I bade my son [*i.e.* Shahjahan] dam it up and make a waterfall . . . This place is one of the sights of Kashmir.'

Shahjahan, who succeeded his father in 1627, was more interested in architecture than horticulture, and added buildings to existing gardens including a black marble pavilion in the Shalimar. Magnificent buildings dating from his reign included palaces with extensive gardens at Delhi, Lahore and Agra as well as the most famous of all, the Taj Mahal. This tomb was built for his wife Mumtaz Mahal who died in 1631. Following the Mughal tradition it stands in extensive grounds, although these gardens have been altered considerably over the years. The original plan of the garden was conventional, with fountains placed at intervals down the central channel and a large raised pool with a cusped and trefoiled

40 A 19th-century photograph of the sacred pool in the magnificent gardens at Vernag, created during Jahangir's time in Kashmir [see also 41]. [IOL 94/1]

41 A manuscript painting of the Vernag gardens dated 1663. [RAS Persian MS 310, ff. 31b–32]

42 A 19th-century photograph of the site of the cascade at Nishat Bagh. [IOL 556/1 (19)]

43 *The cascade bordered by flower gardens at Nishat, in a manuscript painting dated 1663.*
[RAS Persian MS 310, 21b]

border providing wonderful reflections of the building. Water channels at right angles to the main canal divide the garden into the traditional *chahar bagh* scheme. Begun in 1632, it was completed in 1648 and an unusual feature is the positioning of the tomb building at the end of the garden, thus providing an exquisite vista of channels, fountains and reflections. Unlike the long terraced central channel of the Nishat Bagh in Kashmir, which is made spectacular by its series of waterfalls and cascades, the Taj Mahal channel relies on fountains supplied by a sophisticated system of water pipes. The flower beds were planted with roses, tulips, crown imperials, lilies and irises with orchards of mangos, oranges, lemons, pomegranates, apples and guavas. Shady trees such as banyan, plane, cypress, jackfruit and pipal and sweet-scented shrubs including jasmine, champa, oleander and screwpine were widely grown. The flower theme continues in the decorations of semi-precious stones inlaid in the marble of the tomb in the form of sprays, flowers and trees while the outer walls are decorated with flowers in bas-relief.

The Taj Mahal and its garden has been a subject of paintings by Indian and European artists for years. William Daniell painted a version in 1789 of which an aquatint was published in 1801 [*see* 29], whilst an exquisite painting by an Indian artist, dated *c*.1830, appears in a history of Shahjahan [44]. Although it includes somewhat unflattering representations of British officers on the terrace, the painting of the building shows strong European influence.

The concept introduced in the Nishat Bagh, of a pavilion at the far end of a long vista, viewed from below and dominated by a main water channel with waterfalls, chutes and cascades, was reversed during Aurangzib's reign. He succeeded in 1658 and, like Shahjahan, was mainly interested in architecture but, unlike his predecessor, did not create large gardens to accompany his buildings. One who did, however, was his chief architect, Faday Khan, who designed a superb garden at Pinjaur where he was governor. In contrast to the Nishat Bagh, the entrance was positioned above the highest terrace and although planned in the usual way, with a central terraced canal, when it was viewed from above it made nothing like the impact of the Nishat Bagh vista seen from below.

Although gardens were no longer laid out on such a magnificent scale after the decline of the Mughal empire in the 18th century, the tradition was maintained, albeit less ambitiously, by princes and nobles in Central India. They, as well as Mughal governors and high officials, had always taken pleasure in creating gardens for themselves, usually in the *chahar bagh* format, from the late 16th century onwards. They were also patrons of book production and an illustration in a simpler Mughal style, dated 1598, includes a charming and uncomplicated *chahar bagh* [45]. A late

he Taj Mahal at Agra painted by an Indian artist, c.1830.
2157, f. 612a]

n Imperial Mughal miniature, c.1598,
ving a simple chahar bagh. *[Or. 12076, f. 95a]*

47 A simple chahar bagh *illustrated in a miniature painted in Hyderabad in 1760.* [IOL Johnson 37–2]

46 A prince in his garden. This later Mughal miniature (1700) shows the development of the chahar bagh *system into a more complicated scheme of flowerbeds and paths.* [IOL Johnson 1–29]

Mughal miniature (dated AD 1700) of a prince being entertained illustrates the development of the garden, over the course of a century, into a more fussy plan with innumerable small flowerbeds surrounded by paths [46]. A garden in a Hyderabad painting of *c.*1760 is of an altogether simpler design, with its pool, fountain and flanking flower beds [47].

An unusual plan of an orchard included in a British Library manuscript of a poem copied in 1685 in the Deccan, probably at Bijapur, is typical of delicate Deccani paintings. The plan is interesting because the central canal, with its two reservoirs, has no side channels to provide irrigation to the fruit trees. These include fig, mango, pomegranate and citrus, underplanted with poppies, daylilies and narcissus. The channel flows through the gap in the wall and into, or underneath, the end pavilion which has cypresses and willows on either side of it [48].

48 A delicate Deccani plan of an orchard, c.1685. [Or. 338, f. 110a]

In the 17th and 18th centuries some of the princely states remained relatively independent of Mughal rule. This is reflected in their art, particularly in illustrated copies of the Hindu epics, including the *Ramayana* and works that relate episodes in the life of Krishna. Some manuscripts were written on palm leaves or aloe bark.[4] Gardens, trees, flowers and the fauna of the forests are interwoven in the stories and, in turn, serve as backgrounds to the illustrations by Hindu artists. Some paintings include Mughal features against a Hindu background as, for example, an illustration in a copy of the Last Book of the *Ramayana* produced for a Hindu patron at Udaipur. Dated 1653, it includes the Mughal garden plan of pool, fountain and channels in simplified form in an otherwise Indian setting [49].

4 J. P. Losty, *The Art of the Book in India* (London, 1982).

49 *The Mughal* chahar bagh *incorporated in an Indian setting, 1653.*
[*Add. 15297 (2), f. 70*]

50 Gopis searching for Krishna in the forest, in a palm leaf manuscript produced in the early 18th century in Orissa. [Or. 11689 (13a)]

The *Bhagavata Purana*, a collection of stories about the incarnation of Vishnu, contains an account of the early life of the god Krishna and the infatuation of the *gopis*, the wives and daughters of the cowherds. During one episode they think Krishna has deserted them and frantically search the forest, calling on the trees and plants by name for help in finding him.[5] In illustrations to this story, on palm-leaves, each of the trees is named and drawn, in a manuscript produced in the early 18th century at Orissa, on the Bay of Bengal [50]. These delicate drawings which were incised on the leaves with a stylus and then coloured, include fig trees (pipal and banyan), sacred basil, sweet-smelling champa, four jasmines, mango, breadfruit, rose apple and other sacred trees, each one named.

An Assamese manuscript dated 1836 is a copy of the *Brahmakanda* written and illustrated on sheets of aloe bark. It includes a painting of a scene in a forest where Krishna is disporting himself with the *gopas* (cow-herds). Crammed with stylised plants and flowers, animals, birds and insects, set amongst rounded rocks, it provides a joyous natural garden setting for the dancers.

51 A natural garden setting full of stylised plants and flowers, illustrating Krishna with the gopas in the forest. An Assamese painting on aloe bark, 1836. [Or. 11387, f. 3a]

5 J. P. Losty, *Krishna: A Hindu Vision of God* (London, 1980).

68

52 *Kashmiri vegetable growers at work, illustrated with a selection of their tools in a mid-19th century volume.* [IOL Add. Or. 1708]

53 *A gardener making garlands in an early 19th-century painting showing strong European influence.* [Add. 27255, f. 231b]

The crumbling of the Mughal empire and the increasing influence of the British in India in the late 18th and 19th centuries led to gardens being landscaped in a far more English style. Army officers and officials of the East India Company became the patrons of local artists and painting styles became more and more European. One example is a study of a gardener making garlands, one of a series of paintings of castes and occupations commissioned by Colonel James Skinner [53]. The gardener is working in a garden in which a lawn has taken the place of the usual channel. The painting was produced for Skinner in 1825 on his estate at Hansi, 85 miles north-west of Delhi. Another illustration, included in a mid-19th century volume of drawings of trades and occupations in Kashmir, shows a vegetable grower with his implements and examples of vegetables and fruit grown by him; these include rice, radishes, cucumbers, melons, pumpkins, pot-herbs, apples, lotus leaves and flowers and a sheaf of reeds.

Watercolour studies of specimens of Indian flowers and plants by Indian artists were commissioned by Europeans, one of the most notable being the collection formed by William Roxborough, the first official superintendent of the Calcutta Botanic Gardens. European artists, in turn, were commissioned to paint scenes and buildings in India and such artists as Thomas and William Daniell have left valuable records of Indian gardens as they were in the late-18th and 19th centuries.

China

The earliest recorded Chinese gardens were the vast hunting parks of semi-mythical emperors. The wickedness of Jie Gui, last ruler of the Xia dynasty (said to have fallen in c.1763 BC) was expressed in the excesses of his park, where ponds were filled with wine and hunks of meat hung in trees, and the tyrant Zhou, last ruler of the Shang dynasty (which fell in c.1122 BC) was said to have squandered the imperial treasury on parks and gardens where orgies of all sorts took place. The philosopher

55 A lakeside pavilion in the Imperial resort at Chengde, from the Kang xi emperor's poems describing the summer resort, an illustrated copper engraved edition by Matteo Ripa, postface dated 1712. [19957 c.4]

Mencius (fourth century BC), inheritor of the mantle of Confucius, deplored the excesses of Jie and Zhou and frequently pointed to the lavish construction of gardens as an indicator of the barbarity of a ruler. Pulling down houses to make ponds, seizing fields for parks and depriving peasants of their livelihood were aspects of careless rule.

Later emperors continued the tradition. The great summer palaces of the Qing rulers (1644–1911) are the only survivors of these huge imperial enclosures [55] and their vast area contrasts with the better known aspect of the Chinese garden tradition – the tiny gardens crammed with pools, rocks and pavilions that were constructed by the educated class and those who aspired to elegance [54, 56]. Both of these traditions, together with the gardens that were often constructed in Buddhist temple enclosures [*see* 58], had an overwhelming influence on the development of the Japanese garden.

54 Some typical elements of Chinese small-garden design: a pavilion with piled rocks and a tree beside a lotus pool. A scene from the life of Meng jiang nu, the woman whose tears made the Great Wall crumble. Chinese coloured woodblock 'New Year' print, early 20th century. [Or. 5896]

71

56 'Pan Khaqua's garden', a Cantonese export watercolour showing plants in pots and garden buildings, 19th century. [IOL Add. Or. 2127]

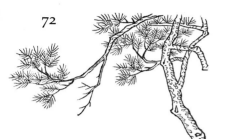

The Shanglin park which lay west and south-west of the capital city of Chang'an (present-day Xi'an) was laid out by the first 'emperor' of China, the founder of the Qin dynasty (221–207 BC) who conquered all the other small states to unify the country in 221 BC. Near his huge palace, built up on an earth core to raise it high above the surrounding countryside, the Upper Grove Garden was part-park, part-hunting reserve. The Martial Emperor (Wu di) of the Han dynasty who ruled from 140 to 87 BC, enlarged the park until it stretched some 100 miles south and west and had ponds dug to improve it. Like its predecessors, the Shanglin park reflected the status of the ruler. Under the Martial Emperor, China's frontiers were expanded. Expeditions were sent out to the north-west, beyond the Gobi desert, to the Central Asian kingdoms of Ferghana and Sogdiana, to expand the empire, consolidate alliances to protect the new borders and bring back the strong and fast 'celestial' horses bred in Central Asia. Though horses were of primary importance for their military use, contact with the outside world also led to an exchange of plants which eventually enriched the gardens of China. The south and the west were also brought under Chinese rule, incorporating the present-day provinces of Guangdong and Yunnan. Amongst the exotic products traded (mainly for silk) with independent states on the borders were animals and birds: camels, peacocks, monkeys, deer [57], bears, elephants, tigers and wolves, and plants and fruits: lychees, camphorwood, mulberry and varieties of peach from Central Asia. The most exotic of these were presented to the Emperor for his Shanglin park which incorporated botanic and zoological gardens amongst the pavilions and pools. Hunts took place in the park, most notably the annual autumn hunt when deer and more exotic animals were massacred in their thousands. In 103 BC, the imperial historian noted that the 'common people' were invited into the park to watch 'competitive games' which included chariot racing, archery and wrestling.

The inclusion of exotic plants and beasts in the park reflected one aspect of imperial garden planning which was to impress Japanese visitors some 500 years later. Filled with the produce of the empire, the park served as a miniature version of the empire. Its wooded hills and pools were the mountains and rivers with their natural inhabitants. In another of his gardens surrounding the capital, the Martial Emperor expanded on the same theme in his lake park. Three small islands in the lake were named after the mythical islands of the immortals which were supposed to lie off the coast of Shandong province. Immortals in Chinese belief were people who through various magical practices had managed to avoid death. Though Taoism is commonly regarded as a philosophical system idealising harmony between nature and man, one sect of Taoists in the Han dynasty developed a whole series of practices including

57 Animals were a common feature of Chinese gardens from the days of the earliest imperial parks onwards, and the pool here was especially dug for these deer. From an illustration in Hong xue yin yuan, *the illustrated autobiography of Linqing.* [15292, f. 1/4]

breathing exercises and the ingestion of (dangerous) potions in the search for physical immortality and eternal life on the islands. The Martial Emperor consulted the leading Taoists about his own immortality and the tall pavilions and halls on the rocky, wooded islands which rose from the lake were said to have been constructed in an attempt to lure immortals inland so that he might learn their secrets. It is not surprising that wealthy merchants of the Han copied the imperial parks for themselves. Yuan Guanghan diverted streams, built up islands of sand in the resulting pool, constructed pavilions and covered walks and stocked his park with yaks, white parrots and mandarin ducks. Executed for his presumption, his animals and plants were transferred to the imperial Shanglin park.

The second ruler of the Sui dynasty (AD 589–618) built a great garden outside his capital at Luoyang. Continuing the tradition of creating miniature islands of immortals established by the Martial Emperor, he had three islands built and covered with pavilions in the middle of the vast lake in the centre of his park. The enclosure was 75 miles in circumference and stocked with golden monkeys, deer and fine trees seized from neighbouring estates. 'Water palaces' lined the pools and dragon-headed barges filled with orchestras of concubines drifted on the lakes between the unfading flowers of artificial lotuses. In winter, when the maple leaves had fallen, tiny silk flowers were tied amongst the bare branches, a practice that is continued to this day in Peking parks. This garden came to the attention of Ono no Imoko, Japanese envoy to the Sui court and is thought to have been part of the inspiration behind the first

58 The Long tan or Dragon pool in one of the major temples outside Peking, famous for its great black carp. The pool is walled and the walls pierced with ornamental openings typical of Chinese garden architecture. From the illustrated autobiography of a Qing official, Linqing, Hong xue yin yuan tu qi (Tracks of a wild swan in the snow), 1847–1850. [15292 f. 1/6]

Japanese imperial parks in the early seventh century. Though the construction of islands in a lake 'sea' continued to play an important part in Japanese garden design, this form of symbolic representation on the grand scale gradually fell out of favour in China and most subsequent imperial parks, whilst still filled with lakes, islands and pavilions, took their inspiration from landscape painting and the small gardens of the south rather than oceans, islands of the blessed and imaginary worlds.

Wall paintings in tombs of the Tang dynasty (AD 618–907) depict gentlemen in black ear-flapped hats and short gowns mounted on fat horses with their tails tied in stumpy plaits, playing polo. Some show ladies in loose gowns seated on rocks beneath leafy trees. Polo was played in the imperial parks of the Tang, whilst more elaborate gardens were constructed for imperial favourites. At the Huaqing springs outside the capital where hot water bubbles endlessly into a series of pools beneath green wooded mountain slopes, the Dark Emperor (Xuan zong) who reigned from 712–756, improved the existing gardens, setting up a miniature island of lapis lazuli in the pool where court ladies floated in lacquered boats, and constructing a marble bath for his famously fat concubine, Yang Guifei. The Huaqing hot springs are still in use and lotuses flower at the corners of the square pool where court ladies boated: 'Amongst the dense lotus flowers, a small boat drifts, Looking for her lover she nods her head and smiles, A green jade hairpin falls into the water'.[1]

Earlier in the Tang, the Empress Wu was the first ruler to establish a 'summer palace' in hills north of the capital where she would decamp

1 Arthur Waley, *The Life and Times of Po Chü-i* (London, Allen and Unwin, 1949).

59 Winter-flowering narcissus, camellia and prunus from Jie zi yuan hua juan (*Colour prints from the Mustard Seed Garden painting manual*), *Chinese coloured woodblock,* c.1679–1791. [15274 a. 1]

with the entire court to escape the heat of the plains. Such 'summer palaces' were to be built in considerable numbers by the later emperors of the Qing (1644–1911) who also moved the court every summer. The Empress Wu's courtiers complained bitterly about the upheaval, especially as they had to live in straw huts in the rural retreat. The desire for escape from the summer heat was also evident in another of the Dark Emperor's garden buildings, the Cool Hall. Surrounded by fountains forming walls of water, cool air was blown in by fan-wheels operated by the movement of water. The seats were cooled by blocks of ice and iced drinks were served.

Disapproval of lavish imperial spending on gardens continued: the poet Bai Juyi, a garden-lover on a small scale, lamented the fate of the elephants in the imperial menagerie whose poor condition due to neglect he contrasted with the tender care lavished on them during the glorious reign of the founder of the Tang dynasty. Bai Juyi's poems are full of garden-related images: as a government official, kept up all night on duty in the palace, he wrote of the stillness of the pines and bamboos in the palace courtyards and when he was serving as governor of Zhongzhou in Sichuan province, he spent his money on fruit trees for the eastern embankment: 'I simply bought whatever had most blooms, not caring

60 A pine and rock in a typical garden grouping, from Shi zhu zhai shu hua pu *(Colour prints from the Ten Bamboo Studio). A Chinese coloured woodblock print, Nanjing, c.1643. [Or. 59 a. 10]*

whether peach, apricot or plum . . . The red flowers hang like a heavy mist, the white flowers gleam like a fall of snow . . . In front there flows an ever-running stream, beneath a little terrace . . .'[2]

His poems contain references to exotic animals like the red cockatoo ('sent as a present from Annam') and those of Du Fu (712–70) describe yet another Tang imperial garden built for the fat concubine, Yang Guifei, where she buried her white cockatoo with coral feet in a burial mound with a proper Buddhist funeral service. Here the customary lake with its three 'islands of the immortals' was overlooked by a terrace planted with peonies, the most fashionable flower of the period.

One of the great imperial garden-builders was the Honorable Emperor (Hui zong) of the Song who reigned from 1101 to 1126 and saw the division of China and the loss of the north to 'barbarian invaders', a disaster which some attributed, as Mencius might have done, to his lavish spending on his garden. Like previous imperial parks, this contained the requisite menagerie with golden pheasants and deer of all

61 The fashion for collecting rocks has been a longstanding feature of Chinese garden design. The varied and ancient rocks in the celebrated Half-Acre Garden taken over by the Qing official, Linqing, were said to have been selected and arranged by Li Yu (1611–1680?), a dramatist and poet, also the designer of the famous Mustard Seed garden in Nanjing [see 59]. From Hong xue yin yuan, *the illustrated autobiography of Linqing. [15292, f. 1/5]*

62

63

sorts and exotic plants like the southern lychee. The park was dominated by the Gen yue or Eastern Peak on whose summit stood a terrace where the emperor could view his capital. The massed rocks forming the Eastern Peak were dotted with curiously shaped stones and lake rocks, 'in various strange shapes, like tusks, horns, mouths, noses, heads, tails and claws', and amongst them were equally contorted pines, their trunks and branches twisted into the form of dragons, cranes and auspicious characters. In his passion for collecting strangely shaped rocks, the 'petromaniac' emperor was reflecting a contemporary craze, which had begun in the ninth century. Travellers, particularly those who ventured to the frontiers of the far south where strange 'forests' of worn limestone peaks dominated the landscape, helped to create the fashion. Vast sums were spent on transporting bizarre rocks ('the best of these were eroded limestone crags')[2] to the gardens of aristocrats and emperors. Li Deyu, a magistrate resident in Luoyang, wrote that he had no need to visit famous mountains for he had his own 'cluster of peaks' in his garden at home [61]. The Honourable Emperor of the Song despatched 'rock convoys' all over China, blocking the Grand Canal and disrupting the movement of the essential grain barges; one of the stones destined for his Eastern Peak, was the Exquisite Jade Rock, now in the Yu yuan (Mandarin Garden) in Shanghai. On its way to the capital, the boat in which it was being transported sank in a storm on the Huangpu river near the small county town which later grew into the city of Shanghai. In the 16th century, when an official called Pan Yunduan was designing a garden for his father, he had the river dredged to recover the Exquisite Jade Rock. Its pitted surface, described as 'crapy, scraggy and holey'[3] is characteristic of the desired type, as is its form. Swelling from a very narrow base, it appears to defy gravity.

Beneath the Eastern Peak, plum and apricot trees were planted in great numbers so that, in spring, the mountain seemed to rise out of a cloud of

62 Discussing philosophy in the rustic hut of a chrysanthemum expert, surrounded by flowers grown in sunken beds. From Hong xue yin yuan, *the illustrated autobiography of Linqing.* [15292, f. 1/2]

63 Writing poems in praise of flowers in the Phoenix tower, with a gnarled tree, a willow and a raised bed for inspiration. From Hong xue yin yuan, *the illustrated autobiography of Linqing.* [152292, f. 1/1]

2 Edward Schaeffer, *The Vermilion Bird* (Berkeley, University of California Press, 1967).

3 Pan Ling, *In Search of Old Shanghai* (Hong Kong, Joint Publishing Company, 1982).

blossom. Pools and buildings clustered at the foot of the mountain which was approached by a road lined with further prizes of the 'rock convoys'. Many of these were personally named by the Emperor, their titles carved in gold letters. The same fondness for naming stones, for seeing elephants, water buffalo, paired swans and human figures in their gnarled forms, continues today. Inscriptions cover the rocks in the gardens on Tiger Hill outside Suzhou and the strange peaks of the limestone 'Stone Forest' near Kunming. Visitors will strain to identify the characteristics of the rocks that have inspired their names and, at the same time, admire the varied calligraphy (one of the most highly regarded art forms in China) that contributes to the interest of the scene.

After the 12th-century invasion of Kaifeng, the Eastern Peak, symbol of imperial unconcern, was destroyed by local inhabitants. The capital of the Song was moved south to the city of Hangzhou, long famous for its beautiful natural scenery. The city lies beside the West Lake (Xi hu) which is surrounded by low wooded hills and is perhaps the best example of a natural landscape that has been constantly embellished by

64 A garden in spring illustrating all the major features of a southern garden; also famous as a site commemorated in a poem by Su Dongpo (1036–1101). From an album of paintings illustrating the stations of the Qian long emperor's fifth tour of inspection in South China; the last painting is signed by Qian Weicheng (1720–72).
[Or. 12895]

man. Man's position in nature and his hand in it is not an explicit theory but it lies behind many aspects of Chinese culture. The holy mountains of the Chinese Buddhists are dotted with temples and pretty pavilions where pilgrims can rest and admire a spectacular waterfall or a twisted pine beside a pointed peak; Chinese landscape paintings very frequently include a rustic hut from where the painter views towering mountains and most Chinese nature poetry includes the poet in the landscape, firmly shutting his wicket gate against unwanted guests so that he can play his zither, drink wine and converse with the moon [62, 63]. Though the Taoists held that nature had its own pattern, to which man should conform and not attempt to alter the inherent balance, the scenery of Hangzhou offers a long history of improvements. To the north and east, long dykes run across the edges of the West Lake: the Bai causeway with a humped stone bridge (Jade Belt Bridge) links the largest of the four islands in the lake to the shore and it is named after the poet Bai Juyi, governor of Hangzhou in 822–25. Bai Juyi did carry out improvements to the lake although he did not, in fact, construct this causeway.

65 'The Ambassador's residence at Canton', showing the garden with rocks, pavilion and pool. Watercolour by William Alexander, 1794. [IOL 959, f. 36/17]

The longer Su causeway with its six small bridges was built by another great poet, Su Dongpo, who also served as governor of Hangzhou in the 11th century. It was built out of silt dredged up from the lake and another of his innovations was the erection of stone lanterns in the lake, set in the deepest part marking the area where it was forbidden to grow any water plants (in an attempt to reduce silting). Lit up at night with candles, together with the moon, they create the illusion of four moons reflected in the water. Such stone lanterns are still an important part of Japanese garden planning; here they survive as an isolated example of what must once have been a fashionable garden feature in China.

The wooded hills surrounding the lake conceal a number of fine temples but were also embellished by free-standing pagodas. Pagodas, ostensibly very Chinese buildings, grew from two origins: the brick or stone *stupas* that were an integral part of Indian Buddhist temples, and the free-standing timber towers built for both defensive and decorative purposes during the Han. Though still often associated with Buddhist temples, pagodas were eventually built as solitary monuments, often set up on hills overlooking towns, for it was believed that they could improve the 'wind and water' or geomancy of an area, preventing floods and other disasters. Multi-eaved, often with upturned eaves and wind-chimes, they are extremely decorative and are perhaps the most common elements in the Chinese garden planning technique of 'borrowing a view', whereby a feature outside a small garden is made the focus of a view from within the garden itself [66, 67]. The West Lake used to be embellished by two pagodas, the Thunder Peak pagoda to the south, which was built in 975 but crashed to the ground in 1925, and the Bao shu (Protector of Virtue) pagoda to the north, first built in 986 which still stands. Printed guidebooks of the 17th and 18th centuries with illustrations of the West Lake all depict a mixture of the natural and the man-made: pagodas above slopes planted with flowering trees, small pavilions and halls on the islands amongst clumps of bamboo and pleasure-boats dotting its surface.

The greatest 'garden' in Song Hangzhou was the West Lake which was open to the public, and the remaining Song emperors, who lived in a huge palace on its shore, made use of the same facility. According to an account recorded in Marco Polo's *Travels*, the emperors had a large park on the lake shore filled with fallow deer, roe deer, red deer, hares and rabbits which they and their concubines would chase with dogs. Heated by the chase, the concubines would then cool off by swimming in the lake whilst the emperor watched from a silk-covered barge.

The Mongols, who finally conquered the whole of China in 1279, were not, despite Coleridge's imaginative description in *Khubla Khan*, garden builders. Khubilai Khan (1215–94) built his new capital at Peking on the

66

67

Chinese model, retaining his earlier stronghold of Shangdu (the 'upper capital' and Coleridge's Xanadu) as a hunting preserve where he could pursue the deer and exercise his falcons. Adopting Chinese plans, there was a lake park in Peking, to the north and west of the imperial palace, which survives today as the Bei hai or North Sea Park. This was largely remodelled by the Qing emperors, filled with pavilions and a number of Buddhist temples, including the great white Tibetan *stupa* which dominates the lake.

It was natural for the horseman-emperor Khubilai to prefer his hunting parks in the Mongol homeland but more surprising that the succeeding dynasty whose name was Ming ('bright'), which was established by a Chinese in 1368, did not see any grand imperial garden construction. The extraordinary character who became the founder of the Ming, Zhu Yuanzhang, rose from a background of extreme poverty and deprivation; his immediate successors were preoccupied with securing their frontiers, and later Ming emperors seem to have become bogged down in the paperwork of government, none having the time or the inclination for relaxation in a vast hunting park. It was another non-Chinese imperial family, the Manchus, who founded the Qing dynasty in 1644, who revived the early imperial tradition of great hunting parks.

Three 'summer palaces' are associated with the Qing emperors. The earliest was the mountain village 'where you can escape the heat' (Bi shu shan zhuang) at Chengde, in the mountains about 90 miles north-east of Peking. In a vast valley with a large natural lake (swelled by melting

66 Waiting in a tower for the moon: the elegant belvedere rising above the trees was built for moon viewing. From Xia Xianggeng, Shao you yuan er shi si xiao zhao tu *(Twenty-four pictures of Wu Xinfu's 'Almost non-existent' garden), 1815. [15323b . 15, ff. 42–43]*

67 Watching a fisherman in a straw raincoat: the perfect illustration of a garden with a 'borrowed view'. The lake lies outside the garden but is visible, complete with rustic boat, from the upper storey of the house. From Xia Xianggeng, Shao you yuan er shi si xiao zhao tu *(Twenty-four pictures of Wu Xinfu's 'Almost non-existent' garden). [15323. b. 15, ff. 12–13]*

68 The imperial library Wen
hui ge (Literary assemblage)
in Yangzhou. Seven sets of
the 36,000 volume imperial
manuscript collectanea Si ku
quan shu (Complete
collection of the four
storehouses) were produced in
the late 18th century and
stored in specially-built
libraries based on a private
library in Ningbo. The
surrounding garden
incorporated fire-preventing
features: a bare rockery near
the building and a
surrounding pool. From
Hong xue yin yuan, the
illustrated autobiography of
Linqing. [15292, f. 1/4]

snow), the Kang xi ('Vigorous and splendid') emperor began the construction of his summer retreat in 1703. A wall some 12 miles long
surrounded a park filled with wooded hills to the west, a lake to the east
and a small area of courtyard living quarters to the south (though these
are low and quite simple, they hardly constitute the humble mountain
village for which they are named). The lake, filled with lotuses in
summer, frozen hard all winter, has a number of small islands in it and is
surrounded by Chinese pavilions and halls, one built specially to house
one copy of the vast imperial collectanea, Si ku quan shu (Complete
treasury of the four storehouses), a manuscript which ran to some 36,000
volumes [68].

As befitted an emperor descended from horsemen, the park was kept
stocked with animals for the hunt, most notably the strange Père David
deer. Named Elaphurus Davidianus after its discoverer, Armand David
(1826–1900), a French Lazarist missionary and naturalist, to the Chinese
the deer were known as 'four differences' (si bu xiang): their horns are like
those of a deer yet they are not deer, they have horse heads but are not
horses, donkey's bodies but are not donkeys and their hoofs are like
those of cattle but they are not cattle. First seen by their discoverer in
1865, the last of the Chinese herd escaped from the deserted summer
palace in 1900 whereupon they were eaten by the starving populace.

Cared for and bred in captivity in England by the Dukes of Bedford, a herd was returned to the park in 1987.

It was in the gardens of the Summer Palace at Chengde that Lord Macartney, the first British Ambassador to China, met the Qian long emperor in 1792. Macartney's secretary, John Barrow, described the approach to the park as much resembling the approach to Luton Hoo in Bedfordshire, 'the grounds gently undulated and checkered with various groups of well-contrasted trees' and the lake and its surroundings, viewed from a 'magnificent yacht'.[4] The islands were differentiated, '. . . one marked by a pagoda or other building, one quite destitute of ornament; some smooth and level, some steep and uneven; others frowning with wood, or smiling with culture'. Later, the embassy was taken to the wooded western part of the park: 'It is one of the finest forest scenes in the world; wild, woody, mountainous and rocky, abounding

4 John Barrow, *Travels in China* (London, 1804).

69 A western view of a corner of a Chinese garden, with piled rocks, bamboo and lotus grown in a jar, in a watercolour by William Alexander, 1793–94. [IOL 959, f. 17/87]

with stags and deer of different species and most of the other beasts of
the chase, not dangerous to man'. Barrow was a discriminating observer,
and he noted one of the fundamental principles of later Chinese garden
design, the importance of garden buildings: 'One thing I was particularly
struck with, I mean the happy choice of situation for ornamental
buildings. From attention to this circumstance they have not the air of
being crowded or disproportioned; they never intrude upon the eye; but
wherever they appear they always show themselves to advantage, and
aid, improve, and enliven the prospect.' He was more critical of some
details, confessing that he did 'not much admire' the lotuses that filled
the lake. 'Artificial rocks and ponds with gold and silver fish are perhaps
too often introduced, and the monstrous porcelain figures of lions and
tigers, usually placed before the pavilions, are displeasing to an European eye; but these are trifles of no great moment . . .'

Nearer Peking, two further Summer Palaces were built by the Qing
emperors. The Qian long (Surpassing sovereign) emperor (reigned
1736–96) oversaw the construction of the most extraordinary imperial
garden, the Yuan ming yuan or Garden of Perfect Brightness, in the
mid-18th century. Fundamentally a Chinese garden on the grand scale,
with garden buildings set amongst hills and pools, the garden was
described by the Jesuit Attiret in 1743, 'Hills have been constructed, 50 to
60 feet high, creating an infinity of small valleys between them. Water is
conducted through a number of artificial channels, and collected in many
spots to form pools and lakes. One travels the pools, lakes and canals in
magnificent barges . . . in all the valleys, beside the water are beautifully
grouped assortments of buildings: courtyards, halls, galleries, gardens
and waterfalls . . . You move from one valley to another, not along a
straight path as in Europe but by zig-zags, winding paths, themselves
adorned with little pavilions and grottoes through which you reach
another valley, quite different from the first, distinguished by its con-
tours or the form of its buildings.'⁵ He also noted the preference for
flowering trees on the slopes [70] and the cunning design of the canals,
bordered with rough 'natural' stones and winding through rocks and
hills, quite the reverse of the neatly bordered, straight waterways of
French gardens of the period. Amongst this grand Chinese landscape,
were a group of surprising buildings, the 'European palaces' built
between 1740 and 1747 by a group of Jesuit specialists, including the
famous painter Guiseppe Castiglione (1688–1766) who designed the
Italianate buildings and Father Michel Benoist (1715–74) who designed
the fountain which cast its water into a great stone shell (one of the few
surviving pieces).

Castiglione's edifices were in a kind of Chinese baroque; rusticated
walls were adorned with columns whose embellishment did not quite

5 *Lettres edifiantes et curieuses . . .
par des missionaires Jesuites* (Paris,
Garnier-Flammarion, 1979).

70 Flowering trees on the slopes: prunus with characteristic spring flowers, magnolia and peony, grouped beside a house. From Hong xue yin yuan, the illustrated autobiography of Linqing. [15292, f. 1/2]

accord with the established orders, as they had swags of stone-carved flowers twisted around them. Such European palaces had no place in the Chinese tradition save to emphasize the grandeur and omnipotence of the emperor; where the Martial emperor of the Han had miniature seas and islands of the immortals, the Qing emperors took European styles into a garden, in a reverse of the fashion for 'Chinoiserie' that was sweeping through Europe at the time, with 'Chinese' gardens at Stowe and a pagoda in Kew Gardens.

The summer palace at Chengde survived, though it was largely abandoned by the later Qing emperors, for after the Excellent and Blessed Emperor (Jia qing) was killed by a bolt of lightning there in 1820, it was considered to be ill-omened; the Garden of Perfect Brightness was destroyed by British and French troops in 1860 in a campaign intended as a show of strength over the Taiping rebellion. The neighbouring summer palace now known as the Garden of the Cultivation of Peace (Yi he yuan) was also sacked (and suffered further depredations at the hands of foreign troops in 1900 after the Boxer uprising) but was twice rebuilt by the notorious and probably murderous Dowager Empress Ci Xi (whose name means 'motherly and auspicious').

There had been imperial parks on this site, in the northwestern suburbs of Peking, since the 12th century but it was the Qian long emperor who relaid the park and extended the lake in honour of his mother's sixtieth birthday in 1750. He had previously used the lake for overseeing naval manoeuvres but decided later to improve it, by adding a 17-arched stone bridge in imitation of the dykes on the West Lake at Hangzhou. Almost all the palaces, pavilions and temples he constructed on the great hill that overlooks the lake were given poetic names associated with his veneration of his mother's great age: the Hall of Goodwill and Longevity, Palace of Joy in Longevity and the Palace of Virtue and Harmony. Behind the hill, he had a mock 'town' created with stone-lined canals imitating the 'Venice of the East', the southern town of Suzhou, which his mother loved. To the east of the hill was a small enclosed garden with a lotus pool at its centre and covered walks and verandahed buildings all round. The Garden of Harmonious Interest (Xie qu yuan) was a reasonably accurate copy of the Garden of Ease (Ji chang yuan) in another southern city, Wuxi, which the emperor had been much impressed by on one of his tours of inspection of South China. All these imitations of southern gardens and scenes mark a distinct departure from the mythical landscapes of the early imperial parks. The growth of importance of the Yangtse Delta in the Ming and Qing in particular had also seen the widespread creation of smaller private gardens [71]. Far from the grand hunting parks of the earlier emperors with their oceans and islands, these were tranquil miniatures, tiny landscapes (sometimes actually designed by painters). The Qing emperors had access to these gardens through their great trips south; whilst inspecting economic progress, they were lodged with their entourage in 'travelling palaces' constructed around the lake at Hangzhou or in specially constructed house-garden complexes characteristic of the Yangtse Delta. On return to the northern capital of Peking, they copied these small, jewel-like enclosures, setting them up amongst the temples and theatres of their grand parks.

The imperial interest in the small gardens of the Yangtse Delta was assisted by the eagerness of the local inhabitants to show off the best of the local style when providing lodgings for the imperial court. One of China's greatest novelists, Cao Xueqin (c.1715–63) was the grandson of Cao Yin (1618–1712), Superintendent of the Imperial Silk Factory in Suzhou, who was responsible for lodging the Kang xi emperor on his tours of inspection of the south in 1699, 1703, 1705 and 1707. To do so, he had a garden palace constructed next door to the factory. Though the construction took place before Cao Xueqin's birth, its scale and magnificence must have entered family folklore for it forms the basis of one of the chapters in Cao Xueqin's great novel *Hong Lou Meng* (usually translated as the Dream of the Red Chamber).[6]

In the novel, when an imperial consort was due to visit Nanjing, the

6 Cao Xueqin, *The Story of the Stone*, translated by David Hawkes (Harmondsworth, Penguin, 1973).

head of the Jia family constructed apartments for her and a lavish garden. Entered through a five-bay gatehouse of plain polished timbers with finely carved lattice windows which stood on a marble platform carved with passion flowers, the garden proper was screened from view by a 'miniature mountain' dotted with 'rugged white rocks resembling monsters and beasts, some recumbent, some rampant, dappled with moss or hung about with creepers, a narrow zig-zag path just discernible between them'. The path led to a 'ravine, green with magnificent trees and ablaze with rare flowers. A clear stream welling up where the trees were thickest wound its way through clefts in the rocks. Some paces further north, on both sides of a level clearing, rose towering pavilions, whose carved rafters and splendid balustrades were half-hidden by the trees' and which overlooked a pool. 'This was enclosed by marble balustrades and spanned by a stone bridge ornamented with the heads of beasts with gaping jaws. On the bridge was a little pavilion.' Further on, 'a cobbled

71 The famous 'Half Acre' garden, laid out in the early 17th century and later inhabited by the Qing official, Linqing, illustrating many traditional features of the Chinese garden: ornamental openings in walls, trees, mock mountain rockery, a pool, potted plants and a garden pavilion. From Hong xue yin yuan, *the illustrated autobiography of Linqing. [15292, f. 1/5]*

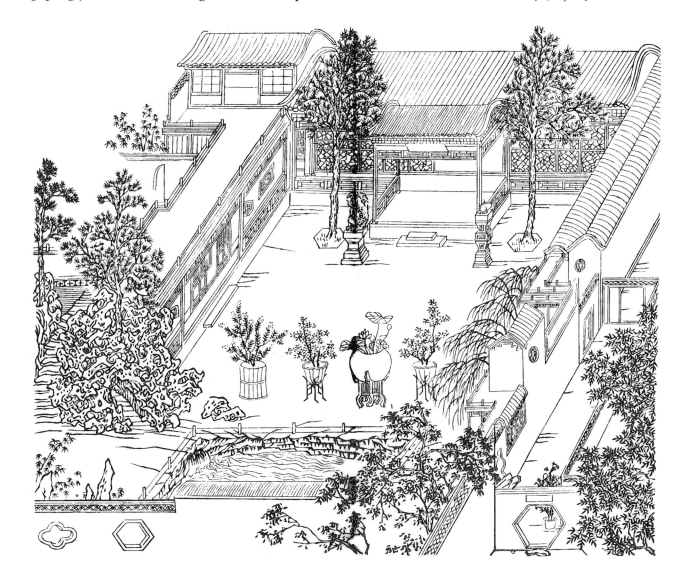

path wound up to a little cottage of three rooms ... a small door ...
opened on to the back garden with its large pear-tree, broad-leafed
plantain and two tiny side courts ... a brook meandered out through the
bamboos.' Other scenes in the garden, revealed as paths turned around
rocks and pavilions, included 'double-flowering peach in blossom' and 'a
moon gate made of bamboo over which climbed flowering plants'. The
balance of plants, water in various forms, buildings and rocks, arranged
in a series of concealed views, is characteristic of the private gardens of
the south. As one character remarks on leaving the gate-house, 'If not for
this hill, one would see the whole garden as soon as one entered and
how tame that would be.'

The point of the chapter in which this description occurs is not to
describe the garden in prose but to watch the hero of the novel, Baoyu,
putting the finishing touch to the whole by finding poetic names and
quotations to be inscribed on rocks and lintels [72]. As her host
remarked, 'By rights, we should ask the Imperial Consort to do us the
honour of composing the inscriptions but she can hardly do this without
having seen the place. On the other hand, if we leave the chief sights and
pavilions without a single name or couplet until her visit, the garden,
however lovely with its flowers and willows, rocks and streams, cannot
fully reveal its charm.' The names were not directly descriptive but
allusive, making a trip through the garden something of a crossword
puzzle as visitors tried to fathom the references. In the largest surviving
garden in Suzhou, the Zhuo zheng yuan or 'Garden of the Humble
Administrator', a name which, like the imperial 'mountain village' hardly
hints at its extravagant extent, the Hall of Distant Fragrance takes its
name from the line, 'a distant fragrance is all the more pure' in a Song
poem by Zhou Dunyi, 'In praise of the lotus', for the hall stands in front
of a lotus-filled pool. Nearby is the Leaning Jade Verandah, beside which
bamboos were clumped and described by the painter and poet Wen
Zhengming (1470–1559), 'Leaning against the columns, a thousand jade
green bamboo stems'. In the same garden, an inscription in the Fan
pavilion reads 'With whom shall I sit in the verandah', taken from a
poem by Su Dongpo, where the refrain continues 'with the bright moon
and a light breeze'. In the Liu Yuan, Garden to Linger In, above a stone
doorway is carved an inscription which reads 'Green bamboo by the
eastern mountains' and through the doorway a single white lake rock
stands in a courtyard planted with bamboo, announced by the
inscription.

The importance of literary texts did not only lie in their significance as
the finishing touch: literary accounts of great private gardens of the past
and the poetic ideal of retreat were also significant. The great growth of
private gardens seems to date from the period of disunion after the fall

72 Choosing poetic names
and quotations to be inscribed
on rocks and lintels. From
Cao Xueqin's novel Hong
lou meng (Dream of the red
chamber), c.1880.
[15326 d. 5]

of the Han in 220 BC. Until the empire was reunited in 580, China was divided amongst frequently warring kingdoms. After the certainty of the Han when the centralized bureaucracy, taking its moral justification and guidelines from Confucian texts, the period of disunion was one of introspection and retreat from the unpleasant realities. Buddhism, a religion of rejection of worldly values, made great strides and cultured gentlemen eschewed the civil service, preferring to gather together in rural retreats, drinking and writing poetry. The 'Seven sages of the bamboo grove' of the third century developed the Taoist ideas of the supremacy of nature and man's small part in the great scheme: the Ruan family of poets accepted their pigs as convivial drinking companions and another member of the group was always accompanied by his servant carrying a spade so that he could be buried should he happen to die in the Bamboo Grove; in south China, the great calligrapher and poet Wang Xizhi (321–79) gathered friends outside Shaoxing to drink and write poetry in a garden setting. One of China's greatest poets, Tao Qian (365–427) who abandoned an official career to take up farming, wrote of his retreat from city life: 'A caged bird longs for its native forests . . . Now

73 A rustic retreat: a 'crazy' pool in the Tanzhe temple outside Peking. Built to imperial order the temple includes a replica of a pool designed for a garden game where guests float wine cups on the water and are compelled to compose a line of poetry as a cup floats by them (or pay the forfeit of drinking it). The game was 'invented' by the calligrapher Wang Xizhi (321–379) at the Orchid Pavilion outside Shaoxing. From Hong xue yin yuan, *the illustrated autobiography of Linqing. [152992, f. 1/5]*

74 *Appreciating snow in the garden. Fur coats, charcoal braziers and hot wine around the frozen pool. From* Hong xue yin yuan, *the illustrated autobiography of Linqing.* [15292, f. 1/4]

I shall clear the land at the edge of the southern wilderness, Embracing simplicity, return to garden and field . . . My thatched hut of eight or nine bays, Elms and willows shade the eaves at the rear, Peach and plum trees planted before the hall . . . I return to nature.'7

A later character who took the same attitude was Sima Guang (1020–86). Dismissed from office, he retired to write the major historical work *Zi zhi tong jian* (Comprehensive mirror of the art of government) and construct his Garden of Solitary Enjoyment. The garden was near Luoyang which is still famous for its peonies and these were included in the garden although the squared herb plots (rather like Elizabethan box planting) and the 'tents' and 'houses' he constructed by planting bamboo in circles and squares and tying the tops together, excited more interest. They are clearly depicted in a painting, The Garden of Solitary Delight by Qiu Ying (c.1494–1552) which was based on Sima Guang's clear account of his work.

The great private gardens of the Ming and Qing, constructed in the pretty towns of the Yangtse Delta, were made for officials and rich

7 My translation but *see* Arthur Waley, *170 Chinese poems* (London, Constable, 1918).

merchants who sought 'the joy of mountain and stream, forest and spring' whilst retaining the material pleasures and resources of the city. Unlike the great imperial parks which were generally constructed outside the city walls, these private gardens were built as functional extensions of town houses [74, 75, 76]. Halls to hold banquets for friends in the garden, extra courtyards, stages for theatrical performances, studios to read or paint in, tall pavilions to admire a distant view, all these were constructed in a garden adjacent to the family house which usually occupied about half the available space. Though retired officials and painters must have taken a personal interest in the construction of their gardens, upwardly mobile merchants, keen to acquire all the trappings of

75

76

scholarly elegance, employed garden designers and resorted to a manual of elegant garden design such as the 17th century *Yuan ye* (Craft of Gardens) by Ji Cheng, which, like other 'style manuals' of the period, tended to didactic pedantry rather than essentially practical advice. Written in a mannered literary style, bristling with poetic imagery, the *Yuan ye* nevertheless stresses the importance of the major elements in a garden: water, rocks and buildings, mentioning plants mainly in relation to these and offering no advice on how to tend them.

The essential natural elements for a garden, water and rocks, were widely available. Water, which often formed the central focus of a garden, was plentiful in the rice-growing Yangtse Delta. In most gardens, if there was no spring within the grounds, local water sources were used, with canals leading water into the garden where it was collected into streams and pools [77, 78]. As the land is flat, there were no natural waterfalls but in the Shi zi lin (Grove of Stone Lions) in Suzhou, a reservoir for collecting rainwater was constructed above the Pavilion for Questioning the Plum and the accumulated water flowed down a series

75 Garden activities included painting, poetry writing, fishing, thinking and aggressive drinking games intended to make others drunk. From Xia Xianggeng's Shao you yuan er shi si xiao zhao tu *(Twenty-four pictures of Wu Xinfu's 'Almost non-existent' garden), 1815.* [15323 b. 15, ff. 40–41]

76 Theatrical scenes on a terrace with rocks, plum and banana beyond. From Wu Cheng'en's Xi xiang ji *(Journey to the West), an 18th-century woodblock edition.* [15271 c. 13]

of stone steps. Water was either 'assembled' in pools or 'dispersed', alternately revealed and hidden by rocks. In the former style, an open pool forms the centre of a garden (as in the Wang shi yuan, Garden of the Master of the Fishing Nets). 'Assembled' water could be 'divided' by creating an artificial impression of a distant source through the construction of a rocky ravine in a corner or adding a bridge. In the small private gardens, it was rare to find a bridge cutting across the centre of a pool for this could have contradicted the desired impression of open space. Low bridges, often of flat stones set at angles to form a zig-zag, cut across the corner of pools. For the same reason, and because open water was

77 Wine and conversation by the water. Two gentlemen beside a lotus pond are attended by small servants bearing a jar of wine and a basket of cakes. From Xia Xianggeng's Shao you yuan er shi si xiao zhao tu *(Twenty-four pictures of Wu Xinfu's 'Almost non-existent' garden), 1815. [15323 b. 15, p. 42]*

valued for its reflective qualities, it was rare to find water-lilies or lotuses covering a pool; they were restricted to the outer edges and carefully controlled. An open stretch of water allowed glimpses of the gold and silver carp, reflections of scudding clouds and the play of wind and rain on the clear surface. Great attention was paid to the banks of a pool which were ideally built up whilst retaining a 'natural' appearance. Earth banks seem to have been preferred during the Ming, but as they were susceptible to rain damage, they were gradually replaced by banks of piled rocks. Creeping plants such as wistaria or small trees were planted in crevices in the rocks and attention was paid to creating a natural descent from a rocky peak down to flatter stones nearer the surface of the water. Some buildings, usually the open pavilions known as 'dry boats', were built directly beside and slightly over the water and surrounded by marble balustrades.

In other gardens, rocks, rather than water, formed the main focus. Emperors like the Honourable Emperor of the Song reflected the passion for collecting strangely shaped rocks, many of which came, if not from further south, from the Yangtse Delta. Limestone rocks, pitted by the action of pebbles in the great lake at Wuxi, were amongst the favourites. They were artificially created, left in the lake for decades and the length of time they took to form added enormously to their price. Single rocks were set in courtyards or in front of halls and where no single rock of sufficient interest could be found, smaller rocks were piled into 'mock

78 Cooling down in the Lotus Pavilion, an open, breezy kiosk to be used in midsummer when the lotuses flowered. From Hong xue yin yuan, *the illustrated autobiography of Linqing.* [15292. f. 1/4]

*79 Paying a visit to the
flowers in the Wang garden,
a famous garden in Jiangsu
province. The dramatic
natural surroundings
contrast with the formal
courtyard groupings and
miniature mountains. From*
Hong xue yin yuan, *the
illustrated autobiography of
Linqing. [15292, f. 1/5]*

8 Edward Schaeffer, *The Vermilion
Bird* (Berkeley, University of
California Press, 1967).

mountains' which towered over streams and could be ascended by
twisting stepped paths [79, 80]. The construction of 'mountains' was a
specialist art: the Lu family of Hangzhou 'piled up mountain peaks and
dug ravines with a skill that rivalled Heaven's'. There were differing
views on methods of construction although the aim was always realism.
Li Yu of the Qing wrote in his *Random notes of an idler*, 'After a lifetime of
travel and seeing all the famous gardens, I have never seen a mountain
which does not bear the marks of joints, chipping or drilling but which,
viewed from a distance, does not look like a real mountain'.[8] Some filled
in the gaps with earth, planted with creepers or trees, others preferred to
leave the stones bare. One of the great rock-piling experts of the Qing,
Zhang Lian, felt that the best method was to start with an earth mound
and cover that with mountains. The similarity of these mock mountains
to the imaginative peaks of Chinese landscape painting was emphasised by the involvement of artists in their design and the fact that they
were usually constructed on the basis of a drawing and a model made of

clay and sand. Wooden piling was sometimes used as a foundation and iron nails, glutinous rice paste and plaster used to join rocks. Though Li Yu claimed that joints were always visible, care was taken to try and conceal methods of construction: when joining yellow limestone rocks, a mixture of iron filings and dark yellow clay from Yixing was used to ensure colour blending. Sometimes the mountains contained grottoes which could serve as rooms, cool in the heat of summer. Particularly where a distant view of a lake or pagoda was possible, tiny pavilions were sometimes placed on top of the 'mountain'. They had to be small, like the tiny Snail Shell pavilion, seven feet in diameter, in the Yi yuan (Suitable Garden) in Suzhou, to complete, rather than dominate, the mountain.

Buildings were the third major element in southern gardens. The house to which the garden was attached, usually took up about half the available space whilst, within the gardens, the proportion of space occupied by further buildings ranged between 30 per cent in small to medium-sized gardens and 15 per cent in the larger gardens where greater expanses of water and mountain were possible. Buildings, as one

80 A lady meets her lover by climbing up an artificial mountain and over a garden wall, from the novel Jin ping mei *(Plum in a golden vase). From a 1933 reprint of a woodblock edition with a preface dated 1617.* [15334. b. 12]

81

81 *A young boy learns to read in a whitewashed garden schoolroom, with bamboo growing against the outer walls: furniture of twisted vine-roots and lattice windows complete the rustic effect. From Xia Xianggeng's* Shao yu yuan er shi si xiao zhao tu *(Twenty-four pictures of Wu Xinfu's 'Almost non-existent' garden), 1815. [15323 b. 15, ff. 2–3]*

82 *Listening to the evening rain on the banana leaves. Banana trees were frequently planted in South China not only for their fruit, but also for their quality of pluvial resonance. From Xia Xianggeng's* Shao yu yuan er shi si xiao zhao tu *(Twenty-four pictures of Wu Xinfu's 'Almost non-existent' garden), 1815. [15323 b. 15, ff. 6–7]*

9 Liu Dunzhen, 'The Traditional Gardens of Suzhou' in *Garden History*, vol. 10, no. 2, 1982, pp. 108–141.

contemporary expert notes, 'provide places from which views can be admired', 'the means by which spaces are divided'[9] and also provide colour with their white-washed walls, grey tiles and dark chestnut timberwork [81, 82, 83]. In the last aspect, they have a close relationship with plants, for the form of bamboo is reflected and enhanced when it is set against a white wall and the whitewash means that plants can gain from reflected light. Halls of all sorts, 'dry boat' verandahed buildings over water, pavilions perched on mountain tops, are all light in construction since the climate of the Yangtse Delta is warm and it is in these garden buildings that the rather exaggerated upturned eaves of southern Chinese buildings are most often seen. Most of the buildings have façades of removable timber lattice panels that can be thrown open or taken out to reveal the garden, or closed so that greenery and rocks are glimpsed through the intricate lattice. Covered walks are also widely used to divide the garden, the walls often pierced with 'flower brick' openings of fanciful shapes – in the form of fans, leaves or plum flowers. As the visitor walks past, these decorative openings offer a glimpse of what lies beyond, like the slow unrolling of a handscroll landscape painting.

In a reverse of the western garden scheme, plants tend to be described last of all in Chinese works on gardens. Two major points were the preservation of large old trees, even when remodelling a garden, and all-year colour from the flowers of the four seasons. Magnolia and peonies were favoured in spring, wistaria, roses and lotuses in summer, chrysanthemum and maple trees in autumn and camellias, *Chimonanthus*

82

83

fragrans, the evergreen bamboo and early flowering prunus in winter. Some of these plants, such as roses and peonies, were best grown in raised beds with carved stone surrounds [85] and others, like chrysanthemum, were often raised in pots and brought out onto verandahs when they flowered [84, 86]. Other 'movable' plants were the small shrubs and trees grown in pots, their roots cut and their stems twisted to form miniatures. The technique, which originated in China where it is known as *pen cai* ('reared in pots') is better known in the west by the Japanese translation, *bonsai*. There is a related form in China known as *pen jing* or 'pot scene' where tiny mountain peaks (pieces of limestone or other rocks collected from famous lakes or mountains) were set in water in flattish earthenware dishes. The tiny peaks were often planted with moss, ferns and tiny saplings and sometimes further decorated with miniature clay pagodas, pavilions or bridges. They were known from the Mongol Yuan dynasty (1279–1368), when they were called little seed scenes, and they may well be older than that. Ming works on the history of Suzhou make it clear that they were a speciality of the area. *Pen jing*, *pen cai* and potted plants were often displayed on stone tables set against the white-washed walls of side courtyards. Though deer were too big for the small southern gardens, bright gold and silver carp were often raised in pools and songbirds in elaborate bamboo cages were brought into the garden to sing (and Manchu aristocrats buried their pet dogs in the grounds of their mansions).

The importance of dividing up even a small garden to provide a series of separate views was fundamental to the plan. Gardens were ideally

83 Supervising the airing of the library: note the potted epidendrum on a stand and the cross-shaped opening framing the bamboo clump. From Xia Xianggeng's Shao yu yuan er shi si xiao zhao tu *(Twenty-four pictures of Wu Xinfu's 'Almost non-existent' garden), 1815. [15323 b. 15, ff. 4–5]*

approached by a narrow twisting path to increase the visitor's anticipation; a method successfully used in the public approach to the Wang shi yuan (Master of the Nets) garden in Suzhou which is, today, approached by the former rear gate. Alternatively, as in *Hong Lou Meng* (the 'Dream of the Red Chamber'), the first scene of a garden was tantalizingly glimpsed through the lattice screens of a gatehouse. Each hall or pavilion had its own 'view', of a pool, mountain or spectacular plant. Side courtyards were sometimes paved with differently coloured pebbles forming tiny pictures of vases of flowers, deer or auspicious designs such as interlocked coins. Bamboos were planted against the whitewashed walls and the central focus of such a courtyard might be a single lake rock or a raised bed of carved stone filled with peonies or roses.

Though the gardens of the Yangtse Delta represented the highest form of traditional garden design, the love of gardens, plants and flowers was not restricted to the south. In North China, where the climate is not conducive to all-year gardening, garden buildings were often painted. In the city of Ji'nan in Shandong province where there are many natural springs, one garden makes use of the constantly moving water as a major focus, viewed from an open pavilion with bright red timberwork and yellow glazed tiles, colourful even on a grey winter day. The same use of brightly coloured painted decoration can be seen in the Yi he yuan Summer Palace outside Peking where even in the Garden of Harmonious Interest, modelled on a southern garden, all the buildings have columns painted red and horizontal rafters painted with multi-coloured landscape scenes. Trees were traditionally planted in the tiny courtyards of ordinary houses in Peking so that 19th century western travellers who viewed the city from its high walls described it as 'a great wood' or *rus in urbe*. Trees or vines grown over a trellis (and carefully protected under straw and clay during the freezing winter) provided summer shade and, since other plants could not be left out all year, some Peking residents set aside one room to over-winter plants, keeping it warm and covering the walls with oiled paper to reduce pests. When the weather allowed, flowering oleanders, single lotus flowers in large pots, fragrant osmanthus, hibiscus and other potted plants were set out in the courtyard, alongside large ceramic jars full of precious goldfish, black, silver and gold.

84 The Qing official Linqing kept editions of his mother's poems in his 'Half Acre garden'. Wisteria frames the windows which have bamboo roller blinds for summer and potted plants stand in the courtyard. From Hong xue yin yuan, *the illustrated autobiography of Linqing. [15292, f. 1/5]*

85 Watering the flowers in raised stone beds. The 'half' pavilion by the wall has a tromp-l'oeil stone-carved landscape and elegant seats with swan's neck backs. From Xia Xianggeng's Shao yu yuan er shi si xiao zhao tu (Twenty-four pictures of Wu Xinfu's 'Almost non-existent' garden), 1815.
[15323 b. 15, ff. 44–45]

86 Ladies in a garden with a climbing plant grown over a frame, potted orchids and a 'pot scene' in the centre background. From a Ming illustrated work included in Zhong guo ban hua xuan (Selection of Chinese woodblock illustrations), 1958.
[15530 b. 67, vol. 2, pl. 96]

85

Japan

87 Ladies in a house, with blinds rolled up to reveal the ajoining garden, from a Japanese manuscript of Yurikawa Daijan, *a tale about a warrior. Colours painted on paper, 17th–18th century. [Or. 13822]*

From the fifth century AD, Japanese gardens were strongly influenced by their Chinese neighbour's parks and planting. Four years after the first Japanese embassy to China, led by Ono no Imoko in 607, the first landscaped garden with a lake was recorded as being constructed in the imperial palace in the capital of Nara (near Kyoto). It would appear that some of the features of this garden were built by a Korean craftsman known as the 'Ugly artisan' because the skin of his face was spotted with white. He built a bridge across the lake, assumed to be a high-arched red-painted bridge in the contemporary Chinese style, and a 'mountain'.

Little is known about the latter structure, though one expert considers that it may have been a sort of fountain made out of a pile of hollow stones that could be filled with water which spouted out through small openings in one of the lower stones. Some suggest that this was a representation of Sumeru, the mountain at the centre of the nine mountains in the Buddhist plan of the universe; thus this early garden anticipates a later form based on temple gardens constructed to represent an earthly version of the Buddhist paradise as described in the *Lotus sutra*. Early Japanese literary accounts describe such mountain fountains as dating back to the Chinese Han dynasty, though they no longer survive in China, and so this example represents the first survival in Japan of garden elements long lost in China.

In this early period, the word that the Japanese used for a garden was *shima* which meant island, firmly establishing a connection with the early Chinese imperial gardens dominated by a lake with islands of the

immortals. Contemporary Chinese garden styles were also reflected in some of the contents of the imperial treasure-house Shōsōin where an eighth-century painted screen depicts a lady sitting on a pitted lake rock beside a tree with a picturesquely twisted trunk. There was also a form of *pen jing* (pot scene) in the collection, made entirely from wood carved to represent a mountainous island, its cliffs cut away by the action of water. Though almost nothing survives of the gardens of Nara, fragmentary references can be gathered from poems of the period which include mention of flowering plants, lakes, willows and plum trees and pleasure boats.

Early in the Heian period (794–1185), an imperial park was laid out with a lake filled by a spring and dotted with islands in the Chinese imperial style. Willows bordered the paths and a large pavilion over-looked the lake. As befitted an imperial park modelled on those of the Chinese emperors, it was used by the court for banquets, boating and sporting events. Another garden, which represents a rare survival, was the Saga-no-in where the Emperor Saga retired in 823. His lake, bordered by cherry and maples, once had a string of five linked 'islands' of rock set in a carefully prepared lake whose floor was paved with pebbles set in clay. A 'cascade' on the north bank of the pool is of considerable interest. Now dry, it has been studied by garden historians who think that it may well have always been dry. Such 'dry waterfalls' became a characteristic feature of later Japanese gardens, made from carefully piled rocks which looked like those over which water tumbled naturally. These were sometimes selected for their patterns, with light stripes suggesting falling water. Ostensibly very much part of later Japanese gardens (distanced from those of the more literally-minded Chinese), the presence of a dry waterfall in the Emperor Saga's garden does suggest a Chinese prototype for he was a passionate devotee of all things Chinese.[1] This is particularly interesting, both since no such dry waterfalls survive in Chinese gardens, and in view of the rather different development of later Japanese and Chinese gardens. The Chinese generally eschewed such devices in favour of real lakes, ponds, streams and cascades, whilst Japan became famous for its metaphorical temple gardens where sand and rocks substituted for mountains and lakes.

A detailed description of a Chinese garden was given in the 18th-century novel *Heng Lou Meng* (the 'Dream of the Red Chamber'), but a group of Japanese works of literature, best exemplified by Lady Murasaki's 'Tale of Genji'[2] (late 10th century) give a much earlier view of courtly gardens. Each of the ladies wooed by Prince Genji lived in a separate estate where a garden was a major feature. For one, he made an autumn garden full of trees whose leaves turned deepest red before they fell and where boulders were set in a stream to increase the dramatic sound of

1 Loraine Kuck, *The world of the Japanese garden* (New York and Tokyo, Walker/Weatherhill, 1968).

2 Murasaki Shikibu, *The Tale of Genji*, translated by E. Seidensticker (London, Secker and Warburg, 1976).

88

89

water crashing through rocks. Another lady was favoured with a winter garden with a bed of chrysanthemum (for the early winter) and many pine-trees which she could admire when laden with snow. By contrast, a summer garden (for yet another of Genji's consorts) contained scented flowers, peonies, roses and orange blossom as well as shady plants: bamboos and tall forest trees formed cool green tunnels around the spring and pool. Lady Murasaki's garden was at its best in spring when its hillside cherry orchards flowered like white clouds and the fresh yellow-green leaves of willows swept the courtyard. She had wistaria and mountain kerria, the former softly draped over doorways and covered walks, the kerria tumbling down over the 'cliffs' that had been cunningly made on the banks of the lake. Such differentiated gardens were quite easily accommodated in the rambling homes of Heian aristocrats. These were made up of a series of buildings, usually connected by covered walks which led the way through landscaped gardens. Manuscript and woodblock illustrations to the great Japanese novels such as 'The Tale of Genji' invariably depict the 'edges' of houses [see 90], the raised verandah, the paper screen walls and the stepping stones, bamboos, streams and twisted pines of the garden beyond [88].

88 A duet between a gentleman playing the flute in a garden and his lady inside on the koto. From Genji Monogatari *(The tale of Genji), woodblock print, 1650.*
[16055 b. 1, vol. 2, p. 23]

89 Accompanied by his servant, a gentleman departs through a garden at dawn. Cockerels and chickens roost in the willow beside a rustic fence. From Ise Monogatari *(The tale of Ise), 1610.*
[Or. 65 c. 1]

104 ORIENTAL
GARDENS

90 The serenity of spring: the edge of a verandah and a garden with scattered petals and rocks. From Ogawa Ritsuo, Chichi no on, a haiku anthology. Japanese coloured woodblock, 1730. [Or. 74 cc. 3]

91 The courtyard of the Shounji (Temple of the Beneficent Clouds), where the central focus is an ancient five-leaved pine, propped up amongst rocks and viewed from the verandah. From Akisato Shosen, Izumi meisho zue (Views in Izumi province), woodblock print, 1796. [16114 d. 1]

92 A lotus pool in a naturalistic temple garden in the Nanzenji, Kyoto. From Akisato Rito, Miyako insen meisho zue (Illustrated guide to Kyoto), 1799. [16114 d. 10]

Princes creep through the garden to visit their lovers, incongruously (given the ostensible secrecy of the event) attended by small servants [89]; they leave billets-doux written on slips of paper folded into origami shapes and pushed under the screen. Ladies, their long hair flowing in waves, seem to wait eternally behind screens, peeping out at the garden below.

Such detailed literary accounts of gardens and their habitués indicate a particular love of brightly-coloured flowers in the Heian period. Though flowering plants were still used with great skill, many later Japanese gardens were more sombre, dominated by the greens of moss, bamboo and pines set off by dark rocks and light sand. In the Kamakura period (1185–1333), larger gardens were constructed with winding pools and hillside walks, in contrast with the enclosures of the Heian era. Even the pools were differently used. During the Heian period, lakes were specifically designed to be viewed from pleasure boats. Many of the rock mountains set in the lakes presented a fine view from the main pavilion but were also designed with coves and cliffs to the rear, visible only from a boat.

The Kamakura era also saw the construction of great temple gardens [91, 92]. Their Chinese antecedents have not survived: the eighth century imperial suppression of Buddhism in China was largely a response to the

南禅境内
まきの
牧護菴

*93 Recommended gardening
tools and a method of moving
large rocks with a windlass.
From Kitamara Enkin,
Chikuzan teizoden (How
to make mountains and
gardens), woodblock print,
1795. [16003 b. 13, garden
section part 2, p. 17]*

*94 Sieve, trowels, mattocks,
mallets and other tools, from
Chikuzan reizoden (How
to make mountains and
gardens). [16003 b. 13,
garden section, part 2, p. 18]*

*95 The raked garden of the
Daitokuji in Kyoto, from
Akisato Rito, Miyako rinsen
meisho zue (Illustrated
guide to Kyoto), 1799.
[16114 d. 10]*

*96 How to construct a
realistic mountain with
numbered stones and trees,
from Chikuzan reizoden
(How to make mountains and
gardens), woodblock print,
1795. [16003 b. 13, garden
section part 1, f. 8]*

growing economic power of the Buddhist church and the vast estates of
the temples were confiscated so that whilst Chinese Buddhist monks and
nuns continue to cultivate flowers and grow vegetables, they now do so
in the restricted space of temple courtyards and tiny garden plots. In
Japan, by contrast, temple gardens are amongst the most famous in the
country and, together with surviving aristocratic gardens and tea-house
gardens, remain major monuments.

The first surviving Japanese garden manual, a manuscript by Tachibana
no Toshitsuna, the *Sakuteiki* (Notes on making gardens) dates from the
Kamakura period. This and the 15th-century manuscript, *Senzui narabi ni
yagyō no zu* (Illustrated designs for mountain, water and hill landscapes)
by the Buddhist priest Zōen, form the basic early literature on garden
construction, antedating surviving Chinese texts. It seems likely that
texts were of more significance in Japanese garden design than in
Chinese. Production of such textbooks continued into the Edo period
(1615–1868) when the very detailed *Tsukiyama teizōden* (Creating landscape gardens) was published which includes details of the types of
trowels, hatchets and pruners to be used and illustrations of how to
move large rocks on rollers using a windlass and pry bars [93, 94]. During
the Edo period, a number of guidebooks to major gardens, especially
those of the temples in the Kyoto area, also appeared, to aid tourists and
inspire designers [95]. Another major Edo gardening manual, *Ishigumi
sono yaegaki den* (Illustrated work on landscape gardening) contained
numerous illustrations, particularly of small tea-house gardens, illustrating an enormous variety of exceedingly similar designs, subtly differentiated by the disposition of the same elements: stepping stones, bridges,
streams, marsh plants, lanterns, rocks and small trees [96].

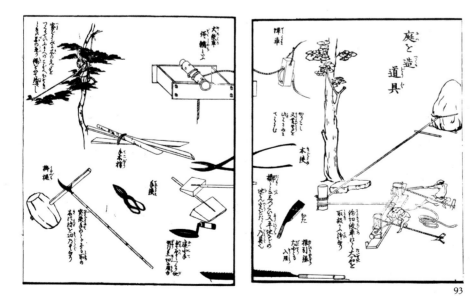

93

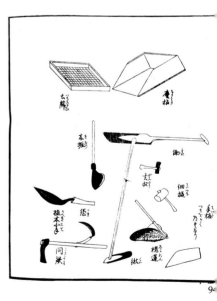

9₄

The *Sakuteiki* was written by an aristocrat who was clearly personally
involved in the practicalities of garden building, recalling Prince Genji
who himself rolled up his sleeves and directed the workmen as they
toiled over rock-moving. In that sense, the text is similar to that of the
later Chinese 'Craft of Gardens' which was also written by a man with
practical experience, despite his constant literary allusions. The first
principle established in the *Sakuteiki* was the importance of visiting
famous sites of natural beauty, to absorb the principles of natural design.
Copying natural scenes became an important aspect of the aristocratic
gardens of Japan and included the very beautiful coastline as well as
mountain sites. In the Korakuen imperial park near Tokyo, laid out on
the orders of the shogun Tokugawa Yorifusa (1603–61), 30 famous sites in
Japan were copied and, later, some famous Chinese views were also

*97 A lonely and romantic
young man in a mosquito
net with a stream and
watercourse outside in the
garden. Illustration by
Sekkosai in* Shinobu-zuri
*(Recollections prints),
Japanese stencil colour print,
Kyoto, 1750. [Or. 81. c. 27]*

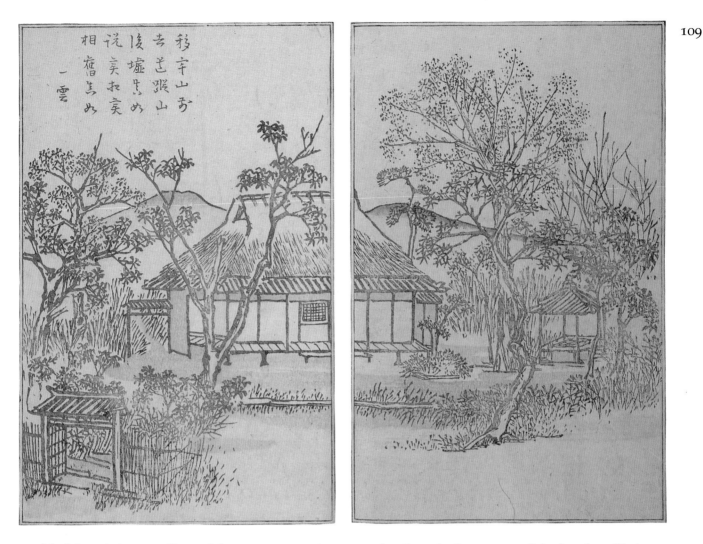

移宇山弖
吉芝張山
後墟点め
说亥扣亥
相奮為み
一雲

109

added in miniature. One of the most attractive reproductions is the copy of the coastal sandbar at Amanohashidate in the 17th-century Katsura imperial villa near Kyoto. The garden version is more winding than the original and covered with twisted pines imitating the wind-blown trees of the coast.

The major section of the *Sakuteiki* deals with the creation of 'mountain streams' which should ideally develop from a rivulet rushing through a deep gully to a broader, eddying stream flowing into a pond. The disposition of rocks and trees was also of paramount importance. Zōen's 'illustrated designs' show exactly how rocks should be placed in different contexts. There are boat-concealing rocks in an otherwise open pool (reflecting the Heian love of boat trips) and there are named groupings of stones. One of the most famous is the 'Buddhist triad' where three stones, the largest at the centre, imitate the trinity of Buddhist images in Buddhist temples. This type of detail is lacking in later Chinese texts and

98 A coloured woodblock depiction of a house in rustic surroundings, from Bumpo Basei, Teito gakei ichiran (Sketches of the neighbourhood of Kyoto), Kyoto 1809–1816. [16112 d. 14, Book 4]

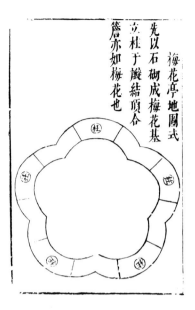

簷亦如梅花也

立杜于簷結頂令

先以石砌成梅花基

梅花亭地園式

99 Plan of a pavilion in the form of a plum blossom. From Ji Cheng's Yuan Ye (Craft of gardens), reprint of a 1635 woodblock edition in a Japanese collection.
[15305 e. 14]

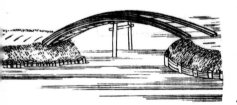

3 David A. Slawson, *Secret teachings in the art of Japanese gardens* (Tokyo and New York, Kodansha, 1987).

4 Ji Cheng, *The Craft of Gardens*, translated by Alison Hardie (New Haven and London, Yale University Press, 1988).

indicates the diverging aesthetic. The Chinese liked stones that looked like things – oxen, lions and cranes – but the Japanese were more concerned with form than appearance. Zōen's illustrations of trees include many described in terms of their line and in illustrations depicting rocks already in position, he notes exactly what sort of tree should be planted where [100]. This absolute attention to concrete detail was an important aspect of training apprentices and contrasts with the air of mystery that grew up around the acquisition of knowledge. The early texts on gardens were described as 'secret texts' transmitting only part of the esoteric skill of garden design. Students in Japan today still have to serve a long apprenticeship of three to five years spent weeding and pruning whilst they assimilate the secret skills of their master through 'body learning' (learning by doing). Then they may be allowed access to the texts which themselves contain injunctions against widespread transmission: 'the illustrations concerning rocks . . . must be kept quite secret'.[3] Secrecy was not part of the Chinese tradition and though the language of Ji Cheng's 'Craft of Gardens' may seem occasionally unhelpful ('There is no set formula for pavilions, nor any rule for their disposition'),[4] there is no danger attached to its content and it was published for the discerning and would-be fashionable gentlemen of 17th-century China. The only remotely similar prohibitions can be found in the Chinese carpenters' 'bible', 'The Classic of Lu Ban', which was a rather different sort of text since it included a large number of spells and talismans to protect (or destroy) buildings.

The twists and turns of Japanese history particularly in the 13th to 15th centuries saw the development of new forms of garden alongside the old. Imperial and aristocratic villas built on large mountain sites permitted the continuing use of a garden form quite close to the Chinese prototypes of the Tang dynasty. These were the 'stroll gardens' where visitors were encouraged to range around the lake or traverse it by boat to see the different set-pieces from a variety of angles. The Eifukuji, laid out in Kamakura by the monk Jogen for Minamoto Yorimoto in 1189, was based on the Fujiwara temple of Mōtsuji which Yorimoto had seen when he led his army against the Fujiwara stronghold. A stream was led down ·to the lake through banks lined by stones and the islands of the lake were linked by scarlet bridges. In the lake itself were groups of rocks known as the 'night-mooring islands' and tortoise island (this latter a rare but popularly used form of a group of stones arranged to look like a tortoise). Such grand imperial parks continued to be constructed, especially with a new vogue for Chinese styles that prevailed in the 14th and 15th centuries. The 'Gold Pavilion' near Kyoto was a version of a Chinese lake-side pavilion and was constructed in 1395 for the Ashigaka shogun Yoshimitsu when he retired. In the Gold Pavilion, he would drink tea

100 How to make a grassy slope, using numbered stones, from Kitamura Enkin, Chikuzan teizoden (*How to make mountains and gardens*), *woodblock print, 1795 [16033 d. 17, garden section, part 1, p. 17]*

brewed from spring water, another innovation introduced from China. The lake beside the pavilion was not meant to be 'strolled round'; its islands and rocks were supposed to be viewed from boats. The rocky groups included a 'tortoise island' like that in the Eifukuji, made of a cluster of stones resembling the shell, head and flippers of a turtle. The association of turtles with longevity probably contributed to their representation in stone and another island in the lake was called the crane island, for cranes were also associated with long life in Chinese and Japanese myth. The crane islands differed from tortoise islands in that they rarely looked much like cranes but consisted of a tall, narrow rock, merely hinting at a long-necked bird peering out over the water. Yoshimitsu continued to improve his garden, particularly with new rocks that were presented to him by his vassals. One, which arrived in 1229, required the strength of 17 oxen to move it. In his acceptance of 'tribute' rocks and use of manpower, Yoshimitsu was no different from other shoguns who constructed their gardens on an appropriately grand scale. Records of such efforts include the use of 1,800 men to move a couple of rocks a few miles, and the suicide of two gardeners when a branch was broken off a plum tree in transit.

101 Different types of garden bridge: rustic, grass-bordered and with a sudden drop at one end to stepping stones below (above) or a smooth curve (opposite). From Akisato Rito's Ishigumi sono yaekiden (*Eight methods of piling rocks to create a garden), woodblock print, c.1827.*
[16033 a. 12, part 1, pp. 28–9]

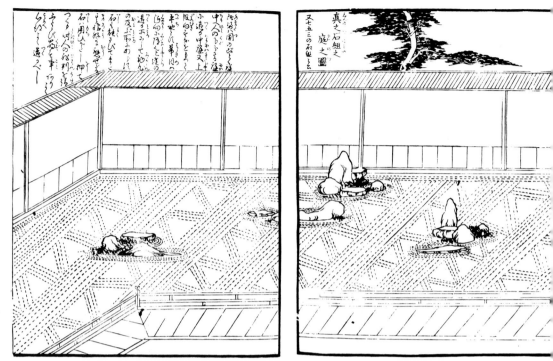

*102 How to make a stone
garden: raked sand between
the stones, with a single pine
beyond. From Kitamura
Enkin,* Chikusan teizoden
*(How to make mountains and
gardens), woodblock print,
1795. [16033 d. 17, garden
section, part 3, p. 33]*

*103 Varying forms of rustic
fencing for tea-house gardens
from* Ishigumi sono
yaekiden *(Eight methods of
piling rocks to create a
garden), woodblock print
c.1827. [16033 a. 12, p. 13]*

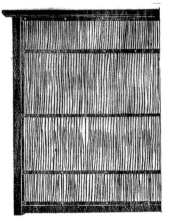

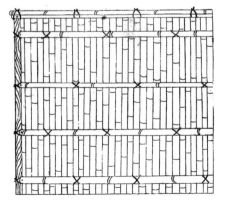

Yoshimitsu's grandson Yoshimasa built a 'Silver Pavilion' in 1482, one of twelve major timber structures in a large hill-side 'stroll garden' near Kyoto. These included a main gate, covered walks, a study, a hump-backed bridge and several pavilions with specific uses: one was for watching football (a game played by long-gowned gentlemen in Song dynasty China and, subsequently, Japan), others for religious ceremonies or tea-drinking. A cascade, called the Moon-washing Spring, fell into the Brocade Mirror Pool and the best view of the garden and the rising moon was from the Silver Pavilion. Yoshimasa's garden, and the later Katsura villa with its lake, bridges, islands, football pitch and other sporting areas, were quite close to Chinese originals but one feature, possibly an accidental survival of the restoration of the Silver Pavilion in 1615, ostensibly associates the Pavilion with the rise of the unique temple gardens. The most extraordinary features of the Silver Pavilion park today are two sand piles. A large cut-off cone of silvery sand is now named the 'moon-facing eminence' and, beside it, a flat, terrace-like pile is known as the 'silver sand sea'. It seems likely that silver sand was used to cover the ground before the pavilion (sand had been used in this way since the Heian period) and that these now sculptured heaps do not represent Zen constructions but were simply the result of building works, subsequently frozen in time and venerated.

Whatever the origin of the 'moon-facing eminence', the raked sand gardens found in Zen temples in Japan are amongst the most remarkable

'gardens' in the world [102]. Small in scale, no bigger than a tennis court, intended to form the main view from a Zen abbot's living room, they indicate the enormous influence that Zen Buddhism had on Japanese garden design. Better known by its Japanese name, Zen, the Chan or 'meditation' school developed in China, partly as a means for lay persons to achieve enlightenment without necessarily leaving home (and abandoning parents and ancestors) and entering a monastery. In Japan, it remained somewhat different from the other sects (its abbots were allowed to marry, for example), though it developed into more of a monastic tradition than it had been in China. The fundamental belief in meditation became associated with practices or 'ways' to achieve the goal of enlightenment and these included the 'way of tea', the 'way of flowers', the 'way of archery'. These 'ways' led to a great elevation of

104 Wine and books on a spring evening beneath the prunus. From Chikudo gafu *(Drawing book of Chikudo), a coloured woodblock print, 1815. [16116 b. 25]*

114

105

105 Different types of garden lantern, From Kitamura Enkin, Chikuzan teizoden *(How to make mountains and gardens), woodblock print, 1795. [16033 d. 17, garden section, part 2, p. 34]*

106 Wash basin beside a tea-house, from Chikuzan teizoden *(How to make mountains and gardens), 1795. [16033 d. 17, garden section, part 2, p. 26]*

107 The disposition of rocks and trees, each carefully labelled so that exactly the same form can be achieved. From Akisato Rito's Ishigumi sono yaekiden *(Eight methods of piling rocks to create a garden), woodblock print. c.1827.*
[16033 a. 12, part 2, f. 16]

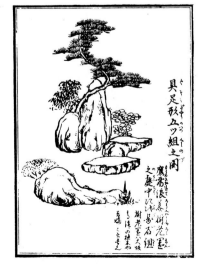

aesthetics, infused by the austerity of Zen. The metaphysical practice of Zen meditation contributed to the development of metaphysical gardening; moss gardens (bare of flowers), 'dry' waterfalls and streams, rocks and swept sand instead of seas and islands, all these were associated with Zen. Austerity and esotericism mingled in Zen gardens. Mossy slopes were kept meticulously free of fallen leaves and other debris, yet one layman who swept a moss garden too assiduously was silently reproved by his abbot who gently shook the branches of a maple in autumn, scattering a few choice red leaves on a green bed.

Perhaps the first 'Zen' garden is the 13th-century Saihōji or Moss temple near Kyoto. This combines a lower garden in the more traditional Chinese-influenced style with an unusual 'stroll garden' in the upper forest. There, a dry cascade of stepped rocks falls from a woodland 'spring' filled with moss, not water, surrounded by low 'kneeling stones'. Later Zen gardens, typified by the small walled enclosures set outside the abbots' living quarters, no longer used the 'stroll garden' principle but were intended to be viewed from a single position, on the verandah outside the main room. Though this single viewpoint plan was widely used in Chinese gardens (in the side courtyards of southern houses) and also during the Heian period, it was developed to a high point in Zen temples. Below the raised verandah in the Daisen'in (part of the Daitokuji temple in Tokyo) is an area of carefully raked sand, striped, piled in island cones. Rocks are arranged to the side and rear of the raked sand; a 'dry' waterfall, a dry 'boat' with a few tiny shrubs planted on and among them. In the late 15th century Ryōanji, the barest of all, five groups of rocks stand in a raked sand sea. The area (the size of a tennis court) is walled and elegantly surrounded by a border of diamond-patterned flagstones and a channel of dark pebbles bordered by paler stones. Above the dark, tiled wall opposite the verandah rise tall green trees.

The smallness of these temple courtyard gardens, as well as the Zen elevation of tea-drinking to an art form with religious connotations, may have contributed to the development of the tea-house garden [*see* 103, 104]. Like the house-garden complexes of south China, where house and garden form a unity, the tiny rustic thatched cottages used for the tea ceremony in Japan were invariably set in a tiny garden courtyard. One authority calls the tea-house garden a 'garden path' for it is a route along which the visitor travels, shedding the cares of the world as he prepares himself for the cleansing ceremony. That it is a route is emphasised by the carefully laid stepping stones or pebbled paths that lead him to the tea-house, through clumps of bamboo, past rock groupings and low shrubs and tiny trees, his way illuminated by stone lanterns [105]. These, consisting of tall stone stems topped by cut-out stones that often resemble small roofed pavilions, probably derive from Tang dynasty Chinese models, though many were imported from Korea. Beside the tea-house is a large stone, either a natural stone with a depression in its upper surface or a specially carved stone, filled with water and provided with a simple bamboo dipper for the visitor to wash his hands [106].

108 A suggested design for a suburban tea-house from Chikuzan teizoden (*How to make mountains and gardens*), *1795.* [*16033 d. 17, garden section part 1, p. 34*]

In the tea-house enclosure, whether a free-standing structure or one of many set in an imperial park, flowers were kept to a minimum, for this is one of the most pared-down 'aesthetic' forms of the Japanese garden [107, 108]. Ferns were planted beside rocks but, at most, only a prunus (for its sparse, elegant flowers in the early spring) or a small-leafed maple (acceptable as a native tree) could be included. Though flowers were thus excluded from the tea-house, in other parts of a large garden, just as in Chinese gardens, flowers could provide a focus. Like the Chinese, the Japanese enjoy the flowers of the seasons, making special trips to gardens famous for a particular flowering plant at the appropriate season. The late winter flowers and plants are the same in China and

109 Pot plants (three varieties of Nandina domestica *by Untei). From* Somoku Kihin Kagami (*Mirror of rare plants and trees*), *Japanese hand-coloured woodblock, 1827.* [16033 c. 3]

Japan: evergreen bamboo and pine which, together with the early-flowering plum, are known as the 'three friends of winter'. Prunus blossoms are known in Japan as 'snow flowers' for their sparse, snowflake-like scatter amongst dark branches, as well as the fact that it often snows as they flower [*see* 112]. One of the great winter flowers, the camellia, native to East Asia, was only planted in Buddhist temples, for the sudden dropping of the red flower at its peak was regarded as ominous (death in the midst of life) to all but Buddhist monks whose life was spent in contemplation of this very notion. Just as in China, the first yellow buds on the willow were to be appreciated slightly later in spring as an indication of a real change in the season and, in mid-April, this is followed by the special Japanese favourite, cherry blossom [*see* 111]. Many of the great gardens of Kyoto, especially the Heian Shrine, specialize in cherry blossoms of all sorts, from the pink fountains of weeping cherries to the cloudlike orchards by the lake. Later came azaleas and wistaria. It is interesting that azaleas were particularly beloved of the Japanese and do not form part of the major seasonal

110 A bonsai establishment in 18th-century Edo (Tokyo). Coloured woodblock print from Ehon Toto meisho (Famous sights of Edo), c.1770. [16114 e. 93]

111 Picnic at Cherry blossom time in Omuro in Kyoto. From Miyako meisho zue *(Illustrated guide to Kyoto), 1780. [16114 d. 11]*

flowerings in their native country, China, though the wistaria was appreciated in both countries. In Japan, the waterside iris was the dominant flower of summer, seen at its best in the Meiji Shrine in Tokyo. Clumps of *Iris kaempferi* are planted in a winding stream, crossed by a low rustic bridge, and set against a background of Japanese maples whose foliage in summer is a plain green foil for the purple iris. In late summer, the morning glory is followed by the Japanese bush clover. Planted in the sand-covered courts of buildings like the Seiryōden imperial palace in Kyoto, the small shrubs are covered with pink blossoms in September and are then cut down to ground level, to promote a bushy growth next spring. Maples, planted on all the hillsides of large imperial parks and sometimes used as a 'borrowed' view, to be admired from the verandah of a hill-side temple surrounded by trees, were the sight of late autumn. Then, when the irises of the Meiji shrine have finished flowering, their 'background' maples assume the foreground. Last of all comes the chrysanthemum.

Pen cai, or *bonsai* in Japanese, the most highly developed Chinese form of miniaturisation, were particularly popular from the 17th century and have been made very much a Japanese art form, tiny, spiky and far removed from the larger, more naturalistic Chinese originals [110]. Though a relatively late introduction, the same sort of lengthy apprenticeship and absorption of tradition specified for garden design was applied to *bonsai*. 'It takes three years to learn to water a tree properly',[5] as one handbook notes severely, before proceeding with instructions on exactly which of the six different types of pruning scissors should be

5 Yuji Yoshimura and Giovanna M. Halford, *The Japanese art of miniature trees and landscapes* (Rutland and Tokyo, Tuttle, 1957).

used on deciduous, as opposed to fruit-bearing, trees. In *bonsai* as in garden planning, a careful study of the natural origin was important. The best *bonsai* trees are pines and junipers which either originate, or look as if they originated, on a barren mountainside or wind-swept shore, their trunks and branches twisted by storms, their growth stunted by thin soils. After this poor start in life, the subject was ruthlessly pruned and wired and set in a 'training pot' in a mixture of fermented cottonseed, fishmeal, lime, soya beans and wood ash. Styles of training were many, and all were laid down. Sixteen types of single-trunk bonsai included 'coiled', 'windswept', 'twisted trunk', 'octopus' and 'clinging to a rock', whilst varied effects were achieved by teasing multiple trunks from a single root or group plantings of two or more saplings. These miniatures were made for individual display and appreciation and are a form quite separate from the fashion for dwarf garden trees which grew up at roughly the same time. Dwarf trees and shrubs in gardens were pruned to keep them in proportion with the garden. As Japan's towns and cities grew more crowded, private gardens were constrained. Where huge forests of pine and maple had been possible in the old imperial estates, the aesthetic of the tea-garden, combined with lack of space, forced a reduction in scale which was carried out with absolute precision.

112 Admiring the early flowering prunus on a riverbank in Kyoto at the Sainenji temple. From Miyako meisho zue (Illustrated guide to Kyoto), 1780.
[16114 d. 11]

Southeast Asia

The luxuriant vegetation of Southeast Asia made gardening something of a negative process, a matter of firm control and intervention rather than encouragement. Though plants and flowers fill the pages of illustrated manuscripts, they are shown largely in their natural place, in forests and groves, as a background to depictions of the animals that figure in many Buddhist legends. Flowers, whether cultivated or wild, were and still are used as offerings in temples and to decorate small shrines with garlands. Locally-produced batik cloth swarms with flowers and foliage and scented flowers such as jasmine adorn women's hair.

As for gardens, many of the houses and temples throughout Southeast Asia are raised above the ground, on high platforms or piles. Raising dwellings protected the inhabitants from floods and snakes, allowed better ventilation and also provided an area that could be used for housing domesticated animals such as cattle and pigs. For these reasons, the area was also kept clear of vegetation, although house enclosures in Bali often had a designated garden area at the rear. When European settlers came to the area, they brought with them their own architecture, somewhat adapted to the local climate, and also the tradition of constructing a garden beside their houses. Yet even the tree-lined suburban streets of European quarters were subject to invasive vegetation, threatening to: 'burst at the seams with a dreadful tropical energy. Foliage sprung up on every hand with a determination unknown to our polite European vegetation ... If you left your bungalow unattended for a few months while you went home on leave, very likely you would come back to find that green lariats had been thrown over every projecting part and were wrestling it to the ground, that powerful ferns were drilling their way between its bricks...'[1]

The over-abundance of plant life did not, however, mean that gardens were totally absent. The palace of the Burmese kings in Mandalay (1857–1885) had numerous gardens consisting mainly of expanses of water carefully bounded with stone embankments and flat areas of neatly clipped grass in which stood tall shady trees. George Bird's *Wanderings in Burma*, published in 1897, offers a contemporary description of the 'royal gardens, containing ornamental tanks and streams of

113 *Natural vegetation from a Thai manuscript of* Mahabuddhagunam, *an illustration of the ten jatakas, late 18th century.* [*Or. 14068, f. 35*]

1 J. G. Farrell, *The Singapore Grip* (London, Weidenfeld, 1978).

water, and laid out with grottos, rockeries, winding paths, rustic bridges and arbours, sheltered by groves of tamarind, cocoa-nut, bamboo and other flowering or fruit-bearing trees'. Bird states that the grounds were laid out by 'one of the many foreigners in the King's service'. Rockeries, rustic bridges and streams recall English garden styles although they are, of course, also present in Chinese and Japanese gardens. The Queen's garden in the same area, altogether a more 'oriental' enclosure, was described in 1907: 'canals and watercourses wind here through little artificial hills and grottos, and long arrays of swooning palms line the broader waters'. In another part of the palace grounds was the 'Queen's summer pavilion', a light, open timber construction built out on piles over the water and decorated with cut-out barge-boards on the gables. Pots of palms and flowers stood on the verandah and baskets of trailing flowers, possibly orchids, were hung from the rafters. The pavilion stood over a pool thickly planted with lotuses.

Though there was a clear appreciation of the restful quality of a plain water surface, where there were lotuses in the palace and moat of Mandalay, they grew thick and unconfined. Some of the pools were traversed by plain timber bridges, set low on the water in the Chinese style. The widespread planting of the lotus in Burmese palace gardens and elsewhere in Southeast Asia, reflects not only the intrinsic beauty of the plant but also its religious significance. For Hindus (Bali is a Hindu stronghold), the lotus is a sacred flower and its significance was inherited by the Buddhist faith which dominates in Burma. For Buddhists, the lotus, its pure pink-tipped flowers rising out of muddy pools, represented a purity that mortals could aspire to, transcending the mire of human existence [114].

Religious and magical beliefs affected the choice of plants cultivated in Thailand. Most people planted 'useful' plants in plots, useful being defined in one work as plants that are 'edible, saleable or are for offering to the Buddha statue'.[2] The last category in particular included scented, flowering plants, such as jasmine and gardenias, although many of the edible gingers have very pretty flowers. Another plant widely grown since it was used in marriage ceremonies was the *Graptophyllum* whose variegated leaves were thought to represent wealth in the form of gold and silver. Medicinal plants were cultivated in the garden: *Aglaia odorata* whose small, scented yellow flowers cure colds and asthma, lantana flowers to be boiled into a refreshing, digestive brew, and herbs and spices including citrus, lemon grass and gingers. Plants such as bamboo (widely used for construction, basket and mat-making) and the edible banana, whose decoratively large leaves were used to wrap foods, were widely planted for their decorative and economic significance; some gardens were fenced with spiky Mother-in-law's tongues; and Muslim

2 Pimsai Amranand, *Gardening in Burma* (Bangkok, The Siam Society, 1970).

cemeteries in Indonesia are always planted with scented *frangipani*.

Throughout tropical Southeast Asia, trees were very important in gardens and surrounding houses to provide cooling shade. It was considered unlucky to plant trees with brittle timber too near houses, a superstition that had a practical foundation in protecting the house and its inhabitants from falling branches, but fruit trees such as mango, banana, papaya, jackfruit, coconut and citrus were favoured. In Thailand, large forest trees were not usually planted in domestic gardens for they were thought to be inhabited by spirits. They could be grown in more 'powerful' places such as temple courtyards where Bodhi trees were common or palace gardens where *Ochrocarpus siamensis* and *Mimusops elengi* were often cultivated for their fragrant flowers that were used to scent clothes.

114 A poor peasant picks lotus flowers from a muddy pond. A frequently depicted scene in Thai manuscripts: the flowers are to be presented to Phra Malai, who will offer them in heaven.
[Add. 15347, f. 19]

The old gardens of the royal Thai palaces were similar in plan to those found in Burma, with well-clipped lawns and trees rather than flowers, and pools bordered by fine stone embankments. A mid-19th century photograph of an unidentified Siamese garden taken by John Thomson[3] shows young men beside a pool with stepped stone embankments. In front of a huge banyan tree are a couple of rugged boulders, between which a slender palm is planted. There is a sense of Chinese influence in the rocks, the carved stone embankments, trees and water, beyond which a building can be glimpsed. Yet the flourishing vegetation and the neat edging of the tank are characteristic of Southeast Asia. Like those in Thomson's Thai photograph, Burmese garden trees were allowed to grow naturally, but the trees in old Thai gardens were sometimes clipped to form strange, gnarled shapes, probably originally influenced first by Chinese *pen cai* in the Sukhothai era (*c.*12th century–1357) and later, in the Ayutthaya period (1357–1767), by Japanese *bonsai*. Favoured trees for clipping included the tamarind, *Strebulus asper*, *Diospyros peregrina*, *Wrightia reliogiosa* with white scented flowers and, for its curiously-shaped roots, the banyan. It would appear that, after the Far Eastern influence, European topiary also had its effect in the late 19th century, for Singapore holly was apparently used to form green menageries on neatly clipped lawns. The Thai aristocracy also enjoyed the Chinese *pen jing* ('pot scenes'), tiny rocks, trees and water arranged in shallow dishes or trays that were placed around the edge of lawns. One of Thomson's photographs (*c.*1865–66) is of a group of Singapore Chinese merchants who lounge beside tables covered in porcelain pots in which grasses, flowering shrubs and foliage plants grow; behind these there appears to be a 'pot scene' with a group of gnarled timbers.

Orchids were particularly loved in Thailand. Special orchid gardens were constructed, with stone flagged floors for the pots to stand on and complex timber lattice walls and canopies. The lattice, often formed into elegant arches, fulfilled many functions in the orchid garden. As orchids require a lot of light but burn easily, the lattice filtered direct sunlight to some extent. They are subject to fungus problems unless well ventilated by the free movement of air through the lattice, upon which it was easy to hang pots and baskets of orchids. Ordinary mortals often hung their orchids, potted in bamboo baskets, from the branches of trees which offered the same filtered light and circulating air.

Whether set beside a simple house or ranged outside a palace or temple, groups of plants grown in pots represented the most widespread form of 'garden' in Southeast Asia. Nineteenth-century photographs show the large clipped trees in raised stone beds that lined some of the paved courtyards of the Thai palaces, interspersed with smaller versions in large Chinese porcelain goldfish bowls decorated with dragons.

3 Stephen White, *John Thomson: a window to the Orient* (London, Thames & Hudson, 1985).

Smaller palms in plain earthenware pots lined the lawns. Thomson's photographs of local grandees include the Governor of Pandam (c.1865–66), seated with an attendant beneath a flowered parasol, surrounded by a variety of pots filled with all sorts of flowers and plants. The significance of potted plants was such that another of Thomson's photographs depicts a very ordinary group of thatched bamboo river huts in Thailand with their inhabitants. In the foreground is a mysterious boat on which is a spectacular, high-footed earthenware pot in which a tree a couple of metres high is growing. Burmese manuscript illuminations show the variety of potted plants set beside homes and temples: great cabbage-like forms alternate with elegant, long-leaved foliage plants. Beside the temples and monasteries with their rows of potted flowers, a vegetable patch is often painted, its contents protected by high wicker fences and by assiduous clearance of the land beyond to prevent jungle incursions.

115 A Burmese monastery in a garden setting from a folding book illustrated with varieties of flora and fauna 19th century.
[Or. 13915, fol. 11]

Bibliography

A number of titles are listed in the footnotes accompanying each chapter; they are not repeated here.

IRAN

E.B.Macdougall and R.Ettinghausen (eds), *The Islamic Garden*, Dumbarton Oaks Colloquium on the History of Landscape Architecture, IV, Dumbarton Oaks, 1976

A.Upham-Pope and P.Ackerman, 'Gardens', in *The Survey of Persian Art*, III, Oxford, 1939

D.N.Wilber, *Persian Gardens and Garden Pavilions*, Rutland, Vermont, 1962

INDIA

Sylvia Crowe, Sheila Haywood, Susan Jellicoe and Gordon Patterson, *The Gardens of Mughal India*, London, 1972

C.M.Villiers-Stuart, *Gardens of the Great Mughals*, London, 1913

CHINA

Sven Hedin, *Jehol, City of Emperors*, London, Kegan Paul, 1932

Maggie Keswick, *The Chinese Garden*, London, Academy Editions, 1978

Alfreda Murck, Wen Fong, *A Chinese Garden Court: The Astor Court at the Metropolitan Museum of Art*, New York, Metropolitan Museum, 1980

Tsao Hsueh-chin, *A Dream of Red Mansions*, Peking, Foreign Languages Press, 1978 (alternatively Cao Xueqin, *The Story of the Stone*, translated by David Hawkes, Harmondsworth, Penguin Books, 1973)

JAPAN

Masao Hayakawa, *The Garden art of Japan* (translated by Richard L. Gage), New York/Tokyo, Weatherhill/Heibonsha, 1973 (Heibonsha Survey of Japanese Art, vol. 28)

Joan Stanley Baker, *Japanese Art*, London, Thames and Hudson, 1984

Wladimir Zwalf (ed.) *Buddhism: art and faith*, London, British Museum Publications, 1985

SOUTHEAST ASIA

Jacques Dumarcay, *The House in South-East Asia*, Singapore, Oxford University Press, 1987

V.C.Scott O'Connor, *Mandalay and other cities of the past in Burma*, London, Hutchinson, 1907

Index